The Story of Architecture

With contributions by Stefan Breitling, Elke Dorner, Andrea Dreher,
Markus Hattstein, Friedrich Wilhelm Krahe, Günter Külzhammer,
Iris Lautenschläger, Katrin Bettina Müller, Katja Reissner

Drawings by Christina Melhose

© 1996 Könemann Verlagsgesellschaft mbH
Bonner Str. 126, D - 50968 Köln

Chief editor: Peter Delius
Editor, layout: Ulrike Sommer
Design: Peter Feierabend
Translator: Susan Cox
Production of the English edition: Goodfellow & Egan, Cambridge
Production manager: Detlev Schaper
Reproductions: Imago Publishing Ltd., Thame
Printed in China
ISBN 3-89508-204-X

Jan Gympel

The Story of Architecture

FROM ANTIQUITY TO THE PRESENT

KÖNEMANN

Table of contents

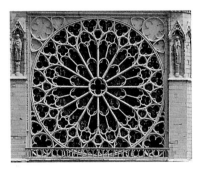

1600 to 1780

1750 to 1840

1840 to 1900

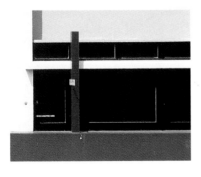

1900 to 1945

Since 1945

Laying the foundations

ANTIQUITY AND EARLY CHRISTIANITY

2900 B.C.–540 A.D.

ARCHITECTURE IN ANCIENT EGYPT 2900–700 B.C.

Building – a basic need and social act

In ancient Greek the architect was known as the "master builder" ("archi-tekton"). Architecture was considered the "mother" of the visual arts, as painting and sculpture often developed in the context of a building project; for example, in the form of murals or friezes. Even magical cult cave paintings served as decorations for dwellings. Unlike all other forms of art, the primary aim of architecture was to fulfil the basic human need for security. Buildings provided protection from the weather and wild animals. Thus, it is almost impossible to escape the evidence of building activity wherever people lived.

However, spiritual and intellectual needs also have a role to play when it comes to building. "The four walls" and "roof over his/her head" separate a human being from the surrounding environment and in doing so create something of individual human proportions. Buildings also change the external environment in which they stand: the yard, the village and the town are artificial environments wrested from nature. Thus, much can be surmised about the person responsible for a building from the way the relationship between the interior and exterior is presented. Does the building have thick opaque or transparent glass walls? Do the entrances, exterior steps, outer courts or fences create a sense of openness or distance?

Several other questions always arise: Who commissioned buildings? Who built them? For whom and for what purpose were they built? What form do they take and which materials were used? Not all buildings are prestigious affairs aiming to impress with their size, volume, style and decorative detail. However, all buildings reflect the spirit of their time, or at least that of the people who commissioned them and the architects who designed them. More than any other human creation, a building represents the social context: building is a social act which nearly always takes place in the social arena. It is an expensive activity and therefore dependent on power and wealth. Hence, elaborate buildings tell a lot about the people and activities important to the ruling group in a given society.

It is no accident that religious buildings have an important role to play in the history of architecture. As history has shown, religion fulfils what is possibly man's most important spiritual need, i.e. the need to bestow (a higher) meaning on existence, to explain the incomprehensible and insufferable, to provide prospects of a higher justice for unatoned wrongs and to offer the comfort of continued life, rebirth or resurrection after death.

Thus, as well as providing shelter for people, since ancient times dwellings have also been built for the gods. In keeping with the elevated position of the latter, these buildings tend to be more durable and impressive than those erected for mere mortals.

EGYPT:

The Old Kingdom (2850–2052 B.C.): The pharaoh is the absolute hereditary king, initially the incarnation of Horus, the falcon god, after the 4th dynasty son of the sun god Re. Famous pyramids built 3rd–6th Dynasty. Sun worship official religion. Hieroglyphics and calendars.

The Middle Kingdom (2052–ca. 1570 B.C.): Unification of Egypt by Mentuhotep II of Thebes. Construction of vast temple complexes in Karnak, the seat of Amon, principal deity of the land.

The New Kingdom (1570–715 B.C.): Egypt becomes a leading power, expeditions to Asia and Nubia, greatest display of power under Queen Hatshepsut, greatest extension of the kingdom under Tuthmosis III. Temple complexes in Karnak, Luxor, Abu Simbel.

The Late Period (715–332 B.C.): Alexander the Great conquers Egypt (332 B.C.).

GREECE:

Ca. 560 B.C.: Peisistratos establishes the great Dionysia festivals in Athens with musical competitions and theatrical productions.

490 B.C.: Battle near Marathon, victory of Athens over previously undefeated Persians, rise of Athens to major political power.

477 B.C.: Foundation of the Attic maritime alliance as a protective force against the Persians.

443–429 B.C.: The age of Pericles: Athens is "democracy by name; in reality, however, the monarchy of the first man".

431–404 B.C.: Peloponnesian War ends the hegemony of Sparta; the Persian Empire emerges as ultimate victor from the international power struggles.

336–323 B.C.: Alexander the Great moves to India: idea of world supremacy, spreading of Greek culture.

Sensuous delight in the use of marble: the Venus de Milo.

ROME:

Ca. 750 B.C.: Foundation of Rome.

218 B.C.: Hannibal progresses across the Alps towards Rome.

45 B.C.: Julius Caesar sole ruler of the Roman Empire.

27 B.C.: Emperor Augustus assumes power as Senate-approved "princep"

54 A.D.: Nero becomes emperor.

70 A.D.: Conquest and destruction of Jerusalem by Titus.

79 A.D.: Vesuvius erupts in Pompeii.

161–80 A.D.: Marcus Aurelius Roman emperor.

313 A.D.: Edict of Milan ensures religious freedom for Christians.

330 A.D.: Byzantium is renamed Constantinople and becomes the Christian capital of the empire.

391 A.D.: Christianity becomes official religion of the Roman Empire; all pagan cults are outlawed.

The Pyramids of Giza (Mycerinus, Chephren and Cheops), Egypt, 4th Dynasty, middle of the 3rd century B.C.

The pyramids of the pharaohs Mycerinus, Cheops and Chephren are visible from far and wide at the edge of the desert near Cairo. Enormous volumes of stone were piled over the small burial chambers of the pharaohs, the culmination of mammoth technical and social projects. Construction of such buildings often took an entire lifetime; hundreds of workers were settled near the building site and many lost their lives moving the stones which weighed many tons.
Stepped structures were erected as an image of social hierarchy and stood for all to see as indestructible guarantors of the eternal validity of Egyptian culture. Awareness of the eternity of death led to the development of a complex death cult as one of the main components of Egyptian culture. The Egyptian tombs are all located on the west bank of the river Nile where the valuable fertile flood plains end and the sun sets over the hostile desert. Each pyramid has a mortuary temple which had its own priests and in which the pharaoh was commemorated.

Sunbeams of stone

As with other advanced civilisations, little remains of the ordinary dwellings built by the ancient Egyptians. The only extant architectural relics of the Old Kingdom are the tombs which served as places of worship.

Egypt's existence depended on the Nile whose annual floods left behind a layer of fertile mud and, far from being disastrous, were therefore life-enhancing. The world view of the people who lived by this quiet stream was determined by this perpetual cycle. Death was seen as a passage to another form of life and this passage was, however, only possible if the body remained intact. Thus, great efforts were made to preserve corpses. The greatest, of course, were reserved for the body of the pharaoh, the king who was regarded as a god. The brain and entrails were removed from the corpse, which was then prepared for burial (this is how the famous mummies originated). Food and other offerings were laid in the tomb. Moreover, the walls of the sacrificial area were decorated with reliefs of harvest scenes and sacrificial offerings in case the "supplies" ran out. Against a background of unchanging ritual conditions, other rooms were often built around the sacrificial chamber so that the dead person would not be deprived of his/her accustomed level of comfort. Sacrificial chambers were always built on the high west bank of the Nile above the actual burial chamber which was con-cealed deep in the rock. Entire houses, palaces and even towns, in which the dead person had lived, were often replicated.

Thus the tomb of the pharaoh Zoser, built in Saqqara between 2780 and 2680 B.C., was conceived as a replica of the pharaoh's palace in Memphis, a compact block with stepped limestone or brick walls. Five rectangular blocks of decreasing dimensions were laid on top of Zoser's mastaba, as these block tombs were known, so that the tower reached a height of approximately 60 metres. The reason behind the introduction of the pyramid may have been to provide greater security for the tomb (and guarantee that the corpse would not be disturbed), or to make the tomb more prominent. The fact that from then on the pharaohs' tombs became monuments can probably be explained by a desire to give visual form to religious symbolism: the stepped pyramid represented a staircase which the dead pharaoh climbed to reach heaven.

During the 3rd century B.C., the pharaohs began to be seen as sons of the sun-god Re and sun worship became the official religion. The pyramids, which had meanwhile acquired a square plan and smooth exterior walls, like the Pyramids of Giza, had become shining columns faced with a shimmering layer of limestone and topped with gold (both these features were eroded with time). They symbolised the sunbeams on which pharaohs were believed to have been transported to Re.

Deir el Bahari, mortuary temple of Queen Hatshepsut, Northern Egypt, 18th Dynasty, ca. 1500 B.C.

The monumental mortuary temple of Queen Hatshepsut lies on the west bank of the Nile opposite the old capital Thebes, and is integrated into the mountainous landscape of the eroded river bank. The central axis of the complex is based on that found in the temple of Amun at Karnak and thus emphasises the close links between the Queen and the god. The rather modest burial chamber and the colonnaded halls are cut into the rock. Avenues of sphinxes, ponds, pylons and rows of trees lined the long path along ramps and terraces to the actual temple. The central structure, the hypostyle hall, is decorated with reliefs on the history of the kingdom and the life of the Queen.

Architectural delight in axes and columns

At the beginning of the Old Kingdom, rooms with ceilings which could not be supported by walls alone were supported by simple square piers without bases and capitals. During the Pyramid era of the second half of the 3rd century B.C., these piers were replaced by columns with decorated capitals inspired by lotus, papyrus and palm trees. This design feature, developed for cult rather than structural reasons, was intended to convey a sense of majesty and eternal worth, and became a typical feature of buildings in Ancient Egypt. The architecture of the New Kingdom, a period of prolific architectural activity lasting from 1570 to 715 B.C., was dominated by axial cult complexes with large colonnaded halls, similar to those found in the Deir el Bahari mortuary temple.

The procession temples in the Nile valley were carved into the rocks west of Thebes and the most famous are the Temples of Amon in Luxor and Karnak. They suggest that the religious and philosophical perspectives of the designing architects were influenced by the surrounding natural landscape. Sloping entrance towers known as pylons flank the entrance in the same way that the rock face encloses the Nile. Obelisks and monumental statues stand in front of the entrance. Behind this is a forecourt surrounded by rows of columns leading through an antechamber into an enormous hypostyle hall, densely filled with columns whose plant capitals are reminiscent of the Nile grove. The complex terminates with a narrow, deep room (the "most sacred") which contained an image of the god for whom the temple was intended as a home (temples carved into the rocks were generally similar in structure). As the New Kingdom increased in prosperity, more and more forecourts and pylons were added in front of the existing ones. Processions crossing these repeatedly extended axes therefore progressed from their own time further into the great past of their country, whose prominent role in the development of the human race ultimately ended with its conquest by Alexander the Great in 332 B.C.

CLASSICAL GREECE AND HELLENISM 800–30 B.C.

The other side of the Mediterranean

Cretan culture, of which the unfortified palaces in Knossus and Phaestros still exist, emerged on the other side of the Mediterranean around 2000 B.C. and had close links with Egypt. The meagre remains of this once flourishing culture demonstrate that without the insights of archaeology and imagination we would be unable to describe the architecture of past eras, because none of the ancient buildings has been completely preserved in its original state. The same applies to Mycenaean culture, which developed on the Greek mainland around 1600 B.C., and whose most important buildings were the citadels in Mycenae and Tiryns. From approximately 1200 B.C. the Dorians conquered the Peloponnese, the Aegean islands and the western coast of Asia Minor (now Turkey). They adopted both Cretan and Mycenaean elements in their culture.

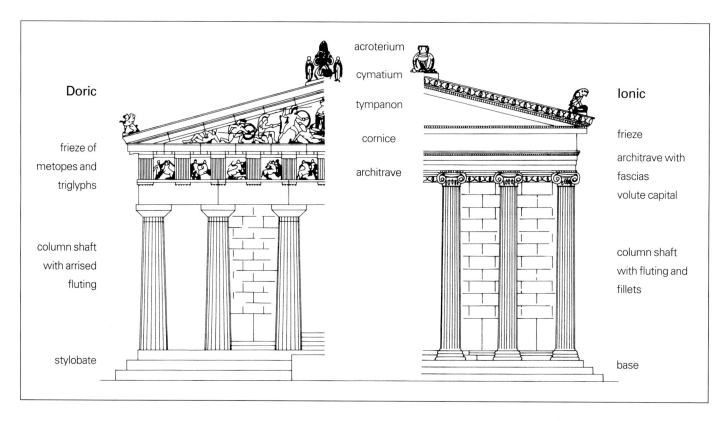

Doric

frieze of metopes and triglyphs

column shaft with arrised fluting

stylobate

acroterium

cymatium

tympanon

cornice

architrave

Ionic

frieze

architrave with fascias

volute capital

column shaft with fluting and fillets

base

This became particularly obvious when a Greek national identity with common myths, cults and festivals began to emerge around 800 B.C. Besides the theatre, which was also used as a shrine, the most important building was the temple. Like the Egyptians of the New Kingdom, the Greeks saw the temple as the dwelling place of a god, whose statue was erected in the interior which was only accessible to priests.

In order to emphasise this core structure, known as the cella, it initially had on one side, and was later often surrounded by, colonnades of timber columns. The columns and clay bricks used in the windowless cella were protected from rain by a gable roof. However, the buildings did not survive the effects of weathering and were replaced by new structures with stone columns and ashlar elements. This gave rise to a rebirth of stone building which had disappeared before the Mycenaean era.

It appears that this new culture also borrowed stylistic elements. For example, the Doric column, and particularly its capital, could well have been influenced by the Lion Gate relief of the citadel at Mycenae. However, the Dorians did not taper their columns downwards, like the Cretans in the Mycenaean citadel, but upwards like the Egyptians, with whom they had contact from the 7th century B.C. onwards.

Restraint and human dimensions

The art of building in stone, however, had to be learned from scratch. In Egypt, as in other advanced civilisations, information about architecture and its techniques was strictly classified. The adoption of a uniform Greek temple style throughout the Mediterranean resulted from the use of a structural technique based on reconstructable mathematical principles. In keeping with the highest ideal of "classical" Greek philosophy – the freedom of the individual – this information was almost freely available. The organisation of the city state, the polis, also corresponded to this model. All citizens – which did not include women, children and slaves – could observe and influence procedures within the city by participating in public assemblies. The defence of the city and a good relationship with the god which protected it was in the hands of each individual, rather than the armies of mercenaries and an independent priesthood.

It is only consistent that in a world based on the emancipation of the people – which of course did not always succeed in fulfilling this noble ideal – the houses of the gods were based not on abstract dimensions but on values derived from the human body. The elements of the Doric temple, both in their individual forms and the way in which they related to the overall structure, were also based on it. The clear tectonics can be traced back to the

The Lion Gate at Mycenae, acropolis, fortification wall with lion relief, ca. 1250 B.C.

The entrance to the citadel of Mycenae, the seat of the Greek king Agamemnon who is mentioned in Homer's Illiad, is decorated by one of the oldest monumental sculptures found in Europe. Two upright animal torsos symmetrically flank a downward tapering column on the powerful relieving triangle above the door lintel. They herald the warlike powers of the Mycenaean nobility.

Epidauros, theatre, ca. 350 B.C.

The semi-circular auditorium of marble seating is cut into the hill, raising the site architecturally. The view of the Peloponnesian landscape beyond the stage is breathtaking. The audience was originally seated on the ground of this open-air theatre. The monumental stone cavea – the auditorium with its concentric sloping stepped benches – was developed in the course of time. Unlike later Roman theatres, the Greek theatre was not a complex building.
Productions staged in the theatres were religious in content, in the service of Dionysos, the god of drama. The theatre at Epidauros belongs to a great shrine to the healing god Asklepios, where the sick could receive help for their recovery. The circular orchestra paved with slabs was initially the exclusive domain of the chorus, which was joined on the stage by actors from the 6th century B.C. onwards. The structure accommodates approximately 14,000 spectators. Pottery vessels were incorporated under the seats to dampen the echo and provide the excellent acoustics for which this theatre is renowned.
The Roman architectural critic Vitruvius appears to have derived his scheme for theatre buildings from this model.

Paestum, temple of Poseidon (or of Hera), 460–450 B.C.

One of the most beautiful and best preserved Doric temples is the so-called temple of Poseidon. Together with two other temples it forms the centre of the town of Paestum, a Greek colony in southern Italy. As the dedication offerings show, the temple was not actually dedicated to the sea god Poseidon but the mother of the gods, Hera.
With the Doric temple, the Greeks realised their classical-humanist architectural ideal on the basis of tectonics and proportioning. All the architectural components are totally logical and relate to each other proportionally. The structure is presented on a base consisting of three steps, the crepidoma. The cella is surrounded by 6 × 13 free-standing columns (peripteral). The loading and supporting elements are clearly distinguished: the massive, upward tapering columns carry the heavy horizontal architrave with its frieze of metopes and triglyphs. The architrave itself rests on rectangular slabs – the abaci – which press down on the echinus, the bulbous layer forming the head of the column. The Poseidon temple is a work of high classical Greek architecture.

original timber version and were further emphasised by the use of colour, possibly inspired by Egyptian models. The fluting on the columns emphasises their function as supporting members and distinguishes them from the smooth masonry of the cella. The way in which the Doric capital mediates between the round column shaft and the angular architrave, with its combination of the bulbous cushion-shaped echinus and flat ashlar abacus, is equally ingenious.

The gradual decline of clarity
Only gods were allowed to live above the human dwellings on the "Acropolis" ("top of the city"). By far the most famous of these Greek citadels was the Acropolis of Athens, with its two main temples; the Parthenon and the Erechtheion. These represent the high point and culmination of the achievements of classical Greek architecture. Whilst the design of the original temples focused exclusively on external effects, with an unadorned cella not open to the laity (the altar was generally in front of the building, on the east side), the Panathenaic frieze on the outer wall of the Parthenon cella appeared to invite the visitor inside at least as far as the colonnaded hall. The design of the cella interior also became more differentiated in that it contained a colonnade along three sides which continued behind the statue. The widening of the naos provided far more space for the statue in the cella than in previous temples.

In the temple to Apollo at Bassae, which like the slightly older Parthenon is ascribed to the architect Ictinus, even the interior walls of the cella are decorated with a sculpted frieze. The side aisles have disappeared altogether; the columns are not free-standing but engaged to the wall by short spurs of masonry. These were necessary to support the cella walls which in turn supported the roof. Therefore the columns were purely decorative and, strictly speaking, no longer columns but decorative elements concealing the ends of the masonry spurs. Thus the previous emphasis on structure shifted to decoration. This temple contains the oldest known Corinthian column, the capital of which is completely surrounded by stylised acanthus leaves which cleverly conceal its load-bearing function. Most columns in the temple at Bassae and the treasury in the Parthenon, which is of the Doric order from the outside, are of the Ionic order.

The Ionic order, which originated in Asia Minor and the Aegean, became more and more commonplace throughout Greece. Doric columns had become narrower and taller with time and this trend continued with the adoption of the Ionic column which was more elegant from the outset. All the features of the Ionic style – the finer fluting with narrow fillets between the flutes, the division of the architrave into three horizontal strips, the scrolls (volutes) on the capitals (which unlike the Doric order did not harshly collide with the architrave) –

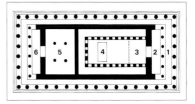

The Acropolis at Athens: view of the entire complex, caryatids in the south porch (Erechtheion) and plan of the Parthenon with **1** pteron, **2** pronaos, **3** cella, **4** cult image, **5** Parthenon, **6** opisthodomos

THE ACROPOLIS

On visiting the Acropolis at Athens in 1911, Le Corbusier wrote: "the Parthenon, this dreadful machine makes everything within a radius of three miles pale into insignificance". The temple of the protective goddess of the city, constructed entirely in white Pentelic marble, is the most famous of all Greek edifices. A fully three-dimensional, spatially complete structure, for many centuries it represented the embodiment of pure architecture. Following its destruction by the Persians in 480 B.C., Pericles had the building restored. Phidias, the famous sculptor, was artistic director of the restoration project. Ictinus and Callicrates are named as the architects of the Parthenon. If a Venetian missile had not hit the Turkish magazine in 1687, it would have been almost completely preserved.

The building is enormous in its proportions: instead of six front columns, the Parthenon has eight. There are six columns in front of the cella antae instead of the usual two columns of the pronaos. Although built in the Doric style, many elements of the Parthenon depart from the standard model. The cella is unusually wide to provide a fitting setting for Phidias's statue of Athena Parthenos, the virgin Athena. The cult image is surrounded by two floors of columns. The separate western part of the cella is the actual "Hall of the Virgins" with four columns forming a square which supported a timber lacunar. The top of the cella walls are lined at a height of 12 metres by a frieze depicting the Panathenaic procession which took place on the main feast day of the goddess Athena, when citizens of the city climbed the Acropolis to bring the goddess a new robe and to commemorate her with processions, a sacrificial meal and sporting competitions. Most of the frieze can now be seen in the British Museum in London. All the corrections and architectural subtleties which lend such a lively dynamism to a classical Greek building can be found together for the first time in the Parthenon. No line is completely straight but strengthened by the addition of a barely perceptible curve. The stylobate, the top step on which the columns rest, has a dome in the centre corresponding to one thousandth of its length. The columns and interior walls lean in slightly to soften the rigidity of the façades. The otherwise straight column shafts bulges, known as the entasis, which makes the supported load almost palpable.

The Erechtheion, another complex on the Acropolis, demonstrates even more clearly that the Greek temple at the end of the fifth century B.C. was no longer intended to demonstrate the sinister omnipotence of the gods, but the beauty and might of humankind. Named after a legendary Athenian king, this building eschews any idealised plan. Instead, the various elevations, i.e. the perspective of the observer from different points, are the key factor in the design.

In the southern porch, the human form actually replaces a load-bearing architectural element. The entablature is carried by free-standing maidens each with one leg forward as if freely striding. These caryatids have often been copied and, particularly in the classical era, came to represent a somewhat formalised recognition of the close links between man and architecture.

were more elegant, decorative and representative. The Artemis at Ephesus (completed ca. 450 B.C.), one of the first and most important Ionic temples, had a double peristyle with 96 columns, a deep entrance porch and an almost Egyptian massing of columns.

Hellenistic pomp

After the Peloponnesian War (431–404 B.C.), classical Greece fell into an economic and political crisis from which it was doubly liberated by the Macedonian Kings. Philip II steamrollered through the country and his son Alexander exceeded all of his plans to unite the Greeks and conquer Asia Minor, creating an empire which extended to the borders of India. The empire brought affluence to the Greeks and cultural hegemony over the entire region. Thus Greek architecture, or at least what remained of it, also spread.

The predilection for excessive effects and pompous staircases became more and more widespread. The fusion of the previously strictly independent elements of the column and the wall to form engaged columns which grew out of the walls

Pont du Gard, Roman aqueduct (275 m long, 49 m high), Gard valley near Remoulins (southern France), late 1st century B.C.

This almost completely preserved aqueduct carries the water for Nômes across a three-storey arch structure over the Gard river bed. The channel, through which the water flowed from the mountains along tunnels to the distribution points supplying the town, is at the top of the structure and was faced with waterproof mortar. The dominion of the Romans was largely based on their engineering feats. Their roads and water-supply structures represent both a demonstration of the strength of their powers of organisation and their technical knowledge.

became typical features of the façade articulation in Hellenistic architecture. Whereas previously the private house was entirely inward-looking and of almost poverty-stricken simplicity, palatial dwellings, colonnaded streets, statues of wealthy citizens and pompous tombs began to appear.

Emancipated man in classical Greece had built temples which did not impose a prescribed spectacle and which respected the freedom of the observer. In contrast, the new architecture increasingly resembled a theatrical production and was intended to overpower the observer. However, although the excess and pomp are undeniable signs of the decline and fall of a formerly thriving culture, the perfection of Greek architecture has remained an integral part of architecture to the present day.

THE ARCHITECTURE OF THE ROMAN EMPIRE 300 B.C.–300 A.D.

The dual legacy

Rome was heavily influenced by Greek culture from a very early stage. The Etruscans, who probably emigrated to northern Italy from Asia Minor, joined the hill settlements on the Tiber to form a single entity and called the settlement Rome. In the third century B.C., already strongly influenced by Greek culture, Rome succeeded in spreading its dominion to Greece and Asia Minor.

The Greeks who lived there were no longer dependent on the city states in the motherland, which the Romans conquered at the beginning of the following century, and had developed an architectural style which was only loosely based on

the classical models. Possibly influenced by the Etruscans, they tended to favour axial orientation and monumentality, crowding several temples on one site, as in the temples at Selinus in Sicily for example.

During the reign of Emperor Augustus, this dual legacy led to the development of an independent Roman style in art and architecture which lasted for over four hundred years. The engineering know-how of the Etruscans in road, bridge and tunnel building was perfected, as was their skill at building arches. The elements of classical Greek architecture were degraded to the level of pure decoration; for example, on the Coliseum where the column orders concealed the load-bearing system consisting of rows of arches on each floor. It is no accident that the Corinthian capital, already very popular in the Hellenistic era, was the most popular of the classical orders in Rome. To make it even more resplendent, richly decorated volutes flourished on top of the wreath of acanthus leaves, converting it to a composite capital. The cornices which protruded at right angles above the purely decorative columns in front of the façade also developed into a typical decorative detail.

The regular street grids of Etruscan towns and Greek colonies were adopted in the area of town planning; however, north-south and east-west axes were added. The forum, based on the Greek agora, which was the centre of public life in the polis, was situated near the intersection of these two roads. The Romans made it into a closed-off square surrounded mostly by longitudinal public buildings such as the basilica (mainly used as a hall of commerce and justice), triumphal arches and temples. Like the Etruscan version, the temples stood on a high

Coliseum, Rome, dedicated 80 A.D.

After the murder of Emperor Nero, the Flavians erected an enormous amphitheatre for gladiatorial games and beast fights on the site of an artificial lake within a rambling villa built by Nero. This was the first stone amphitheatre to be built in Rome and replaced the previously commonplace temporary timber structures. An ingenious system of staircases, similar to those found in today's stadiums, made it possible to clear individual levels very quickly. Entrance was free. Each social group was seated according to its social rank. The exterior four-storey ring wall reaches a height of 50 metres and consists entirely of travertine blocks. The semi-columns on the piers between the arches have Tuscan capitals on the first floor, Ionic on the second and Corinthian on the third. This vertical arrangement of the classical orders was to become a very important feature in Renaissance palaces.

podium with an open flight of steps leading to the entrance, whilst the back and side cella walls were plain or decorated with engaged columns.

Town planning activity was also evident in the magnificent theatres, stadiums and thermal baths. The villa, with its gardens, intricate terrace complexes, colonnaded halls and porches – some of which extended into the sea – showed the significant status of the private sphere. A considerable increase in city dwellers also created the need for high-density high-rise accommodation which marked the birth of construction on a mass scale.

Expression of power and compulsion for expansion

Architecture was an expression of power for the Romans. The government commissioned the construction of civil buildings everywhere by the army: it had a monopoly on natural construction materials and bricks were produced by state-owned brick works. The fact that the arch became the most formative element in Roman architecture is symptomatic of this: whereas the colonnades used in the Greek peristyle conveyed a sense of tranquillity and stasis, the rows of arches (arcades) were forceful and dynamic. The arches strive upwards only to return again and again to the earth to form the beginning of a new arch, thus propagating themselves over any distance. This gives them an expansive dimension, extending into the distance, which is consistent with the compulsion for expansion which reigned during the Roman Empire. It succeeded in conquering extensive areas, to which it exported its architecture, constructing long-distance roads and boring deep into the landscape with its piping, which ran partly through aqueducts, conveying spring water across long distances to the towns.

By applying vaulting and dome techniques to ever larger dimensions, the Romans succeeded in creating enormous spaces without intermediary supports. Their version of today's most common building material, concrete, which they manufactured using lime, rubble, water and volcanic sand from nearby Pozzuoli, was indispensable to this development. For example, the dome of the Parthenon was constructed using concrete, although for structural reasons it is almost impossible to tell from the outside. The first great religious building of Ancient Rome, this centrally-planned building was completely inward-looking.

The interiors of most public buildings also showed the Roman predilection for axial orientation. This effect was reinforced by the decoration, especially the majestic paint work. Otherwise, much of the prestigious and majestic architecture was a matter of appearance rather than reality; marble facing, mosaics and stucco work often concealed cheap brick, rubble and imitation stone.

In subsequent centuries, Roman architecture was characterised by gigantic proportions and increasing magnificence. The third century, however, brought an insecure period of external threats, crises in state finances and the internal collapse of the empire, which was ruled by a succession of rapidly-replaced emperors who were often at loggerheads.

EARLY CHRISTIAN AND BYZANTINE ARCHITECTURE 300–540

Christianity is recognised as the official religion

Emperor Diocletian tried to put an end to the power struggles by dividing the Roman Empire among four equal rulers. Following his retirement, however, the conflicts were rekindled and in 312 Constantine I emerged as the sole victor. Part of Constantine's ruling strategy was to bring about a reconciliation with the Christian church, which had previously been vehemently outlawed. Christianity, which had a particularly strong following among the poor, offered a mystical power which the empire lacked, although the hierarchical structure of the church gave it a certain transparency. The price paid by the Christian church for its promotion to official religion by Emperor Theodosius in 391 was to relinquish its hitherto sacrosanct refusal to engage

Pantheon, Rome, 118–25 A.D.

The impressive simplicity of interior of this building, which stands in the heart of the Campus Martius and was dedicated to all gods, arises from the fact that its diameter is the same as its height. It is lit from a single circular opening in the crown of the coffered dome, which forms a perfect hemisphere with a diameter of exactly 43.3 m. The walls of this brick building are encrusted with thin marble slabs. Volcanic rubble was added to the mortar to reduce the weight of the dome. Support is provided by a system of relieving vaults and arches concealed within the masonry. The Pantheon, which is surrounded by buildings on all sides and has a gabled façade, originally looked like a normal temple.
Pantheons also functioned in the Hellenistic era as temples of the ruler who had himself represented as an equal among gods. With this building, Emperor Hadrian replaced a building from the time of Augustus and demonstrated his ideological links with the founder of the Empire.

S. Sabina on the Aventine Hill, Rome 422–32

Following the Edict of Milan, numerous large Christian buildings were constructed in the 4th century. They were modelled on the interiors and additive design principle of Roman public buildings. In addition to the Early Christian centrally planned buildings, which were mainly built as memorial churches on the sites of martyrs, graves (martyria) and baptisteries, places of assembly for congregations – ecclesiae – were also required. These were generally modelled on the Roman basilica.

One of the best preserved examples of these Early Christian basilicas is S. Sabina on the Aventine Hill in Rome. The low side aisles are separated from the nave by rows of arches supported by Corinthian columns. A large clerestory is perforated by semicircular arched windows. The timber roof structure is open. The altar stands in a semicircular apse which is decorated with mosaics. Simplicity and an abundance of light are typical features of Early Christian buildings.

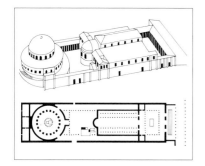

Church of the Holy Sepulchre, Jerusalem. Begun under Constantine in 326

Elevation and plan
From left to right: sepulchre rotunda (two-storey ambulatory, three-storey domed central building), courtyard with arcades, five-aisle basilica, atrium.
The Church of the Holy Sepulchre was a model for numerous centrally planned buildings until well into the Middle Ages.

San Vitale, Ravenna, 522–47

Octagonal, centrally planned church built by Justinian, Emperor of the Eastern Roman Empire, is the acknowledged model for Charlemagne's palatine chapel in Aachen, Germany.

in violence, a development which also brought the empire's armies some desperately needed manpower.

The church, of course, needed buildings which reflected its new status. This can be explained not only in terms of the desire to make a statement about its new position of power, or the fact that former places of prayer were now too small. The old temples were only open to priests – ordinary people paid homage to the gods from outside – and the Christians needed spacious buildings where their congregations could assemble. Early Christian architecture developed a wide variety of models and solutions based on existing architectural forms: emperors' mausoleums served as models for martyr's shrines, thermal baths as baptisteries and the originally secular basilica – halls of justice and commerce, assembly rooms and venues for appearances by the (god) emperor when he held court – became the Christian basilica, a church. The most important innovation imposed on these models was the need for a clear longitudinal emphasis along the nave to the altar and bishop's seat. Thus the concept of the rectangular building with uninterrupted longitudinal emphasis was born. The Early Christian basilicas also had a short transept to the east of the nave (later extended to give the cruciform plan of the Romanesque churches). The precise history of the emergence of this plan is unclear. It is possible that the new architectural features reflected a shift from the notion of a god in the form of the Roman emperor to

the idea of the Christian God: it is therefore possible that the plan of the church as place of assembly was developed from the plan of the emperors' fora, the market places which were the centre of public life.

In the early days of Christianity as the official religion, existing temples were often rededicated for use as churches. In many cases old foundations and mismatched columns were also used for the new churches: the old buildings and their architectural features were now allowed to serve the "real" God.

The Roman Empire may well have placed great emphasis on pomp and splendour in its heyday, but all that adorns the exterior of the Emperor Constantine's audience hall in Trier (early 4th century) are blind arcades enclosing two rows of otherwise unadorned semi-circular arched windows. Early Christian basilicas were equally modest. The baldachin-covered emperor's platform in the apse was replaced by the "Lord's table", the altar. Early basilicas were often built on the sites of saints' graves. Singers stood in the area in front of the altar which is why this part of the building became known as the choir.

The domed buildings of the "second Rome"

Due to confusion caused by the migration of peoples, Italy was no longer able to exercise much influence within the western half of the Empire, which had been divided in 395. The centre of power, and hence of architectural development, shifted to

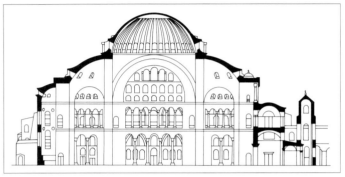

Anthemios of Tralles and Isidoros of Miletus, *Hagia Sophia*, Constantinople, 532–37, interior (left), elevation (top), longitudinal section (above)

HAGIA SOPHIA

Heavenly light floods the interior of the "Church of Holy Wisdom" in Constantinople, now known as Istanbul. When the Emperor Justinian saw the completed building for the first time, he is reputed to have said "Solomon, I have outdone you!"

The meaning of architecture underwent a transformation in Early Christian times. Individual forms and types may have been adopted from ancient architecture but they were reinterpreted. Buildings were now intended to declare the glory of God so the whole – like the parts – assumed a symbolic meaning. The fact that Justinian sees himself, along with his architects Anthemios of Tralleis and Isidoros of Milet, as a counterpart to the Biblical King

Solomon, who built the great temple in Jerusalem, shows the importance assumed by the Biblical tradition. The central plan and longitudinal emphasis are combined in a unique way. The powerful pendentive dome rests on four piers, the horizontal thrust of which is abutted to the east and west by half-domes and to the north and south by a system of arches. Two walls which are perforated by numerous windows and arches filter the light. The static significance of individual architectural elements is not emphasised. The inner walls are sheathed in shimmering polychrome mosaic like a reflection of God's love. Unlike ancient Greek architecture, this architecture finds fulfilment in the presentation of its inherent laws; its purpose is to make religion capable of being experienced on a symbolic level; the architecture carries the meaning.

the East. In 330, Constantine established the second capital of the empire in the small city of Byzantium, renaming it Constantinople (Istanbul since 1930). Constantinople subsequently became the metropolis of the Eastern Roman or Byzantine Empire. The model of the circular Roman temple – the outstanding example of which is the Pantheon in Rome – was adopted and developed in the East, especially when Justinian I began trying to restore the power and influence of the old empire. The most important domed buildings of this period are San Vitale in Ravenna, which was the seat of the Byzantine governor in Italy, and the Hagia Sophia in Constantinople.

Lightness and elegance replaced the mass and power of "old" Rome as the predominant impression conveyed by these buildings. More and more arches and domes were balanced on top of each other for structural as well as aesthetic reasons: lateral ambulatories and semi-domes acted as abutments for the thrust of the main dome which, like all arched or vaulted structures, exerted a lateral thrust on the columns or walls. The domes of Constantinople, the "second Rome", symbolised the cosmos and heaven. The centrally planned churches became an architectural model which has, in part, remained the prescribed model for Christian churches in the East to the present day.

Influence and
independence

ISLAM

622–1600

Modest spatial requirements

The Hagia Sophia was the architectural expression of Emperor Justinian's dream to confer the greatness of the old Roman Empire onto the Byzantine (Eastern Roman) Empire. Despite this highly effective gesture, a threat to the empire emerged ca. 570 in Mecca with the birth of Muhammed, who went on to build a new religion and empire which gradually eroded the power of Byzantium. Islam brought considerable political power to its prophet, who succeeded in uniting the tribes on the Arabian peninsula. Within one century of Muhammed's death in 632, the caliphs (Arabic for "followers") had established an empire which extended from Spain to India.

Unlike the Christian God, Allah (the Islamic name for "the god") is never depicted in visual images. Allah should never be imagined as having a human form and figurative representations are absolutely forbidden under Islamic law. Muslims tend to assemble for prayer in the mosque on Fridays at noon, even though their faith does not actually stipulate that they must come to the building. The five daily prayers can be said anywhere, facing Mecca and following ritual washing.

The architectural ambitions of the new religion were initially extremely modest. Neither the Prophet nor the "Four Orthodox Caliphs" appear to have commissioned the construction of larger buildings. In addition, the Arabs had for the most part been divided into nomadic tribes and had not developed a major architectural culture. Therefore, buildings from older religions were often converted to mosques in the colonised areas.

Competitive splendour

The situation was different in places invested with a particular symbolical significance (The Dome of the Rock, Jerusalem), or where the new religion encountered other majestic religious buildings, such as those built by the Christians in Syria. The Umayyads felt challenged by them. The Great Mosque in their capital city, Damascus, became the architectural model for all houses of god in the Umayyad dynasty.

The original model for the mosque is acknowledged to be the Prophet's house in Medina. It was a place of private and collective prayer, political assembly and negotiation, a centre of theological education and court of justice, a home for the homeless faithful and even a hospital. It finally became the burial place and seat of government of the caliphs. Individual parts of the mosque were eventually designed or reserved for most of these functions, which helped them to preserve their importance.

Based on the fundamental Arabic dwelling with its covered hall built on palm tree trunks, the mosques consist of a colonnaded hall (haram), the back wall (qibla) of which faced Mecca. The qibla was distinguished from the other walls by a niche (mihrab) which was usually crowned by an arch and flanked by columns. It was the place where the prayer leader stood. Columns or piers in the haram were usually linked by rows of arches which ran parallel (and in some cases perpendicular) to the qibla wall. The aisle leading to the mihrab was accentuated by its greater width and, in some

---

622: Muhammed's emigration from Mecca to Yathrib-Medina ("City of the Prophet"); beginning of the Islamic era.

630: Return of Muhammed to Mecca. He cleanses the city and the Kaaba, the old Arabic deity, of the worship of false gods; the new teaching triumphs in Arabia.

632: Muhammed dies in Medina.

632–61: Era of the "Four Orthodox Caliphs"; rapid spread and establishment of Islam; codification of the teaching of Muhammed.

661–750: Umayyad Dynasty with Damascus as capital; consolidation of a unified Arabic culture and the Islamic empire.

710–11: Beginning of conquest and Arabic colonisation of Spain.

756–1031: Emirate (since 929 Caliphate) of Cordoba ruled by the Spanish Umayyad; high point of Islamic art and culture in the West.

750–1258: Dynasty of the Abbasid caliphs with Baghdad as capital; suppression of Arabic and predominance of Persian culture in art and science; cultural high point under Harun al-

Rashid (786–809) and al-Mamun (813–833).

909–1171: Shiite opposition caliphate of the Fatimides in Cairo; new impulses for Islamic art.

1256–58: Invasion of Persia by the Mongols; conquest and destruction of Baghdad.

1453: The Turks conquer

Constantinople and establish the Ottoman Empire (the Balkans, North Africa, Mediterranean islands); Turks become a major European power.

1501–1722: Safavid dynasty in Persia; new high point of Islamic art.

1526–1858: Islamic Empire of the Great Mughal in India; independent artistic school; decline in the 18th century.

Mosque decoration with flowers: Islamic ornamentation.

The Dome of the Rock, built under caliph Al-Malik, Jerusalem, 687–92

The Dome of the Rock (Arabic: Qubbut as-Sahra) is a political-religious creation which the caliph built with the aim of making Jerusalem the religious centre of Islam (instead of Mecca and Medina). He commissioned an octagon with a centred plan (without orientation to Mecca) to be built over the rock, which the Jews honoured as "Mount Moriah", the place of Abraham's sacrifice, and which Muslims honoured as the legendary site of Muhammed's ascension into heaven. The old Temple of Solomon is also reputed to have stood on this site. Thus, in the Dome of the Rock, Abd al-Malik planned a common symbol for Judaism, Christianity and Islam.
The octagon is inscribed by two concentric ambulatories which were intended for ritual processions (like those around the Kaaba in Mecca). The inner circle is crowned by the powerful gold dome. There are four gates facing the four points of the compass. The exterior of the octagon is decorated up to window level with slabs of Turkish faience. Valuable ornaments, crowns and symbols of dominion are depicted in the interior. The Syrian-Byzantine architects who built the Dome of the Rock in a conscious spirit of competition with the Christian monuments in the city, appear to have been familiar with ancient and gnostic numerical symbolism and implemented it geometrically in the design. The Dome of the Rock was converted to a Christian church during the rule of the Crusaders (1099–1187).

cases, greater height. In front of the prayer hall was a courtyard surrounded by colonnades, with a fountain in the middle for ablutions and a tower from which the faithful could be called to prayer (minaret).

In its efforts to compete on an architectural level with other religions, Islam adopted formal elements and sometimes even existing structures from late ancient, Early Christian, Persian, Sassanian, and Indian architecture. However, the interiors of the Islamic buildings remained relatively unimpressive: Islamic religious philosophy does not provide the mosque with a focal centrepiece comparable to the altar in Christian churches. The Great Mosque at Cordoba (785–late 10th century), which is seen as representing the crowning achievement of the Umayyad style, was extended from its original form of a simple colonnaded hall with outer court until it had 19 longitudinal and 35 transverse aisles. There was no regard for symmetry in the addition of these aisles, so the mihrab no longer remained on the central axis. As it merely indicates the orientation for prayer and the place where the imam stands, the mihrab does not have to be on the central axis.

However, the Great Mosque at Cordoba, eventually deformed through the insertion of a church following the Catholic re-conquest of Spain, did have a degree of opulence. Its enclosure wall was decorated with door panels, the arcades of the prayer hall were embellished with decorative strips, and elegantly intertwined bays melted into domes. Experts from Constantinople were brought to Cùrdoba to build the mosaics.

After 750, the Umayyads could only hold on to their power in Spain and established their own caliphate there. The rest of the Islamic Empire, which slowly declined from the second half of the 9th century, was ruled by the Abbasids, who founded a new capital at Baghdad in 762. Under the Abbasids, Sassanian architectural forms were imported from Persia. This can be seen in the Great Mosque at Samarra with its tunnel-vaulted hall (iwan) opening out onto an inner courtyard. Four such halls on each side of a square courtyard constituted the typical form of the madrasa, in which the (religious) instruction given in the mosque originally took place. This, combined with the introduction of domes from the 11th century onwards, changed the architecture of the mosque, above all in Persia.

Spiral Minaret, Great Mosque of Samarra (Iraq), 848–52

The 55-metre-high brick minaret stands on the central axis north of the largest fortress-like mosque in the Islamic world, which was built in 850 and could accommodate a congregation of over 100,000 for prayer.
Its form is based on the ziggurat in Babylon and probably reached Islam via Sassanian Persia.

Alhambra, Court of Lions, porticoed ambulatory, fountain, Granada, Spain, 14th century

The palace of the Nasrid princes in Granada is acknowledged as the most important example of Islamic palatial architecture. The Court of Lions, built between 1354 and 1391 and named after the basin at its centre, which rests on water-spouting stone lions, is the most famous part of the palace.
The photograph shows the axial view of the courtyard from one of the pavilions which stand at both ends of the complex. Small fountains softly bubble in these pavilions and the water is led from them to the centre of the courtyard through two channels.
The courtyard is completely enclosed by a portico, the pyramid-shaped roof of which rests on slim columns joined by slightly pointed arches. The skilfully carved plaster and ornamentation on the arcades emphasise the floating charm and delicate decor of the entire structure.

THE GREAT OTTOMAN ERA 1400–1600

The challenge of Constantinople

The Alhambra palace in Granada, built in the 13th and 14th centuries, was the residence of the last Muslim princes in Spain. It was a vast dream-like complex full of reflective pools, gently rippling fountains and buildings whose contours were blurred by stalactite vaults and other decorative details.

By the time Islamic rule in Spain had finally been superseded by the Reconquista in 1492, a new Muslim power had already become established at the other end of the Mediterranean. In the 11th–12th century, the Turks had progressed from Central Asia to Asia Minor and in the 14th century their dominion extended to the Balkans. Over the next decades it extended to Tunisia, the Arabian peninsula and north of the Black Sea. The Empire ruled by the Ottoman dynasty was crowned in 1453 with the conquest of Constantinople.

This brought a new flourishing of the city today known as Istanbul. The city which had been the "second Rome" and centre of orthodox Christianity, now became the capital of a Muslim empire. Naturally, this was reflected in its architectural appearance. The scale was obvious: the Hagia Irene and, even more so, the Hagia Sophia.

Happily, experience with domed structures went back as far as the 12th century. Thus the basis already existed for the Ottoman alternative to colonnaded mosques, which had previously only had small domes. Its high point was not reached until 1539 when Sinan, for whom the Hagia Sophia

was something of a fixation, was appointed court architect. Having built several other mosques, Sinan constructed his masterpiece – the Great Mosque for Sultan Selim II. This was not in Constantinople, which was already overcrowded with large domed mosques, but in Edirne, previously Adrianople, the first Ottoman residence in Europe. Here, Sinan towered domes and semi-domes on top of each other creating a building which, as a result of its height and compact structure, is monumental and weighty in effect. The slender pencil minarets, a typical feature of the Ottoman mosque, provide an elegant contrast with the vast domed central structure.

Clearly defined as opposed to elaborately staged spaces

The heyday of the domed mosque, which also represented the high point of Islamic architecture, disintegrated with the Western Renaissance, in which the dome played an equally important role. However, the Islamic houses of god were completely different from their Christian counterparts. Spatial sequences, the staging of depth and the dome as an artificial heaven could be omitted, as the mihrab did not have the significance of the altar.

Thus Sinan was not concerned with the creation of overpowering, elaborately staged spaces but clearly defined spaces. This is why the interiors of his mosques have nothing of the complexity of their exteriors. Here, the space does not consist of intertwined architectural elements but is enclosed by smooth shells and walls perforated by a multitude of windows without elaborate frames. It

Sinan: the Great Mosque for Sultan Selim II, Edirne, Turkey, 1570–74

The mosque for Sultan Selim II is the last great work of the legendary Ottoman architect Sinan, who was over eighty years old when it was built and called it his masterpiece.
Sinan chose a wide rectangular courtyard from which the mosque rises at the back as if from a mould. It is flanked by four minarets which shoot up to the sky like pencils. They enclose a dome which is 32 metres in diameter and lies over a room based on the Kaaba cube in Mecca. This room is raised above eight powerful octagonal pillars. The refined sobriety of the homogeneous prayer hall creates an impression of axial orientation through the location of the mihrab opposite the entrance hall. Thanks to Sinan's impressive manipulation of light, the entire building seems flooded with sunlight; it is seen as the greatest achievement of Ottoman architecture.

TAJ MAHAL

The Taj Mahal is a majestic mausoleum, which the Shah Jahan (ruled 1628–58) commissioned in commemoration of his wife Mumtaj Mahal, who died in childbirth. The shining white marble building stands outside the garden of Shahar Bag, as Shah Jahan wanted to be buried in a similar black marble mausoleum which he planned to have built on the opposite bank of the Yamuna river. In 1658, he was supplanted by his son Aurangzep who destroyed his father's plans and buried him beside his beloved wife in the Taj Mahal.

The complex is accessed through a red sandstone gateway which provides a conscious contrast to the white marble of the mausoleum. Having entered the complex, the observer faces the powerful mausoleum from a distance. The building is reflected in a long pool of water in the foreground.

The Taj Mahal has a square plan with slanting corners. A high tambour supports the enormous onion dome, which is 28 metres in diameter and 65 metres in height. Each side of the tambour is flanked by a 20-metre-high longitudinal hall (iwan), the frame of which exceeds the ceiling height. Pavilions on both sides of

the main dome form a pyramid-like link which gives the central building an upward thrust. This is reinforced by the four corner minarets which do not detract from the dominance of the central mausoleum. The Taj Mahal is strictly symmetrical on all sides and its transparency gives many nuances of colour with the movement of the sun during the day.

The interior of the mausoleum is defined by the planned procession of pilgrims and the central tomb chamber, which also links the four ancillary rooms on the diagonal axes of the building. The burial chamber is covered by a semi-dome, above which the second enormous onion dome rises. The latter is, however, only visible from the outside. A large unused blind space lies between the two domes.

The architect of the Taj Mahal is not known by name, a fact which has given rise to speculation. There is also much debate as to the extent to which the Taj Mahal can be seen as a fully independent building of the Indian Moghul tradition, and to what extent it was influenced by the Timuridic mausoleums and the Persian-Safavidic onion domes.

is decorated with mosaics, geometric or floral planar ornamentation or with decorative scripts. These are abstract forms developed because of the ban on figurative representation, which are important in terms of their contribution to the overall impression of mosques. All this has proved sufficient to inspire Western observers to use the terms "fairy tale majesty and beauty" in describing the most famous and typical works of Islamic art. These terms are revealing. Texts, illustrations and films, which located the stories from "A Thousand and One Nights" in medieval-Islamic architecture, have led to most members of Western civilisation

being reminded of the imaginary world of fairy tales when they see such buildings. The architecture of the East is ultimately alien to them. This association is so deeply rooted that the European and even Early Christian architecture which was adopted, further developed and propagated by Islam seems alien. Most Westerners would probably identify the Hagia Sophia, once the greatest Christian church, as a mosque – even without the minaret which was later added. Islam left its architectural traces in Europe. However, its influence on European architecture is reflected almost exclusively in ornamentation.

Castles for God and
His Emperor

THE
ROMANESQUE
PERIOD

750–1250

CAROLINGIAN AND OTTONIAN ARCHITECTURE 750–1024

In the bosom of the Church

The (Western) Roman Empire, which had been in decline for some time, finally collapsed under the pressure of invasions by migratory peoples. The demise of this powerful regime marked the beginning of a period of great insecurity in large parts of Europe. The areas previously ruled by the Romans were subdivided between many rulers who often only succeeded in holding on to their power for relatively short periods. The state, justice and technology, i.e. the entire organisation behind human communities, disintegrated under these conditions. Living standards declined significantly and the development of the cities stagnated. All of this had a direct effect on cultural, and, in particular, architectural activity.

By contrast, the power of the Church was not limited to a few decades of rule and a relatively small geographical area. On the contrary, it was now able extend its influence over the entire territory of Europe. Following the demise of the Western Roman Empire, the Church became the most important promoter of culture.

The monasteries built by the Benedictine Order, founded in 529, played a particularly important role. They acted as cultural outposts in the often almost uncivilised locations in which they were situated. Ancient books were copied and translated, research and teaching were carried out, and even lay people who did not belong to the monasteries were given instruction in a wide variety of disciplines. Many of the monks, who normally specialised in particular crafts or academic disciplines, were advisors to princes. The monasteries also owned land to ensure their economic survival, another factor which contributed to their power. It was not uncommon for monasteries to serve as refuges from external threats in times of political instability when the rule of the fist often reigned supreme. For this reason, settlements tended to be built near them.

The legacy of Rome claimed

The political, economic and cultural influence of the Church was further enhanced when a powerful state entity emerged in the 8th century with the Frankish Empire. The alliance between the Church and this empire was later extended further by Charles the Great. This gave the Pope a certain degree of independence from the Byzantine Emperor. In return the Frankish King received legitimisation of his rule from the head of the Church. This pact reached its pinnacle during Christmas 800 when Charles the Great was crowned emperor by Pope Leo III in Rome.

The aim of linking up with the Ancient Roman Empire, which became more obvious with this re-establishment of the Western Empire, was also expressed in architecture. Apart from buildings which had been erected within or by the Byzantine Empire (for example in Ravenna), little of major, permanent or monumental importance had been built in Europe since the decline of the Western Roman Empire. The monumental stone building was revived under Charles the Great as a reflection both of the competition with Byzantine monarchy, which was still in its prime, and the claim to the legacy of high Roman culture. Due to the alliance between clerics and the crown, this revival was restricted almost exclusively to the construction of

751: Pippin succeeds the Merovingian ruler Childerich III as the first Carolingian King of the Franks.

800: Charles the Great is crowned emperor by Pope Leo III.

1066: William the Conqueror defects King Harold II at the Battle of Hastings and is crowned in Westminster.

1073: Pope Gregory VII's ban on religious appointments by lay people (appointment of bishops and abbots by the secular ruler) results in the investiture row with the emperor.

1077: King Henry IV succeeds in repealing Pope Gregory VII's ban through the pilgrimage of Canossa and in doing this reinforces his power in the German Empire.

1096: First crusade for the conquest of Jerusalem and dissolution of the power of Turkish Islam initiated by Pope Urban II.

1098: Abbot Robert of Citeaux founds the Cistercian order.

Around 1100: Jousting tournament spreads from France as competitive sport played by knights. Hildegard von Bingen, abbess and scholar fights irregularities in the church, writes religious and scientific works.

1119: Foundation of the first European university in Bologna (Paris ca. 1150, Oxford 1163, Salamanca 1218, Cambridge 1229).

1122: The Concordance of Worms brings a definitive end to the investiture row when Henry V declines investiture powers.

The Battle of Hastings as depicted on the Bayeux tapestry: King Harold is struck by an arrow.

1147: Bernard of Clairveaux starts 2nd crusade under Hohenstaufen King Konrad III.

1155: Frederick I crowned emperor Barbarossa in Rome.

1170–1220: Flourishing of courtly literature with Chrétian de Troyes, Wolfram von Eschenbach and Walther von der Vogelweide.

1215: English barons force King John I (at Runnymede) to grant the Magna Carta which recognises the privileges of towns, free movement of merchants, freemen's right of inheritance and free selection of bishops by the clergy.

1232: Emperor Frederick II makes his court in Palermo into the centre of Italian cultural life and grants important rights of sovereignty to the clerical and secular princes in Germany.

Ca. 1250: Carmina Burana, collection of medieval German songs.

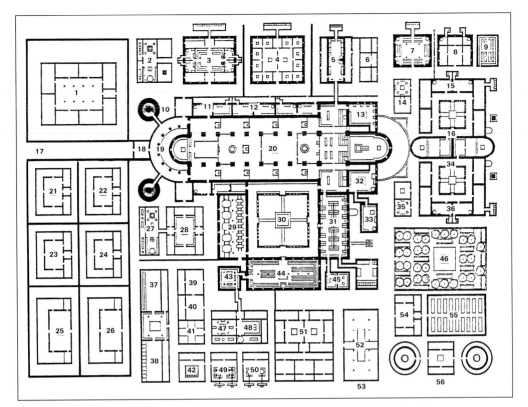

Parchment plan of a monastery
St. Gallen, ca. 820

1 house for the retainers of distinguished guests 2 farm buildings
3 accommodation for distinguished guests 4 external school 5 Abbot's house 6 farm buildings 7 slaughter house 8 doctor's surgery and pharmacy
9 herb garden 10 bell tower 11 porter
12 school head 13 library 14 bathroom and kitchen 15 hospital 16 cloister
17 entrance 18 reception hall 19 *choir*
20 monastery church (*basilica*)
21 servants 22 sheep raising 23 pigs
24 goats 25 mares 26 cows
27 kitchen 28 inn 29 store room and wine cellar 30 cloister 31 dormitory and heated room 32 sacristy 33 host bakery
34 cloister 35 kitchen 36 novice school
37 horses 38 oxen 39 cooperage
40 wood turner's workshop 41 barn
42 malt kiln 43 kitchen 44 refectory
45 bathroom 46 cemetery 47 brewery
48 bakery 49 crushing mill 50 mill
51 various craft workshops 52 threshing floor 53 corn barn 54 gardener's house
55 vegetable garden 56 poultry raising

The monastery plan shows the constituent parts of a Carolingian monastery to the last detail. At the centre of the complex stands the spacious monastery church with two free-standing round towers in front of the west façade. The cloister, from which the dormitory and refectory can be accessed, adjoins the southern end of the church. The size of the dormitory can be estimated at 12.5 × 28 m. The Abbot's residence, infirmary, wine cellar with individual barrels, barns and stables for different animals are all depicted in detail.
The plan of St. Gallen is unique for its time, i.e. early 9th century, as no other plans have survived which are earlier than the 12th century. The Benedictine order, for whom this plan was drawn up as a model for all monasteries, preserved many ancient building traditions, above all those concerning the organisation of life in a community. It is not known whether a monastery complex was ever built exactly on the basis of this plan.

churches and monasteries. There was, however, a price to be paid by the Church for this development: the pact involved making concessions to "secularisation". To put it in a more positive perspective, one could say that the Church became more involved with the Christian representation of this world as opposed to the next.

In architectural terms, this development was expressed in the emergence of the "double-ended" church plan. Evidence for this can be found as early as the plan for the St. Gall monastery church. The fact that a plan was drawn up for this entire monastery complex shows that planned construction was indeed re-emerging. The organisation of various functions in the monastery site is also telling: the craftsmen's houses, workshops and barns are located on the west side of the site and the novice school, hospital and cemetery are in the east. Thus, in accordance with the traditional eastern orientation of churches, all "secular" matters are located in the west, whereas "sacred" functions are found in the east.

It therefore comes as something of a surprise to find that, in addition to the choir at the eastern end of the building, many churches now had an additional choir on the western side. This was initially explained in terms of greater interest in the worship of saints and relics. It was the view at the time that in order to pay homage to two patrons, a second main altar was required, which had to have the corresponding architectural form – i.e. a second choir. The "double-ended" plan, to which a second transept and a second crossing tower were also

added, soon became a symbol of secular power claims. The two towers on the complex west façade, which subsequently became quite common, were dedicated to the archangels Gabriel and Michael. According to holy scripture, the latter led the army of angels during the division of Heavenly Jerusalem. Installed thus on the western side of the church, Michael was intended to prevent the evil of the world from penetrating into the church building. The upper-storey chapels above the entrance, which were dedicated to Michael or Salvador, were also intended for the adoration of the angels. The throne of the emperor or king was situated at the western end of the church. Seated opposite the main altar, the ruler was presented as the earthly ally of the Archangel Michael.

In view of his position of power, it is hardly a coincidence that the first such "staging" of the role of king or emperor took place under – and for – Charles the Great. The Palatine church at his residence in Aachen had a large portal structure on the exterior: a setting for the monarch who took his place here, literally with the heavenly power at his back. San Vitale in Ravenna, the former residence of the Roman Emperors which Theoderic, the first great German founder of state, made his own after his triumph over the Western Roman Empire, is acknowledged as the model for this chapel. As a centrally planned building with galleries, the Palatine church at Aachen became not only the model for palace churches up to and during the 18th century, it was also adopted as a model for the westworks of the great churches.

Odo von Metz: *Palatine chapel*, octagon in the Aachen Cathedral with so-called "Throne of Charles the Great", ca. 800

The skeleton of the Palatine chapel at Aachen, which Charles the Great commissioned as an addition to his palace, was completed in 798 and consecrated by Pope Leo III in 805. It now forms the central core of the cathedral. The architect Odo von Metz based the chapel on San Vitale in Ravenna which originates from the first half of the 6th century. The octagon is inscribed in a two-storey sixteen-cornered structure. The upper storey with the throne was intended for the Emperor and his retainers.
Aachen became the centre of the Frankish Empire under Charles the Great. The chapel is today seen as the most important example of Carolingian architecture.

The origins of this design feature can be explained by the fact that Frankish rulers resided in different places throughout their empire and did not want to build palaces. The Emperor and his court increasingly availed themselves of monastery churches, to which a westwork had been added. This usually took the form of a square shaft flanked on three sides by galleries; the side facing the actual church remained open. As the shaft was always lit by a window above the lean-to roof over the galleries, the westwork was crowned with a tower and was higher than the nave and side aisles.

To provide a fitting presentation of the court entourage in the chapel, the seats were allocated on the basis of rank. In Aachen, the emperor could reach his gallery by climbing the spiral staircase in the corner towers of the westwork. The choir stood in the gallery above him.

Poised between the secular and spiritual ruler

The westwork stood facing a series of structures in the east. These structures were dominated by the crossing tower which rested on four arches above the intersection of the transept and the nave. This meant that the choir had to have its own bay, which emphasised the differentiation of the "excluded" (i.e. clearly delineated), crossing with its four transverse arches from the nave, and which, like the latter (and the westwork), formed a space of its own. This series of structures replaced the former

longitudinal emphasis running straight from the entrance to the choir.

Thus, the crossing became the basic module. Given the level of technical expertise available at the time, all that could be built above it was a tower resting on four arches of equal dimensions, i.e. with a square cross-section. Clear, almost symmetrical complexes emerged with naves symbolically spanning the area between the eastern structures which served the spiritual ruler, and the western complex, which served the secular ruler. St. Michael's in Hildesheim is an outstanding example of this architectural model, which was mandatory for all churches under the Ottonian, Ludolfing and Saxon rulers who succeeded the Carolingians in 919.

Contained, strong, weighty and sombre

It is important, however, not to imagine that all Romanesque buildings were mere copies of a strict model. For example, the Palatine church in Aachen and San Vitale in Ravenna, on which it was modelled, have little in common when it comes to the details; the significant features were the basic form and spirit of the building. Thus the interior of the Palatine church is far more contained, strong, weighty and sombre than San Vitale. There are no curved niches but an octagon clearly defined by the pillars and arches at ground-floor level.

Contained, strong, weighty, sombre – these adjectives can be applied to Romanesque architecture in general, or at least to that of the early Romanesque period which spread throughout Western and Central Europe with the Carolingians. The term "Romanesque", first used in the 19th century, is not entirely accurate and can be misleading. A quick glance shows that these buildings had little in common with those of Ancient Rome. Romanesque architecture was not only found among the Roman peoples, i.e. those who had been influenced by ancient Roman culture. The Frankish Empire joined areas ruled by Rome for centuries with others in which comparatively uncivilised Germanic tribes lived. An attempt was made in late-19th century Germany – mainly for nationalistic reasons but not without justification – to replace the term "Romanesque" with "Germanesque".

The Romanesque style on the whole seems like a reaction to times of confusion and decline: its sobriety and coarseness would appear to reflect the loss of affluence and knowledge suffered during this period. The churches and monasteries look like fortresses with their thick, heavy walls. This powerful earthy impression is further evoked by the horizontal emphasis achieved with the help of round arch friezes, triangular gables, cornices, blind arches and blind arcades, extensive reduction of window size, usually rather flat decor and rejection of plaster. The effect of the stone is pure, the tectonics almost primitive: the structures seem clearly defined but modest and simplified.

The Corinthian capital which was the favourite of the Classical orders in the Roman Empire was covered with so much sumptuous decoration that its supporting function was almost completely concealed. By contrast, the Romanesque cushion capital – a mixture of a cube and a sphere which optically links the round shaft and square abacus – demonstrates with almost rude directness that it forms the transition from the support (the column) to the load (the arch). Its sides were initially bare.

The spatial impression evoked by the series of structures in Romanesque churches is static, sober and almost awkward. The crypts, which were increasingly added beneath the choir to house the tombs of the highly respected dead and growing cult of relics, increased the impression of disintegration. The altar area had to be raised to accommodate them. On the other hand, these series of structures with their complexes of transepts, towers and apses, which were generally based on liturgical requirements, gave Romanesque architects the opportunity to create an external image of majestic, richly structured "heavenly castles" or "godly palaces".

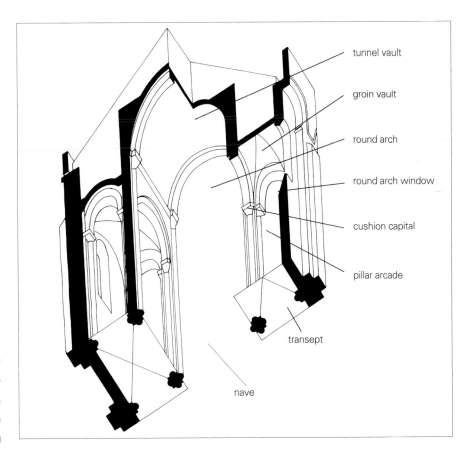

Poitiers, cathedral, 1166–14th century, isometric projection.

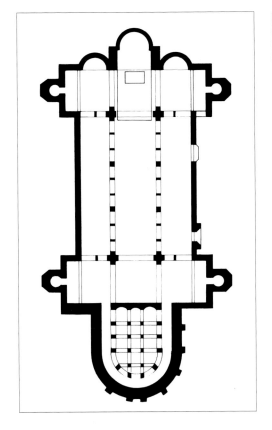

St. Michael's, Hildesheim, 1010–33

St. Michael's in Hildesheim, Germany, for which the corner stone was laid by Bishop Bernward in 1010 and which was consecrated in 1033, is the most uniform and complete existing Ottonian church. The painted timber ceiling originates from the 13th century. The plan, the eastern alignment of which is shown in the photograph, shows the equilibrium and rationality of the structure. The main entrance is concealed in the ambulatory of the second choir on the western side above the crypt; four other entrances provide access to the church from the monastery to the north and the town to the south. The square crossing is the central element of the plan, as both the length of the nave (three squares) and that of the transepts (one square on each side) are based on it. The crossings are marked by four powerful pillars which alternate with pairs of columns. The doubled alternating system of supports evokes a rhythmical, rather than static, spatial quality. This is further emphasised by the arches with their alternating red and white strips of stone.

Together with the cathedral, St. Michael's monastery church forms the centre of the early medieval cathedral city.

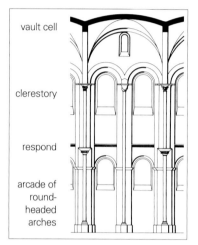

vault cell

clerestory

respond

arcade of
round-
headed
arches

Speyer Cathedral, begun between 1024 and 1033, consecrated in 1061. Groined vaulting of the nave and transept 1056–1106 (cf. photograph)

Three zoned wall articulation of Speyer Cathedral following conversion of the building in the late 11th century (cf. diagram)

Speyer Cathedral was a symbol of imperial power for the Salian (Frankish) emperors who ruled from 1024 to 1105. The impressive, massive, yet aesthetically clear, architecture of both the interior and exterior emphasise the self confidence of Emperor Henry IV (1052–1106). Henry IV was constantly involved in disputes with the Popes of his time who postulated the primacy of the Pope over the Emperor. The desire to erect a monument in stone to German imperial dignity and worth, as demonstrated by Speyer Cathedral, can only be understood against this historical background. The Salian emperors were laid to rest in the crypt of their cathedral.

THE HIGH ROMANESQUE PERIOD UNDER THE SALIANS AND HOHENSTAUFENS 1024–1260

Majestic imperial cathedrals as an expression of opposition to the Pope

The efforts made by Romanesque architecture to achieve greater heights of monumentality and representation were most prevalent in the former eastern area of the Frankish Empire, where the western empire was continued by the Salians and – from 1125 – the Hohenstaufens. Imperial cathedrals like those in Worms and Speyer represent the pinnacle of Romanesque architecture. Against the background of a growing conflict for supremacy between the Emperor and the Pope, these cathedrals demonstrate the monarch's claim that the Church would continue to have a role to play in what was called the "Roman" empire but was, in fact, under German rule.

Thus the Romanesque style became more and more refined, and consequently more expressive, up to the end of the 11th century: the growing mastery of construction techniques also contributed to this development. The earlier churches, most of which were flat structures spanned by timber roofs – which usually burned down at some stage because the interiors were lit using candles and torches – were gradually replaced by vaulted stone structures.

Vaults exert a strong lateral thrust which requires the support of massive exterior walls. The vaulting of the naves gave rise to the replacement of columns by powerful pillars. Other columns (vaulting shafts) were built in front of these pillars and the transverse arch which supported the vault rested on them. The most simple form of vaulted structure – groin vault built above a square – was realised using the so-called crossing square plan. This was a square plan based on the crossing square as a module, on which all Romanesque basilicas are based. As each side aisle was usually half the width of the nave, there were two small squares on each side of the large central square. This provided a structural opportunity for the use of the existing technique of alternating system of supports: as each pillar had to support both the central vault and the side vaults, they became thicker and stronger.

Towards the end of the Romanesque period ribs began to replace the groins on the groined vault. The ribs, which were initially massive with semi-circular diameters, were later divided into numerous grooves. The ribs supported the load and transmitted it to the pillars, and this allowed the construction of lighter structures. The breaking-up of the wall mass was also achieved through optical features: gallery floors (triforia) were introduced above the arcades in an effort to articulate the wall surface. Unexpected optical finesse was achieved through the introduction of larger windows, small rows of apses carved into the walls of the choir apse, blind arches and more sculptural decorations, paintings and frescoes. Carolingian and Early Romanesque massing was replaced by more vertical, delicate, divided forms and spaces.

The religious orders: opponents of secularisation

Different approaches, many supported by the church, were developed in opposition to the idea of imperial representation in church buildings. The rivalry between the architectural styles aimed at formulating a clear church-related response to the expression of secular power with similarly impressive effects.

The majestic serial structures of the Romanesque period were not the only means of taking sides in this dispute. The Catholic Benedictine order of monks, for example, returned to the style of the simple Early Christian basilica. However, in view of the tension between the Emperor and the Pope, circles loyal to the head of the Church did not believe that it should simply submit and take second place to the pomp and splendour of the imperial cathedrals.

The Abbey church of Cluny, which was built between 1088 and 1130 as the northern seat of the order, which generally supported the Pope, is an extreme example of the Romanesque complex. It has two eastern transepts, two crossing towers plus four other towers and a two-storey ambulatory choir with radial chapels. It is significant that this eastern complex clearly dominated the two western towers, and the antechurch which was added at a later date.

The most radical break with this architectural style was made by the Cistercians, who split with the Benedictines following a major ideological dispute in 1098 and quickly became established all over Europe. Their allegiance to a pure, non-material religious faith was expressed not only in the poverty and asceticism of their lifestyle but also in their church buildings. The abbey churches of Clairveaux (founded in 1115) and Fontenay (1139–47) were built on the same plan and became models. This plan consisted of a simple nave terminated by a transept, which in turn was terminated by a small rectangular choir. There was no decoration or

SAINTE FOY

In 866, following a number of failed attempts, a monk from the Benedictine Abbey in Conques finally succeeded in appropriating the remains of the early Christian saint Fides (Foy in French) and bringing them back to the Abbey. The saint's relics soon gave rise to miracles in their new home in the monastery.

In the 9th century the relics were given a valuable gold shrine in the form of the enthroned saint.

The pilgrimage church of Sainte Foy is situated in a remote valley near Conques on the route to Santiago

Following a miracle in 985, the shrine was embellished even further: it is the only one of many such churches which has been preserved to the present day. As a station on the pilgrimage to Santiago de Compostela, the relics quickly brought the monastery great fame and fortune.

The new abbey church, which was started in 1050 to replace the existing Carolingian building, was influenced by this turn of events. The most important part of the church, the choir, was completed by 1065 and the relics were ceremoniously deposited in their new sanctuary.

The church was completed up to the west façade by the end of the 11th or early 12th century. As was often the case with medieval churches, the two towers were not completed, being added in the late 19th century. Despite this, the building was a remarkable artistic entity; it is well preserved and unadulterated by later alterations.

Sainte Foy at Conques, a village in the southern French region of Aveyron, is the smallest representative of a group of pilgrim churches which were situated on the main route of the pilgrim trek to Santiago de Compostela, and were important places of pilgrimage in their own right. They included St. Martin's in Tours and St. Martial in Limoges, which no longer exist, and the churches of St. Sernin in Toulouse and that of Santiago at Compostela itself, both which still stand. These

Tympanum sculpture above the main portal depicting the Last Judgement

churches all have shared characteristics: a wide nave flanked by side aisles. All the side aisles have quadrant vaults in the galleries which buttress the nave and transept vaults. For safety reasons, there is no clerestory in the nave; the interior is lit indirectly by large windows in the aisles and galleries. The galleries in Conques and the other pilgrim churches were to have been continued along the front of the transept. However, in the end it was decided that a passageway would suffice. The ambulatory choir with radial chapels, which had just been developed in France, was used to terminate the eastern end of the church. This meant that the liturgical functions were concentrated in the main choir and gave the faithful the opportunity to walk past the relics, which were housed in a correspondingly located crypt beneath the choir. In Conques, which was planned as an attraction for pilgrims, the relics were displayed in the more practical location of the choir – predicting a custom later introduced with the Gothic tradition. There was no crypt which was otherwise typical of the Romanesque churches. This meant that the crowds of pilgrims could use the choir ambulatory more comfortably. The three apses on the ambulatory and the four on the eastern side of the transept were used for the many masses celebrated by the monks.

The exterior view of the choir reveals a charming graduation of stereometrical elements which culminate in the octagonal crossing tower. The clarity and harmony of the articulation and the strong vertical emphasis of the interior are equally impressive. The nave and transept have the same two-storey elevation: very high arcaded openings to the transepts, above which there are large round-headed openings with free-standing load-bearing columns reaching up to the gallery floors. At the arcade level, semi-columns alternate with rectangular responds from one bay to the next. This rhythmical system is not found in any of the other pilgrim churches. The responds "serve" the transverse arches which optically support the vault. In the sanctuary, the choir apse, slim columns support stilted arches, above which there are two rows of arched galleries each with seven arches, of which three are pierced. In the lower row, they open onto an unlit arch above the

The church interior: view along the naturally lit main nave to the altar in the east

choir ambulatory; in the upper row they allow daylight to enter.

Even if Sainte Foy, like most Romanesque churches, seems bare and colourless today, it is important to try to imagine the rich, colourful, pompous and varied interior which would have fascinated the pilgrims with its multitude of new and captivating impressions. The capitals and corners were designed like imaginary animal figures, described by the French art historian Focillion as figures from a horrific collective nightmare. The arches and walls were covered with biblical pictures and texts, and tapestries hung on the otherwise bare and hostile walls. The church's treasures and riches were not hidden behind locked doors but displayed on the altar in all their pomp and majesty.

The tympanum, i.e. the arched gabled area above the main western doorway of the church, with its figurative high relief depiction of the Last Judgement which promises reward for believers and punishment for non-believers, is sophisticated and highly effective. The blessed, who sit on the right of Christ (i.e. on the left-hand side of the tympanum), and the damned in hell on the other side, are strongly emphasised in the three-tier relief. An unusual feature of this tympanum is the profusion of Latin inscriptions; various events from the life of St. Fides are also depicted. These were no doubt pointed out to the pilgrims in sermons.

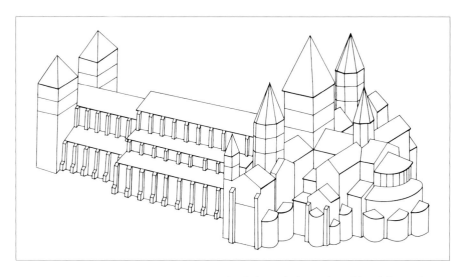

Cluny, Abbey Church III, 1088 beginning of new building by Abbot Hugo. Reconstructed sketch of the basilica which was almost completely destroyed in 1807

Cluny was the most important Benedictine monastery north of the Alps. The "Cluniastic reform", which had widespread architectural reverberations, originated here. Above all, the emphasis of the orientation of a church with the assembled altars at the eastern end can still be recognised in this third and significantly more complex church building. Westworks and choirs at the western end were, by contrast, strongly condemned.

stained-glass windows; the ashlar of the walls was carefully hewn or plastered. The Cistercians did, however, soon relax the rules governing their lifestyle and architecture. Nonetheless, the ban on towers was upheld: the bells were housed in a timber turret.

ALTERNATIVES TO IMPERIAL ARCHITECTURE

Italy – torn between loyalty to the emperor and a sense of urban identity

As a result of the demise of the Western Roman Empire and the expansion of the Arab empires, which led to a temporary blockade of international trade with the East, Italian towns were in crisis. The political and cultural centre lay north of the Alps – despite the fact that Northern Italy and Rome, and later the entire peninsula, belonged to the Frankish (and later "Roman-German") Empire. This was to provide the link with the ancient Roman Empire.

The political disunity of Italy is reflected in the completely heterogeneous development of architecture in the different regions. During the 12th and 13th centuries, however, the further development of the Early Christian basilica tended to be favoured rather than that of the Romanesque church. The basilica-based churches generally had three aisles without transepts or towers, and the west façade was merely the terminating wall of the nave.

Despite this simplicity, some magnificent buildings were created, such as San Miniato al Monte in Florence (begun in 1018, façade from the 12th century). Here the flat inlay of dark and light marble created the illusion of a rich plastic articulation of fluted pilasters, a dwarf gallery and blind arcades, doors and windows. This design feature was common in Tuscany. The location of the crypt slightly below the altar and open to the nave, which raised the altar significantly, was equally common in the rest of Italy. The open timber roof truss, the apse mosaic and the coloured marble inlay on the interior walls of the choir and clerestory were such an obvious link with the late antique tradition that the Florentine architecture of the 11th and 12th centuries is most often referred to as the "Protorenaissance". This is because it predicts the early Italian Renaissance of the 15th century, which also theoretically moved towards ancient times.

Influences from oriental architecture can be found in other northern Italian ports and trading cities which became rich and powerful during this time. The domed building, reimported from Byzantium, spread through northern Italy from Venice. San Marco, the royal chapel of the Doges who ruled the city in the lagoon, was itself a successful example

Campo dei Miracoli (Cathedral, bell tower, baptistery and cemetery), Pisa, 11th–14th century

The architectural history of the Campo dei Miracoli began in 1063, with the laying of the foundation stone for the cathedral, which was consecrated in 1118. Although the remarkable ensemble of buildings was built over several centuries, it was possible to achieve an impressive uniformity, probably through the use of the same building material of white and coloured marble and the repetition of architectural features. The lively, light architecture and the elegance and grace of the omnipresent arches is vaguely reminiscent of Moorish-Norman forms. The decision to locate the complex – which would no doubt have achieved the same degree of fame even without the leaning tower – not at the centre of the urban life of the maritime and commercial town of Pisa, but in an isolated location on the periphery, further heightens its monumental effect.

of this architecture: two three-aisle basilicas super-imposed one upon the other, with domes, rose in splendour over the naves, the crossing and the choir. Dome-like structures also appeared elsewhere, for example in San Ambrogio in Milan (1117–55), where two of the six bays were linked with the help of a large groin vault. However, the dark impression evoked by this building arises partly from the fact that the side aisles are almost as high as the nave and there is thus no clerestory. Italian vaulted buildings were often lower than their German counterparts and usually seemed cave-like and gloomy. The façades offered a similarly archaic picture. San Michele in Pavia, which had the prestigious role of the coronation church of the German emperor in Lombardy, like San Ambrogio has a powerful stone façade in which windows, entrances, a cross and rough relief bands seem to have been carved almost arbitrarily. The dwarf gallery under the roof ridge of the gable slope is the only element which provides some light relief.

The work done in Pisa is of a completely different mood. Construction of the ensemble, consisting of the cathedral, bell tower, baptistery and cemetery, began in the 11th century when the imperial city was at the peak of its power. However, the project was not completed until the 14th century. Despite this, the homogeneity of the complex was preserved by use of the same materials and design features throughout: blind arcades and column galleries towered on top of each other break up the cathedral façade and the bell tower exterior (the famous "leaning tower of Pisa") in a way that is as exhilarating as it is simple.

Scandinavian timber churches

A completely independent version of the Romanesque style originated in Scandinavia. As in other parts of Europe which were not converted to Christianity until after the middle of the 1st century, most churches here were timber structures. Regional tradition and the fact that timber was a widely available local material probably had as much of a role to play here as the minimal cultural influence of the major southern and central European empires at the beginning of the 2nd century. Secular rulers in Scandinavia did not feel any compunction to celebrate and preserve their power for posterity in monumental religious buildings.

This does not, of course, mean that the Scandinavian stave churches, like those built in Heddal from the 11th century onwards, were primitive structures. On the contrary, their structural systems were highly complex and the buildings themselves presented richly diverse elevations. The

static and sculptural qualities of the timber were cleverly exploited (including carvings on gables and doors) thanks to the skills acquired in the rich ship-building tradition. The staves (corner post columns) extended from the floor to the ceiling and generally stood at the sides or corners of the main rooms. Sometimes they were also in the centre; the complex structure which braced them on all sides was clearly visible and logical in its order. In this the stave churches were similar to early Romanesque stone churches. The division of the interior space into ambulatories and aisles was clearly reflected in the exterior form, as each spatial entity had its own roof. The towering steep roofs crowned by roof ridges with protruding dragons' heads represented the creation of an individual architectural style which has little in common with those of other regions.

France paves the way

Events in France, which was as fragmented as Italy following the decline of the Frankish Empire, proved decisive for the further development of Western architecture. Because a central secular force like the empire no longer existed, very different schools of architecture were able to develop. Their main concern was the problem of vaulting, which could only be approached on an experimental basis. As structural calculations had yet to be developed,

Heddal, stave church, near Notodden (Telemark, Norway), built in the mid-13th century, restored 1952–54. View of altar and elevation

Norway, the land of timber, very much went its own way when it came to the construction of churches between 1000 and 1300. Some 1000 stave churches were probably built there during this period. These churches, which were built entirely of timber, take their name from the vertical pillars which make up the structural frame.
Various roofs stagger the building up to the sky; this effect is heightened by three peaked ridge turrets. The almost picturesque architecture, the variety of warm wood tones and the rich carvings, combine to give this church a unique charm. The covered ambulatory in the interior made it possible to hold processions in winter.

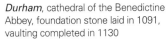

Durham, cathedral of the Benedictine Abbey, foundation stone laid in 1091, vaulting completed in 1130

Durham Cathedral is a Romanesque basilica with a transept featuring ribbed vaults (the first definite example of this type of vaulting in Europe), thick walls, supports and articulatory elements carrying the vaults.

Santiago de Compostela, pilgrimage church, Puerta de la Platería, ca. 1075–1128, numerous conversions

Despite its late Baroque envelope, the pilgrimage church in Santiago de Compostela, the last station on the St. James's pilgrim trek, is an excellent example of Romanesque architecture and architectural sculpture in Spain. The Puerta de la Platería (silversmiths' gate) on the southern transept is the only strictly Romanesque part of the façade.

experience and trial and error were the main methods and these often resulted in collapsed structures.

Church requirements also played a more important role than during the imperial empire. Thus the church at the important place of pilgrimage, Santiago de Compostela, was a clearly articulated longitudinal building with a homogeneous interior: the altars were grouped to the east so the clear orientation to the Almighty was recognisable. The west had merely the double façade which, having a prominent entrance, only served to emphasise the eastern orientation. The town is in Spain but the project was probably started by a French architect. As a three-aisle galleried basilica with transept, eastern choir, a barely emphasised crossing and a monumental double-tower façade in the west, it corresponded to a type developed in France.

Norman churches were also based on this model, of which St. Etienne in Caen (ca. 1070) is a prime example. The Norman school of architecture was, however, more successful in its experiments with the articulation and division of the walls. For artistic and technical reasons this led almost unavoidably to the development of the groined vault – because a tunnel vault divided only by transverse arches could not have matched the ground floor arcades formed using gradations and semi-columns so that no smooth wall surface remained. Around 1100, ribs were drawn under the groins of the arches, heralding a development in the direction of the Gothic style – optically if not structurally. This led to the aesthetic linking of wall and arch articulation.

Durham cathedral was built between 1091 and 1130. It is one of the many churches built in England following its conquest by the Normans in 1066, and is similar in layout to St. Etienne. Many typical features of English churches over the following

centuries can be found here: the combination of cathedral and monastery church which was unusual on the Continent, the isolated situation raised above the river Wear and the new form of transept basilica, which involved the shifting of the transept further into the centre of the building through the extension of the choir by four bays to the east. Durham has the first definitively dated rib vault, and the vaults over the side aisles were replaced with flying buttresses as abutment for the nave vaults. However, it was yet to emerge that this structure could be used to make the vaults lighter. The seeds of the Gothic period were clearly planted in Santiago de Compostela as in St. Etienne and Durham. However, it was the architectural school of the Île de France that later made it into an architectural style which would soon spread throughout the Western world.

CASTLE ARCHITECTURE IN THE MIDDLE AGES

The middle ages saw the era of feudalism, a system of land ownership by the nobility which over the centuries became more and more complex. The system, based on an intricate hierarchy extending from the vavasour to the sovereign and characterised by complicated interdependencies, is barely comprehensible today. At the top of the feudal system was the prince or king, or in Central Europe the German Emperor. The central figure of feudalism was, however, the knight; an armoured and heavily armed mounted warrior, a kind of mercenary whose expensive equipment was paid for by the work of the vassals on his land, or fiefdom. The knight was the backbone of the feudal system of the lower nobility. The warrior could only become a knight following dubbing or knighting; this applied also to the superior nobility. The condition for elevation to knighthood was generally a proven record in war.

Castles and ruins of castles all over Europe bear witness to the existence of the warring nobility, which increasingly sought protection in fortified stone buildings. These buildings soon, however, assumed a further function as dwellings. To facilitate protection, sites were favoured which were difficult to access, the favourite being the tops of mountains and hills. In low-lying areas, which did not offer such sites, moats had to suffice as protection for the castle.

Castle architecture for knightly dwellings probably started with the construction of residential towers on artificial hills known as mottes. These towers were initially timber structures but were later built in stone. They played a particularly important role in England, where they were known as keeps and formed the centrepiece of many Norman castles. The White Tower in London, which was built after 1066 by William the Conqueror, is an example of such a keep. The rest of the castle complex was later added around the spacious keep. This was also how the Norman keep at Rochester developed.

In France, the towers and usually uninhabitable mountain keeps were known as donjons. The most important of these stands at Courcy in Picardie. With a diameter of 30 metres and height of almost 60 metres, it was the biggest of the circular towers. Circular towers were less

common because square plans were easier to divide up. In Germany around 1100, earlier in Western Europe, castles began to be built which were enclosed by an enceinte, within the protection of which the residential and farm buildings were erected. If the space inside the walls proved insufficient, the farm buildings were built in what was known as the Vorburg (i.e. structure in front of the castle), which more or less resembled a farm enclosed by a wall. For geographical reasons, however, many castles consisted only of the central residential unit and did not have a Vorburg. In these cases, an estate or farm belonging to the castle can usually be found nearby, which was staffed by the serfs and contained the stable of the knight's valuable war horse.

The variety of the external shapes and plans of castles is astounding and makes it almost impossible to classify them, as form was determined by geographical position. Knights tended to prefer castles with regular shapes like those which are most common in low-lying areas.

The stereotypical image of the medieval castle always includes an enceinte and a tower. This is not far from reality as around three quarters of all castles had a main tower, the castle keep. In most cases there was also a residential structure at the enceinte, the "palas" (living quarters) and other less important buildings. The word "palas" may evoke the image of a palace; however, the residential quarters in most castles, particularly those of the lesser nobility, were quite modest. The only room to be heated in the early Middle Ages was known as the "caminata". Ovens first appeared in significant numbers from the mid-13th century. Minuscule windows which were locked in winter allowed little light to filter into the interior, which was consequently dark and cold. The weakest point of a castle was always the

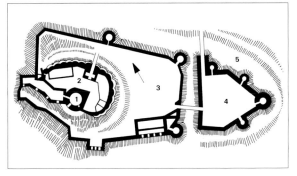

King Richard Lionheart: Château Gaillard, above a loop in the Seine, ca. 1200 (photograph)
Plan of the castle (diagram) with **1** donjon, **2** keep, **3** ward, **4** Vorburg, **5** trench/moat

gate, a gap in the enceinte. In the late Middle Ages attempts were made to increase its security by adding further buildings around it.

At the height of the Middle Ages there were approximately 13,000 castles in the central region of the German Empire. If West and South Europe are included in the calculations, this number increases to between 25,000 and 30,000. This may seem an unrealistic estimate. However, it becomes more plausible when one considers how feudalism was linked with the castle as the dwelling place of the ruling class. Castles began to lose their importance in the 15th century with the invention of firearms and the decline of the knighthood. No more castles were built after 1500 and existing structures were often converted into palaces.

The above-mentioned Vorburg was almost always built on one side of the main castle and was often significantly bigger than it. This can be seen from the plan of Château Gaillard. It also has a barbican, a type of fort, which was linked to the main castle by a (draw) bridge. The castle keep had an unusual drop-shaped plan.

Realistic paintings from the 15th century – for example by Durer – show many castles with widely varying proportions and shapes, and also show how strongly the landscape was once defined by large numbers of castles. As the castle surroundings were generally cleared of vegetation to remove cover for potential attackers, they could be seen from far and wide. Farmers and civilians may have hated them as symbols of noble rule. The romantic image of castles and knights did not emerge until the 19th century.

Norman Keep, Rochester, before 1140

Focusing on this world

GOTHIC

1130–1500

CLASSICAL CATHEDRAL GOTHIC IN FRANCE 1130–1300

From solid to skeletal structures

It is extremely difficult to put an exact date on the transition from Romanesque to the Gothic style. Art historians fondly engage in disputes as to whether Durham cathedral should be classified as late Romanesque or early Gothic, or perhaps should belong to a transitional style. Terms such as "Romanesque Early Gothic" have also been suggested. The term "Gothic" itself originally had rather dubious connotations: it was used derogatorily in the 16th century by the Italian painter, architect and art critic Vasari: the (West) Goths had brought about the ultimate demise of the Roman Empire and, in Vasari's opinion, were absolute Barbarians. In some places, the term Gothic expressed the epitome of contradiction and lack of taste as late as 1800.

The fact that the Gothic style originated in the Île de France, the area around Paris, is undisputed. This area was the power base of the Capetians, who had replaced the Carolingians as rulers of the Western Frankish Empire in 987 with the election of Hugo Capet as King. When they succeeded in re-uniting the country under their rule in the 11th century, this area became the centre of French cultural and scientific development.

Of all building types, the cathedral is seen to epitomise Gothic architecture to the present day. It was the symbol of the new power of the French kings and spread throughout France along with the influence of the crown. With its King's Gallery on the façade, and as the site of royal coronation and entombment, it lends visual legitimacy to the royal claim to power (like the imperial Romanesque cathedral). However, it also embodies the philosophy of society and is an expression of the political and theological world view of all the members of the society in question. These people no longer were involved in the construction of cathedrals as the fulfilment of a mandatory task, but in the conviction that they were working together to erect a symbol of their faith, their town and themselves. The pride of the guilds was on display for all to see. The anonymity of the Middle Ages was abandoned; portraits of patrons and inscriptions provide numerous reminders of the architects, artists and citizens involved in the project. The design of the cathedrals speaks the language of all social classes – their symbolism, above all the figures and window images, can be understood by everyone from intellectuals to simple people. Even if different sectors of society interpret them in different ways, they still fulfil the same purpose.

Of the many Romanesque schools of architecture in France, some continued to work in the traditional style up to the mid-13th century. The school in the Île de France developed the style which eventually replaced the Romanesque style in France and ultimately the entire Western world. The abbey of St. Denis near Paris is acknowledged as the building which launched the Gothic style. Between 1140 and 1144, Suger, the abbot of St. Denis, replaced the old narrow choir with a new one. The new choir

---

Ca. 1250: Medieval division of the "liberal arts" into "trivium" (grammar, rhetoric, dialectics) and "quadrivium" (music, astronomy, arithmetic, geometry).

1254: Royal Chaplain Robert de Sorbon establishes the school of theology in Paris (known as the Sorbonne from the 14th century).

Ca. 1260: According to the theory of alchemy, metals consist of mercury, sulphur and salt and can be transformed into each other (with the help of the "stone of wisdom").

1275: Marco Polo reaches Peking.

Ca. 1300: Pharmacy is recognised as a profession in Germany, spectacles are produced in Italy, glass windows gradually spread, the foot-operated loom is invented, the mechanical clock with stop wheel is invented in Italy; masses in Bruges, Antwerp, Lyons and Geneva become very important events.

1302: Pope Boniface VIII issues the Papal Bull "Unam sanctam"

(formulation of the Papal claim to world rule).

1309: Pope Clemens V transfers the Papal see to Avignon ("Babylonian imprisonment of the church").

1311: Dante starts work on the *Divine Comedy.*

1318: Development of a new system of payment. A law on the transfer of money (giro bank) is passed in Venice.

1339–1453: "Hundred Years War" between England and France; Joan of Arc liberates Orleans and succeeds in setting up the coronation of Charles VII as King of France (1429); she is imprisoned by the English and burned as a witch (1431).

1347: Outbreak of the plague in Europe.

Ca. 1350: Division of the English parliament into the upper house (House of Lords) and lower house (House of Commons) which is given right of petition.

King Charles V (the Wise, 1364–80) moves to Paris; miniature from the French chronicle by Jehan Foucquet, 1472.

1353: Boccacio completes his collection of stories, the *Decameron.*

1356: Emperor Charles IV confirms the sole right of the seven German

Princes to elect a king in the "Golden Bull".

1378–1417: The Great Schism with opposition Popes in Avignon and Rome marks a nadir in papal power.

1415: Czech reformer Johann Hus is burned as a heretic.

1445: First book printed by Johann Gutenberg in Mainz, Germany.

1447: Foundation of the Vatican library.

1481: Beginning of the inquisition in Spain. The secular ruler must implement death penalty as the church "does not thirst for blood".

1492: Discovery of America by Christopher Columbus; Martin Behaim designs the first globe.

was more spacious, free, dynamic, colourful and bright. This reflects an essential feature of Gothic architecture: the discovery and consequent re-evaluation of the choir as an important religious focus. As was the case with the Carolingian nave in St. Denis, in many cases the nave was left unchanged and simply extended through the addition of a larger and more complex choir. The choir of St. Denis has a double ambulatory with chapel niches which open directly on to the ambulatory and are not separate structures. The former individual chapels were replaced by light, open, curved structures, which are fused with the outer ambulatory and give the exterior wall of the choir a wave-like form.

This plan was so irregular that it could no longer be adequately served by groin vaults. Pointed arch rib vaults were identified as a suitable alternative. Vault ribs already existed in Romanesque architecture and had been used mainly by the Normans, although usually for decorative purposes. In St. Denis, the ribs were given a structural function for the first time. It was possible to build the ribs first and then fill in the surface between the ribs (the cells). As the cells no longer had any structural purpose to fulfil, it was now possible to reduce their bulk to a minimum. This meant that not only were the vaults easier to build, but the weight of the entire structure was also significantly reduced.

Moreover, pointed arches exert a weaker lateral thrust than the round-headed arches of the barrel vault. The round or square structural pillars were surrounded by responds – semi-columns which continued in the ribs to buttress or transmit the thrust from the vault.

It is important to remember that for Abbot Suger all these technical details had a significance beyond their abstract structural functions. He saw a symbolic and mystical significance in each detail: the columns were apostles and prophets which "carry" Christianity and Jesus was the keystone linking one wall with another. What is fascinating about all of this from today's perspective, is that this belief caused a virtual revolution in architectural style.

All these technical innovations made it possible to give the church interior a completely new look. The new choir of St. Denis no longer consisted of separate introspective spaces built simply in a sequence. It was a single large uniform space. To heighten this impression of unity, the crossing was no longer emphasised in the interior and the transept was sometimes omitted, the side aisles continuing into the choir ambulatories.

This optical impression of spatial uniformity was, however, accompanied by an extreme dissection (division) of the contours. The introduction of the rib vault and the flying buttress system made it possible to reduce and perforate the wall mass to

St. Denis, abbey church near Paris, *choir*, consecrated in 1144

The abbey, which originates from the 7th century, was converted from 1137 onwards by Abbot Suger. The first parts of the church to be reconstructed were the double-tower façade in the west and the choir in the east. The planned nave which would join the two parts was not built until the 13th century in the high Gothic style. The upper part of Suger's choir was also redesigned in the high Gothic style. Of the original choir only the pillars, ambulatory, radiating chapels and parts of the crypt are extant. St. Denis was the burial church of the French kings and their tombs can be found in the choir and transept. The double-tower west front with its dynamic articulation is also very important in terms of the trend it set for the development of Gothic cathedral architecture. The wide portals had deeply carved jambs which were decorated with columns and figures of kings and queens, sibyls and Old Testament prophets. Gothic cathedral sculpture has its origins here. The rose window also features here for the first time. The sculptures and precious interior fittings were for the most part destroyed during the French Revolution. A few objects can today be found in the Louvre. Parts of the west front were restored to their original form during restoration work undertaken in the 19th century.

an extent which was hitherto impossible. The walls became largely superfluous from a structural perspective. The nave of Chartres cathedral, which was built from 1194 onwards, became the model for the three-layered interior elevation: above the high nave arcades there is a low gallery (triforium) which is in turn crowned by a high clerestory. The remaining surface is further divided up by the ribs, composite piers and decorative details.

Exterior walls were sealed by huge windows which did not, however, admit bright daylight. As it was not technically possible to produce such enormous panes of glass, the windows were instead filled with small pieces of glass held in place by lead frames (leaded glazing). Enormous painted or stained glass images were usually created in strong but sombre colours which glowed all the more because the interior was only barely lit. This completely new, unreal light (*lux nova*) was very important to the faithful because the windows, like the rosettes, carried theological messages: the sacred origin of the images was apparent from the way in which the light filtered through them. Like the *biblia pauperum*, the illustrated Bible for the poor, the windows conveyed the Biblical message to the illiterate and those who could not afford expensive bibles.

It is important to keep in mind the colour of Medieval architecture in this context. Gothic cathedrals were all richly painted inside, giving rise to a highly effective interplay of windows, walls and "sky" (often actually showing a sky with stars) which is often difficult to imagine when considering how they appear today.

Thanks to their new form, the observer no longer perceived cathedral interiors as consisting of heavy, bulky materials but as tightly spanned – and thus all the more fragile – skeletal structures, filled in with majestically shining coloured leaves. They had become shrines of light. This is demonstrated by the illuminated altar which represents the focal

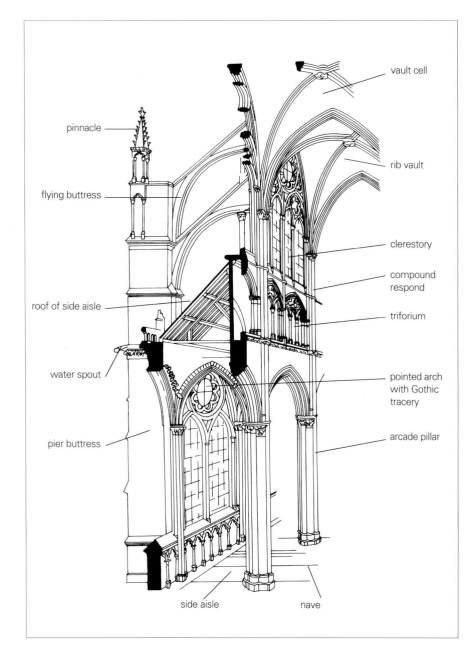

pinnacle

flying buttress

roof of side aisle

water spout

pier buttress

side aisle

nave

vault cell

rib vault

clerestory

compound respond

triforium

pointed arch with Gothic tracery

arcade pillar

The Duc de Berry's Book of Hours (*Très riches heures*), ca. 1415, month June, with the old royal palace and the Sainte-Chapelle

The Sainte-Chapelle, Paris, consecrated 1248, upper chapel

King Louis IX of France, the Saint, commissioned the Sainte-Chapelle as a monumental shrine for relics which he brought back from Byzantium (crown of thorns, relics of the Crucifix). Extensive piercing of the wall with coloured, light-flooded windows reaches its pinnacle here. The images on the stained glass panes depict Christ's Passion, the history of the relics which are stored in the chapel, and scenes from the Old Testament. In Suger's choir at St. Denis the columns represent the twelve apostles; in the Sainte-Chapelle the apostles are also represented by sculptures on the columns. The tribune with the reliquary shrines, which were destroyed during the French Revolution, stood in the centre of the choir. The Sainte-Chapelle also served as the palatine chapel. The upper chapel was reserved for services for the royal family who had direct access to it from the palace. The lower chapel was used by the rest of the court. The miniature from the Duc de Berry's Book of Hours shows the Sainte-Chapelle between the buildings of the royal palace on the Île-de-la-Cité, Paris's oldest centre.

point in the Sainte-Chapelle cathedral in Paris, an outstanding example of this spatial concept.

A secular-clerical architecture

The fact that this new effect is referred to in terms of a "spatial concept" clearly shows that it was not merely based on structural innovations, but was also an expression of aesthetic aims. St. Denis was an abbey church. However, its first architect, Abbot Suger, was a close advisor of King Louis VI and the Sainte-Chapelle was built as the palatine chapel for the palace of Louis IX. A mutually beneficial relationship developed between the religious and secular powers. The Church became increasingly involved in secular matters, just as the French monarchy used the Church, or the theological world view it postulated, to represent itself politically.

The emerging philosophy of scholasticism reflected this productive relationship between the church and the crown. Knowledge was systematically recorded for the first time in the form of encyclopaedias. At the same time, a method was developed which made it possible to dialectically prove the truth of divine revelation using this knowledge. However, like all new things this movement faced resistance. The mystics staunchly rejected the idea of proving the existence of God and instead sought to experience God.

The cathedrals of the time very clearly expressed this contradictory notion which was still very much fuelled by faith. The new technical possibilities are linked in "God's skyscrapers" (Le Corbusier), with the vision of creating a colourful imaginative representation of *Heavenly Jerusalem* because – as in the Biblical Revelation of St. John the Divine –

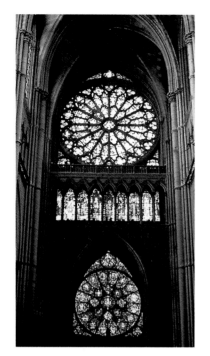

Reims, cathedral, interior view of the west front with large rose window, triforium and portal rose, ca. 1280–1300

Reims cathedral, where the French kings were crowned, is famous mainly for the west front with its prominent rose window. In all cathedrals, the architectural form and visual representation of the rose window were combined, to form a symbol of Christian order and the cosmos permeated by complex theological ideas.

Gothic man imagined heaven in the form of a heavenly architectural structure.

Pointed arches and composite columns may have been developed for structural reasons, but they were also intended to convey the impression of steep arrows aiming up to heaven. This vertical wall articulation makes the already unusually high churches seem even higher. Romanesque inertia, mass and weight are replaced by an apparent dispersal of the bulk through denial of the material, dissolution of the walls and the creation of a delicate skeletal structure soaring up to heaven. It is interesting to note that the Gothic style had spread throughout the West by the mid-13th century, when the "Roman-German" Empire declined after a lengthy struggle with the Pope. This marked the end of the idea of a universal unified empire and the equal status of secular and religious powers.

Community projects in the thriving towns

The 12th and 13th centuries were characterised by strong growth in population, economy and trade. Conversely, during the 14th century Europe fell victim to the plague, Jews were persecuted and widespread revolts by farmers and peasants were mainly caused by the decline in economic prosperity. The Hundred Years War raged in France. The new mendicant religious orders (Franciscans, Dominicans) lived a life of poverty, but unlike their predecessors no longer settled in remote, relatively uncivilised areas. Instead they became involved in charitable work in the towns and cities. By

extending the geographical scope of their activities, they came to exercise a strong influence on the piety of the people.

From the end of the 12th century, new towns were established everywhere and existing towns grew both in physical size and importance. As the town represented the perfect community, Christian kings saw it as their duty to found towns and in this way lead their subjects to God. The silhouette of medieval towns clearly illustrates the contrasting positions of secular and religious power: the cathedral, bishop's palace, king's palace or residence, arcades and houses of the guilds and commercial associations towered over the low residential buildings; the town hall and the church often competed for the highest tower. With perhaps as many as 200,000 inhabitants, Paris was the most populous city of the late Middle Ages after Milan.

After the isolated monasteries and their churches of the Romanesque period, the most important architectural task during the Gothic period became the construction of the cathedral. This stood in the centre of the town or city and was often the symbol of its identity. Its construction frequently represented the combined efforts of the inhabitants of the town and its surrounding area, who contributed to the project in the form of either money or labour. No effort was spared when it came to fulfilling this task which invariably took generations to complete. However, many Gothic cathedrals – and particularly their towers – remained unfinished, because the

Notre-Dame, Paris, 1163–ca. 1197, view from the south

Notre-Dame, the construction of which was initiated in 1163 by Bishop Maurice de Sully, is an excellent example of an early Gothic cathedral. The most important features of this era are the four-layered elevation (arcade, gallery, triforium, clerestory), the round pillars and six-part system of vaults. The elevation was modernised at a later date when the triforium and the clerestory were combined. The open buttressing system is presumed to have been used for the first time in Notre-Dame, giving rise to the extremely daring system of wide flying buttresses. The transept façades with large rose windows and portal figures were added when the transept was extended between 1245 and 1270. The royal gallery on the west façade is also an important feature. It was the first such gallery to be built on a cathedral front and depicted an idealised genealogy of the French kings. It was destroyed during the French Revolution and the ruins can now be viewed in the Musée de Cluny, Paris.
Notre-Dame was restored during the 19th century by Viollet-le-Duc. The large ridge turret originates from this time.

projects were overtaken by time, enthusiasm waned or the money ran out.

Special associations of church builders and artisans were formed for the organisation and management of these major building projects. The associations consisted of all the artisans involved in the construction of the church and a director. His role went beyond the technical scope of the artisan to encompass the aesthetic function of the architect, right through from the design phase to actual construction. This marked the beginning of the gradual emergence of the creative individual in place of the anonymous artist of the early Middle Ages. Cathedral associations were subject to the authority of the bishop and similar associations also existed for urban churches and monastery buildings. Experience and regulations were documented in the associations' books, to which only members of the association had access. The only surviving copy of such a book from the Middle Ages was compiled by Villard de Honnecourt. With its numerous diagrams, it gives us great insight into the varied artistic activities of such a church-building association. However, the scope with regard to the planning and construction of buildings was still rather limited. While triangulation provided a process for calculating proportions, and static knowledge was becoming more widely available, the latter was still based on empirical values and a mathematical system had yet to be devised for calculating stress and thrust. Thus the collapse of buildings was still a frequent occurrence, especially when the dissolution of the walls, the delicacy of the structure and its height were taken to excessive lengths.

Construction and ornament

As cathedrals usually stood in the narrow confines of small towns, which were often enclosed by fortresses, the side elevations and choir were not usually visible from very far away. Hence, the sole focus of the exterior was concentrated on the west façade, where the main entrance was located. This was further emphasised by the location of the building's only towers on the west front. Priority was given to the design and decoration of the interior, which was implemented to the highest standards in artistic precision.

One of the most striking features of the exterior of Gothic cathedrals is the way in which the mass required for support of the load-bearing frame was banished from the interior. To avoid building the side aisles too high to provide the support necessary to counteract the lateral thrust of the vaults (which would have restricted the size of the clerestory windows), support was provided by flying buttresses

Chartres, cathedral, consecrated in 1260, central west portal (ca. 1145–55)

The King's Portal of Chartres cathedral represents the high point of early Gothic French sculpture. It symbolises the "*porta coeli*", the gate leading to heavenly Jerusalem. Its theological programme combines with that of the two side portals to form a single unit.

The column figures represent characters from the Old Testament. The tympanum contains an image of the apocalyptic Christ surrounded by symbols of the four Evangelists and 24 elders: Christ is the way to the eternal life in the next world. In St. Denis and Chartres, large statues independent of the architecture reappear for the first time since Antiquity. The robes worn by the figures look similar to those depicted on antique models. The pose and gestures of the figures still seem rather archaic and distant, but it is possible to detect the first signs of emerging individualisation.

The cathedral was renovated in high Gothic style from 1194 onwards. The early Gothic west portals, however, still exist in their original form.

which hovered freely above the roofs of the aisles, often spanning several floors, and which opened out into solid pier buttresses at ground level. This system was first used on a larger scale in the cathedrals of Laon and Paris (Notre-Dame).

The pier buttresses were crowned with small towers (pinnacles), more arrows pointing to heaven. These too were broken up by decorative details: climbing plants (crockets) scaled their spires and terminated in the finials, foliated ornaments which blossomed towards heaven. With time the decorative detail in classical cathedral Gothic became more and more abundant, intricate and differentiated, and seemed to overrun the entire building, or at least the remaining slivers of masonry.

Roses, ivy, thistles, maples and vine or oak leaves were initially reproduced in stylised form and later with greater realism; on the crocket and foliage capitals of the pillars, and on the corbels, keystones, cornices and balustrades. Animal figures also featured extensively in the decorations, with the result that the entire church became an image of a paradise-like habitat for all types of living species.

More important, however, was the design of the portals (which were terminated by triangular roof-like gables), because the symbolical message could be seen to undergo a transformation. During the Romanesque period, sinister and depressing fears of the last judgement dominated such depictions. The illiterate were familiarised in this way with the horror which threatened the sinners and unfaithful, and the paradisiacal ecstasy which awaited the good Christian. By contrast, the repertoire of the

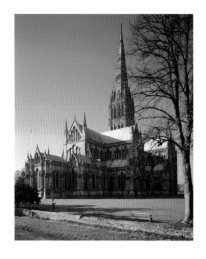

Salisbury, cathedral, 1220–ca. 1265, view from the north east

The fact that this cathedral was built from scratch gave enormous scope for the design, as it was not constrained by existing structures. The construction period being relatively short for its time also ensured a degree of uniformity in the design.
The three-aisle basilica has two transepts, a choir ambulatory and Lady's Chapel. A cloister and chapter house adjoin the building to the south. In contrast to the spatial unity of French cathedrals, the staggering of the structure makes it easy to read the functional spatial division both from the interior and exterior.

Gothic stone masons was based, in accordance with the scholasticists' insights, on a "factual description" of the divine. This was reflected in particular in the royal portals. In Chartres, for example, kings and queens of France are depicted wearing Biblical attire and stand next to the apostles and figures from the Old Testament. This image was fuelled by the desire, expressed in a prayer from the coronation rituals, that the king would have the virtues of Old Testament kings bestowed upon him. The funnel-like staggering of the portal jambs, which had already been tried out during the Romanesque period, created an optical pull to the cathedral interior and also provided additional space for jamb statues and the decoration of the socle area. The columned west portal of Chartres cathedral marks the beginning of the re-emergence of three-dimensional sculpture.

Whilst the colour and Biblical motifs selected for windows were based on a deep symbolism, the actual division of the windows was, nevertheless, based on abstract forms. Moulded posts, mullions, divided the window surfaces into narrow vertical sections, which terminated above in pointed arches. The spandrel between these arches and the pointed arches of the windows was filled with tracery. During the early and high Gothic periods this consisted of symmetrical circular forms known as trefoils, quatrefoils and cinquefoils, depending upon the number of circles or clover leaves (rayonnant style). The strict geometrical patterns were later replaced by more dynamic interlaced forms (mouchettes, flamboyant style). The same devel-

opment can be observed in the tracery balustrades and in some cases in the large rose windows on the main west façade. These rose windows, which symbolised the sun, allowed light to filter through to the cathedral interior.

THE GOTHIC STYLE IN ENGLAND 1200–1500

Continuing the Norman traditions

It was mainly thanks to travelling architects that the style developed in the Île-de-France became known outside France. Guillaume de Sens (an architect from the Sens church building association) was mainly responsible for the reconstruction of the burned choir of Canterbury cathedral. In doing this he brought the Gothic style to England where it developed to eventually rival the French Gothic. What emerged in England was a combination of Norman architecture, which already incorporated many Gothic trends, and the new style. This resulted in the development of something completely independent of the French style. Unlike the continent, large churches in England were generally built outside the towns, as illustrated by Durham cathedral. The English Church saw itself as an established territorial church and its cathedrals tended to be attached to monastic residences on the peripheries of towns, rather than the bishop's seat in the town centre. Thus it was the custom to build large cathedral complexes with "castle gates" on all sides, and a cathedral chapter house integrated into the periphery of the complex.

Lincoln, cathedral, begun in 1192, view of the nave to the east

The stellar vaults along the nave immediately attract the eye of the observer on entering the cathedral from the west portal. The ribs above each of the bays combine to form a star. Viewed from one of the pillars, the effect is that of a fan. The central rib extends the entire length of the nave right up to the crossing. The walls emphasise the horizontal articulation of the three levels. Galleries above the ground-level arcades also have arcades, which open onto the roof of the side aisles; these are crowned by the clerestory. The three responds in front of the wall terminate on brackets above the pillars and do not correspond in number to the ribs in the vault; they are conceived for a traditional rib vault. The number of responds does not correspond to that of the ribs until the Angel Choir. The actual choir has a strange asymmetrical rib vault which can probably be ascribed to the influence of Bishop Robert Grosseteste, a scientist who was particularly interested in optical phenomena.

Other typical features of Gothic churches in England included a far greater emphasis on the horizontal proportions, which was not reflected in the height of the buildings, and the straight eastern termination of the chancel, to which the lady chapel (chapel dedicated to the Virgin) was added. In continental Gothic churches, this was closely integrated into the overall system of the building, as the central chapel among the chapels radiating from the choir ambulatory. As in French cathedrals, the addition of a chapel at the choir end of the church caused the shifting of the crossing to almost the centre of the entire complex. Although this feature received little or no emphasis in the country of birth of the Gothic style, in England it became the pivotal focus of the church. Rectangular structures were added on all sides and it was crowned by the tower vault.

The central role of the crossing was also generally reflected in the exterior. Salisbury cathedral (which like Lincoln cathedral has double transepts) does not have a double-tower façade. The west front merely has two small corner towers similar to those which terminate the transepts and the choir. These towers do not soar above the nave roofs. The dominant feature is the 123-metre-high crossing tower. The high shaft of space which it creates is particularly effective in the interior. Unlike in France, there is no spatial unity; division of the wall surfaces is based on decorative rather than structural motifs. Hence, independent adoption of the French model took over from the Early English Gothic style (of which Salisbury is an example) around 1250 and became known as the "decorated style". In the classical French Gothic cathedral, the structural methods used were clearly exposed and the decorative details were based upon them, emphasising their effects. The continuous ridge ribs of the fan vaults in Lincoln and Exeter cathedrals have no load-bearing function whatsoever. Instead, they form part of a decorative detail consisting of sharp graphical lines which also divide up the thick pillars and arcade arches. The optical dematerialisation achieved in this way is, however, inadequate. The responds of the fan vaults do not take off from the abacuses of the arcade pillars, or even rest on floor pedestals, but arise from brackets which hang freely beneath the spandrels. This absence of continuous vertical lines stretching from floor to ceiling emphasises the spatial effect evoked by the squat nature of the building. The impression created is not one of a delicate, upward-striving skeleton held together by lines of force, but of a complex structure consisting of many individual parts and layers, which is nevertheless extremely stable and massive.

The "perpendicular style", which emerged in the mid-14th century and is found in Gloucester cathedral, is the logical continuation of this trend. In Gloucester, a complex regular network of ribs was added to the vaults, which were clearly devoid of a structural function. This left little scope for further development: the box-shaped spatial form remained unchanged, only its decoration could be varied endlessly. This architectural style exercised a decisive influence for several centuries in England and also spread back to France and the late Gothic period with its "flamboyant style".

Gloucester, cathedral, view from the south-west

Construction of this Romanesque abbey church, which was extended and "modernised" several times, initially started in 1089. At the beginning of the 14th century the south side aisle, and in the 1340s the southern transept, were given new windows with tracery in the flowing lines of the decorated style. A net vault was also added to the crossing. Over the following decades the choir, north transept and cloister were redesigned in the perpendicular style, which involved covering the wall and vault surfaces with a dense lattice of decorative details. The crossing tower, a prominent feature of English Gothic cathedrals, originates from the 15th century.

Holy Cross Cathedral, Nordhausen (Thuringia), mid-14th century

During the 14th century, the basilical nave was replaced by a three-aisle hall in numerous Romanesque, early and high Gothic churches in Germany. This was also the case with the cathedral in Nordhausen, where in the mid-14th century a three-aisle five-bay hall was added to the choir, itself consecrated in 1267 and vaulted around 1300. Initially the converted hall structure was temporarily covered with a flat roof. Construction of the vaults started in the 16th century and was not completed until the 19th century. Responds on the composite pillars had simple low bases and capitals decorated with leaves, while the vaults had star and parallel ribs. The uniformity of the space in Nordhausen is somewhat undermined by the capitals between the pillar responds and vault ribs. The responds and ribs do not always relate logically as is the case, for example, in the Wiesenkirche in Soest. The lengthy construction period made it impossible to achieve an ideal uniform spatial impression; the church clearly consists of elements from different eras.

Cathedral of St. Peter and Mary,
Cologne, begun in 1248, completed in
1322, 1842–80 final completion; view of
choir from the east

The Cologne cathedral chapter decided to
build a cathedral in the French high Gothic
style to accommodate the steadily
growing stream of pilgrims who came to
visit the relics of the Three Wise Men.
The choir was linked with the nave on
completion and used for services.
Cologne cathedral is modelled on Amiens
cathedral. It has a five-aisle plan and the
single choir ambulatory adjoins seven
radiating chapels. The tripartite wall
articulation, consisting of arcades,
triforium and clerestory, is also based on
Amiens. Early 14th century paintings on
the glass windows depict the history of
the Three Wise Men whose shrine is
located in the crossing. The structure of
the radiating chapels, ambulatory and
choir, which are spanned and staggered
between the open buttressing, is easily
detected from the exterior.

THE GOTHIC STYLE IN GERMANY 1250–1500

The development of the hall church

The French Gothic style was adopted very
hesitantly in Germany because it was here that the
Romanesque style was most popular. For example,
the cathedral in Limburg on the Lahn shows the
combination of new Gothic decorative elements
with a spatial concept which is firmly rooted in the
Romanesque era. The foundation stone of Cologne
cathedral was laid in 1248, the year in which the
Sainte-Chapelle was completed. Two years later
work commenced on the construction of the nave
of Strasbourg cathedral. It is not surprising that the
most faithful adoption of French cathedral Gothic
can be observed in the Rhineland area (Elsass was
then part of German political and cultural territory).
Many German architects had completed their
apprenticeships in Laon or Amiens, Paris or

Beauvais and there were close links between Paris
and Cologne. However, the construction of Cologne
cathedral was abandoned in 1560 and not taken up
again until 1842; it was completed in 1880. The west
front of Strasbourg cathedral was also designed in a
form which deviated from classical French cathedral
Gothic, although the plans corresponded to it. In
general, a direct adoption of the French style can
only be observed in a few individual cases. It was
often simplified, for example in the wall structure or
in the omission of the choir ambulatory and the
radiating chapels. The "Gothic" effect was mainly
achieved by raising the height of the side aisles to
that of the nave. A French model for this development also existed in St. Peter's cathedral in Poitiers,
begun in 1166. On the other hand, the process of
dividing up a space which cannot be roofed in one
fell swoop by constructing intermediary supports is
one that goes back to ancient times and is
extremely obvious.

This rendered the complicated system of free-
standing buttressing redundant, and created a
further open space more uniform than that familiar
from classical cathedral Gothic. As can be seen in
Soest church, an excellent example of a hall church,
the choir ambulatory was often built to the same
height and width as the central choir and the
transept was eliminated. Hall churches with raised
naves but no nave windows also emerged. In these
churches, in order to take advantage of the
enormous roof truss towering steeply above all the
aisles, the nave was also raised (the pseudo-basilica
originated in this way). This plunged the upper
section of the nave into darkness, an effect contrary
to the aim of this new concept to create a space
which was brighter, clearer and even more serene
than that of French Gothic cathedrals. Pillars no
longer consisted of a central core surrounded by
circular responds, but were either fused to a single
unit with flat responds or were completely round.
The rest of the walls became flat surfaces at the
same level as the windows, which were glazed in
brighter colours. The exterior was also uniform. Pier
buttresses fused with the exterior wall grew out of
the bases of the chapels. These exterior pier buttresses surrounded the entire building and supported the powerful pitched roof.

Hall churches – the most popular type of church to
be found in Germany from the mid-14th century –
were not usually cathedrals (bishops' churches) but
collegiate or parish churches (the main churches
in towns). The clearly organised interior and
compact exterior were not the products of pure
chance but reflected an altered understanding of
the church building. For the Cistercians, in particular,

the church no longer represented a model of *Heavenly Jerusalem* but was a place of prayer. The sermon assumed an increasingly significant role within the religious service. People living in the towns, particularly traders, increasingly devoted their time and energy to this world, in which they did business, acquired their wealth and often sustained business relationships over wide distances. The "other world" was by no means dismissed as unimportant, but it gradually lost its repressive dominance in the minds of the people.

Hall churches still soared up towards heaven but the previous ecstatic reach was replaced by a quieter, softer and more harmonious gesture. The balance between life in this world and the next (an imminent development reflecting the germination of Renaissance thought) also found expression in the increased importance given to the external appearance of the church – proud towns and cities with self-confident citizens paid greater attention to the importance of conveying a suitably prestigious image.

Instead of a pair of towers, hall churches often had only one tower, which in some cases was added asymmetrically to the nave. It was often disproportionately higher than the nave and its position was sometimes dictated by town-planning considerations. In the case of St. Martin's in Landshut (1387–1498), for example, the tower is located on a bend in the main street.

More complex secular buildings, which reflected the town, its significance and its affluence, also became increasingly common. Town gates, town halls, commercial buildings (shops) and – from the 14th century onwards – residential buildings, were increasingly built in stone. The cathedral may have represented the central community building during the high Gothic period, but was later replaced by an increased interest in living and working quarters. The bay window or oriel, from which the street could be comfortably observed in both directions, is a typical structure of the late Gothic style. It reflects an obvious focus on the goings on in this world. However, in almost all cases secular buildings reflected in some way the form of religious buildings, as is clearly shown by the town hall in Louvain, Belgium. Deliberately irregular complexes, which gave the impression of having sprung up on their sites at random and were intended to present a "picturesque" image, also became popular towards the end of the Gothic period. Rich with ingenious detail, like star or net vaults and the unusual e.g. corkscrew-like arches and pillars, they represented a trend which ran counter to the earlier desire for simplicity and clarity. As was the case in England,

they are evidence of a predilection for pure, playful decoration.

Northern German brick or backstein Gothic

Another version of the Gothic style developed in north Germany. Due to the efforts of the German order of knights who organised the crusades for the Christian conversion of Eastern Europe and the association of Hanseatic trading towns, this area culturally encompassed not only the Netherlands but also the entire southern side of the Baltic Sea and the Baltic provinces. As in some areas of south Germany, natural stone was scarce in this region. However, unlike the south, no effort was made to clad or plaster the brick which was used instead of natural stone. Instead, architects concentrated on achieving an architectural effect using brick. Initially brick churches were of almost Romanesque massiveness, like St. Mary's in Lubeck, but increasing efforts were made to reproduce the (decorative) forms of classical cathedral Gothic with ashlar and brick. For structural reasons, it was not possible to pierce the walls to the same degree as with natural stone. This was partly compensated for by the simplification and abstraction of the articulation; blind arches and blind tracery disappeared and the inset wall was whitewashed. This created a strong contrast with the red, green, blue or black glazed brick surfaces and buttresses. Light relief was provided by the use of different coloured burned and glazed bricks, and the combination of decorative terracotta elements to form friezes. All these methods were used to create an independent form of Gothic which, despite its magnificence, retained a certain sombre and sober note. This in turn reflected the character of the Northern Germans who developed it.

THE GOTHIC STYLE IN ITALY 1250–1450

The shift away from religious architecture

Italian Gothic deviated even more strongly from the French model than the German version. As already mentioned, the term Gothic was coined in Renaissance Italy and had negative connotations. It is not unusual for an era to be critical of the one which preceded it. However, even at the height of the Gothic period, there was actually little enthusiasm for it.

The beginning of Italian Gothic is marked by a building constructed for Emperor Frederick II, the last Hohenstaufen and last emperor in the ancient sense. Frederick II ruled from Italy and had the Castel del Monte, which looks more like a castle

St. Mary's, Lubeck, 1250–1350

Due to the lack of natural stone, a specific form of the Gothic style, backstein Gothic, was developed in north Germany. The powerful church of St Mary in Lubeck is a particularly good example. An urban parish church, it aimed to compete in size and form with a cathedral.
The construction material gave rise to a reticent flat articulation of the façade, the uniformity of which is not undermined but emphasised by the coloured glazed and moulded bricks.

Castel Del Monte, Puglia, before 1240–ca. 1250

The Hohenstaufen Emperor, Frederick II, had the Castel del Monte built as a hunting lodge. The design is of prismatic clarity. The two-storey structure rises above an octagonal plan. The corners are also emphasised by the octagonal stair turrets. The castle is accessed through an ancient style portal. The influence of the Gothic style can be seen in the plan and in individual decorative details in the interior.

Palazzo Pubblico (town hall) Sienna, 1297–1348

The Tuscan town of Sienna has one of the most important town halls in Italy. The wide façade with its high bell tower demonstrates the self-confidence of the medieval urban community for all to see. The city fathers had a square for public assemblies built in front of the town hall, and prescribed a uniform façade design for the neighbouring buildings.
The façade strikes a delicate balance between the horizontal and vertical emphasis, and between an inviting and distant note. The large halls in the interior are decorated with important frescoes – historical and memorial images. Allegorical representations of the "Good Regiment" and the "Bad Regiment" by Ambrogio Lorenzetti (1338–40) can be found in the Sala della Pace (hall of peace). They were intended to remind the city fathers to ensure the basis of Christian faith for the well-being of the town and its inhabitants. The theme is also taken up in the chapel anteroom and evoked in allegories of virtue and portraits of famous historical role models.

than a palace, built on a hill in Puglia around 1230. With its completely regular form, representative image and obvious identity as a secular building (the chapel was not in any way prominent or emphasised), it was an exception among castle buildings. It is only classified as a Gothic building on the basis of a few decorative elements. This style did not spread beyond the Hohenstaufen castles until the following century – probably as a result of experiences from the crusades to the east.

This ultimately led to the construction of magnificent residential palaces like the Ca' d'Oro in Venice, the construction of which began around 1420. The self-confidence of the Italian towns and cities and their (rich) citizens had already resulted in the construction of town halls which broke with the dominance of the religious buildings. The Palazzo Pubblico, Sienna town hall, with its massive sealed walls, crenellation and high tower conveying a strong sense of urban power, resembles a castle and served as a model for many other town halls and residences.

The popularity of palace architecture is even more prominent in the case of Venice town hall, the Doge's Palace. As head of this city state, the Doge had the rank of a prince. The façade of his palace (1309–1443) consists of a closed surface with rhombus-shaped decorations into which seven large plain windows are carved. These rest on two floors of completely open arcades, the lower of which have the widest openings. The way in which the bulk of the building increases from the bottom

to the top seems contradictory. In this, the Doge's Palace goes even further than the Ca' d'Oro, where the part of the facade pierced by arcades and loggias progresses horizontally to the more closed part. Both buildings illustrate the important role played by the surface in the Italian interpretation of Gothic ideas. To an even greater extent than in Germany, the wall surface is prevented from looking like an inert Romanesque mass and appears like a thin light partition.

The ascetic architecture of the mendicant orders had a strong influence on Italian church architecture. For example, the Franciscan church of Santa Croce in Florence, which was built between 1294 and 1442, consists of a flat-ceilinged rectangular nave; there are no towers and the transept terminates with a small apse in the east. Not surprisingly, given the emphasis placed on simplicity by the orders of the time, the model here is the Early Christian basilica. Thanks to the extensive width which almost exceeds the height of the nave, and the high, wide arcades, the spatial impression created is of an enormous uniform hall. At 34.5 metres, the height exceeds that of Notre-Dame in Paris. However, this is not at all obvious, due to the width of the hall church and the horizontal emphasis created by the continuous bracket cornice above the arcade arches, which are the sole source of vertical emphasis in the building. The consistent flatness of all the walls also emphasises the uniform character. There is hardly any decoration, no carving and perforation, no division.

On the way to a more "human" architecture

Italian Gothic tended to pursue the development of its own architectural traditions rather than adopting French models. Thus the west fronts of the churches for the most part remained simple walls terminating in the nave, and the bell tower was always built beside them. The façades continued to be faced with coloured marble. As in the cathedrals at Sienna and Florence (where the west front was not built until the 19th century), standard patterns used in Romanesque churches were sometimes executed in three-dimensional form and adapted to the new forms of decoration.

The Florentine cathedral, Santa Maria del Fiore (1296–1446) demonstrates that the Italians continued to prefer wide, sprawling and clearly defined spaces. Its plan is that of a short nave which terminates in a kind of trichora or cloverleaf plan. It is vaulted and has composite pillars. However the spatial effect is almost identical to that of Santa Croce as the arcades between the central and side aisles are wide open, and the responds are flat projections on the relatively low pillars. The arch is separated from the arcades by a powerful bracket cornice which interrupts the powerful upward thrust with a strong horizontal accent. The powerful dimensions of the space can be recognised on a comparative level: the spread of four bays in Florence cathedral approximately corresponds to that of twelve bays in Salisbury cathedral and ten in Amiens cathedral. Despite this, the space in Florence, which is not divided up but consists of smooth composed surfaces, is clearer, more tangible and earthly. The dome, classified as Renaissance, merely acts as a crown on the spatial achievement of the entire building.

The middle classes in Italy rose to power and affluence earlier than their German counterparts, developing a different style of piety which is reflected in the transformation of architecture. The religious was no longer seen as the counterpart of the secular. Thus the Italian Gothic style already contained the seeds of the Renaissance. Whilst on the other side of the Alps large Gothic cathedrals continued to be built, and while north German backstein Gothic reached its height in the 15th century, a new epoch with a new architecture was already under way in Italy.

Bartolomeo Bon: *Ca' d'Oro* on the Grand Canal, Venice, 1421–40

The Ca' d'Oro, with its richly gilded marble façade, is a good example of the transitional style from Gothic to Renaissance in Venice.
The tracery screens on the first and second floors, the windows and balcony railings, are clearly late Gothic in form, whereas the colonnaded hall in the ground floor and the small square windows on the right wing are Renaissance. The palace is incomplete, the missing left wing giving rise to the asymmetry in the façade.

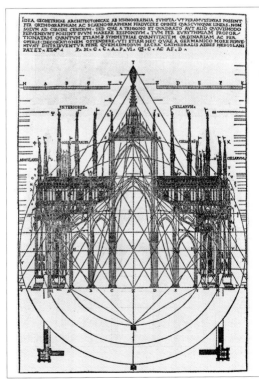

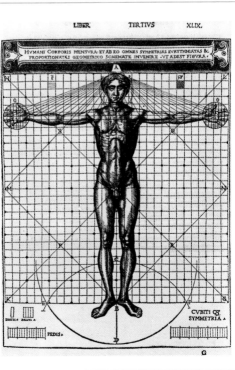

Vitruvius – edition of the Cesariano (Como, 1521); the orthographia (elevation) of Milan cathedral and the Vitruvian figure

The painter, architect and engineer Cesare Cesariano (1483–1543) completed the first translation into Italian of the ancient architectural tract by Vitruvius in 1521, and accompanied it with detailed commentaries and woodcut illustrations. The representation of Milan cathedral and the Vitruvian figure illustrate the transition from Gothic to Renaissance. Cesariano applies the ancient principles of construction described by Vitruvius to Milan cathedral and demonstrates them on the Gothic triangulature (use of triangles to determine architectural shape). In the Vitruvian proportional figure, Cesariano develops in parallel to Leonardo da Vinci the relationship between the proportions of the human body, the cosmos and architecture. This was later to exercise an important influence on architectural theory and practice during the Renaissance.

The divine harmony of this world

RENAISSANCE

1420–1620

FLORENCE AND THE EARLY RENAISSANCE 1420–1500

Discovering the world and man

It may be possible to detect some evidence of the presence of the Gothic style in the transition from the Romanesque to the Renaissance in Italy. However, it cannot be said to have had a major impact. With its urban palaces, clearly defined spaces and tranquil, horizontally accented forms, the Italian architecture of the Gothic period already carried the seeds of the movement to follow. It is therefore justifiably referred to as the Proto-renaissance.

The rich and self-confident Italian city states were ruled by neither the clergy nor knightly nobility with its abstract ideals, but by the middle classes. In Italy these were more a nobility with strong middle-class values, such as "tangible" virtues of diligence, craftsmanship and thrift. Having achieved their position of power and affluence through trade, these people had developed a different kind of piety. Unlike their Christian counterparts of the Gothic period, they did not long for a rapid journey through this "miserable" earthly existence and instead became involved in discovering the beauty and harmony of the world.

Humanism emerged during the 14th century. It believed in and promoted the idea that the natural sciences need no longer be based on religious principles (dogma) but on the objective observation of nature, reason and experience. This brought to an end the former identification of faith with knowledge. The burgher emerged along with the priest as an upholder of culture and civilisation, and universities severed their dependency on the Church. This marked the beginning of a lengthy process of secularisation. Indeed, the basis and approach for various developments which took place during the Renaissance often took centuries to be realised. Rationalism, democracy and human rights, modern science and technology, banking, economics based on the principle of maximum gain, and the perception of building as an art would all be inconceivable were it not for this remarkable period, which marked the end of the Middle Ages and the beginning of modern times.

The original aim of the new movement was far from the "secularisation" of human existence. On the contrary, the world was seen as a heavenly creation and an effort was made to understand the laws of nature as a way of understanding the harmony behind it. It was also believed that harmony and beauty in art resulted from the application of specific rules. The reconsideration and rediscovery of ancient Greek culture was an almost inevitable consequence of this belief. Humanists were already calling for the revival of the Italian cultural tradition. People learned Greek and Latin – the language of ancient Rome which had previously been almost exclusively reserved for the clergy. They sought, translated and studied ancient documents, surveyed and reconstructed ancient buildings, excavated sculptures and re-erected them.

The only literary source on ancient architecture available to the humanists was a treatise consisting of ten books on architecture compiled from around 25 B.C by the Roman military engineer and

---

1434: Cosimo de Medici becomes ruler of Florence and establishes the "Accademia Platonica" in 1459.

1497: Vasco da Gama discovers the sea route to India.

1498: Girolamo Savonarola is executed in Florence for his opposition to autocratic Medicis and the immoral Pope Alexander VI.

1510: The Fuggers, the commercial rulers of Augsburg, run the world trade society.

1514: Niccolò Macchiavelli writes his *Principe* (The Prince), a portrait of a clever and powerful Renaissance ruler.

1517: Martin Luther publishes his 95 theses in Wittenberg, the beginning of the Reformation in Germany.

1518: Adam Riese's first arithmetic textbook is published.

1519: Luther contests the Godly origin of the papacy and the infallibility of the Councils. The Italian painter and intellectual Leonardo da Vinci dies.

1519–22: Magellan circumnavigates the earth.

1521: The Pope bans Luther at the Diet of Worms.

1527: Conquest and plunder of Rome by Emperor Charles V's troops ("*Sacco di Roma*").

1528: Baldassare Castiglione publishes the treatise *Cortigiano* which describes the "*uomo universale*" as the typical Renaissance man.

1534: Luther's complete translation of the Bible is published. Ignatio von Loyola founds the "Society of Jesus" (Jesuits) which becomes the main defender of the Catholic church (especially during the Counter Reformation).

1536–41: Michelangelo paints his fresco "The Last Judgement" in the Sistine Chapel.

1555: The "religious peace" of Augsburg regulates faith in Germany and finalises the schism.

Plato and Aristotle deep in conversation: Raphael's *The School of Athens*, 1510–11, fresco, Stanza di Raffaelo, Vatican, Rome.

1564: William Shakespeare is born in Stratford-upon-Avon.

1565: Dutch revolt led by William of Orange and Count Egmont against intolerant religious rule in Spain.

1571: Spanish and Italian fleets break the maritime power of Turkey in the Battle of Lepanto; Spain achieves dominance in the Mediterranean. Giovanni Palestrina musical director of St. Peter's, Rome.

1588: Defeat of the Spanish Armada in battle against the English fleet under Sir Francis Drake.

1605: *Don Quixote* by Cervantes is published.

1616: Gallileo's Copernican writings included in the Index.

architect, Vitruvius. Vitruvius's treatise had continued to be recorded down through the Middle Ages, but found a much wider audience during the Renaissance. In addition to essays on architectural history and construction theory, Vitruvius drew up a definitive job description for the architect, which included a plan for his education and training. He also dealt with town planning, various building materials, the effect of colour, civil engineering and mechanics. By describing the universe as an architectural structure, he derived laws for the cosmos and architecture. The technical terms from this, the only existing ancient textbook on architecture, are still in use today.

The "Renaissance" ("rebirth" – a term also used to describe the renewed flourishing of a style, fashion or philosophical perspective) of antiquity was less concerned with a precise imitation of ancient architecture than with rediscovering the philosophy and world view of ancient Greek and Roman civilisations.

Experiments in Florence

Florence was the indisputable forerunner in developments leading up to the Renaissance. This thriving, ambitious and critical republic had gradually worked its way up to a prominent position in Europe through trade, commerce and banking. The Pazzis, Medicis and Pittis supported all artistic endeavours which created a distance from the recent inglorious past and which helped to spread a sense of optimism with regard to the future. Leading citizens were counselled by humanists or themselves pursued humanistic studies; the combined pursuit of public service and intellectual activity is one of the distinctive developments of this period. The desire to establish a modern way of life which linked up to the rich cultivated legacy of ancient times led to a comprehensive revival of the arts.

It was under these fertile conditions that Renaissance architecture developed in Florence and the surrounding state of Tuscany. Filippo Brunelleschi's dome for Florence cathedral, which was begun in 1420 and, strictly speaking, merely represents the culmination of a Gothic construction task, is acknowledged as marking the beginning of this new era in architectural history. The use of the double-shelled structure made it possible to design the exterior and interior of the dome independently of each other. Thus the inner dome was low, as suited the proportions of the Gothic cathedral interior, while the outer dome was higher and slimmer, reaching in absolute tranquillity and harmony to the crowning lantern. The load-bearing ribs were concealed between the shells. It

therefore differed from standard structural practice in Gothic buildings in that the structural elements were not exposed.

The appearance of a building was not merely seen as an expression of structural requirements and abstract systems of proportion but above all as an expression of the architect's design concept. It was the architect's job to "make God's ideas visible" and thus follow "heavenly harmonies" of beauty. The form of the Florence cathedral dome was initially defined in a model and with time this became standard practice in the design of important buildings. The architect provided an individual artistic service and always had the overall appearance of the building in mind. He no longer saw himself as an anonymous craftsman – as was the case in the Middle Ages – but as an independent creative artist, an individual.

This concept of individual artistic genius also spread to painting and graphic arts. Portraits and representations of other forms and events, displaying a degree of realism which had never existed before, began to appear alongside the religious paintings which had hitherto almost completely dominated this area of the arts.

As part of this trend, for the first time since antiquity, the dwelling place became a focus in architecture in the 14th century. The self-confident upper-classes in Italian towns wanted prestigious residences

Florence cathedral, ca. 1294–1467, dome by Brunelleschi, 1418–36 (axonometric projection based on Sanpaolesi)

The powerful dome of Florence cathedral is seen as a technical masterpiece of its time. The extension of the cathedral choir which was built in the 13th century by Arnolfo di Cambio was not completed until the addition of Brunelleschi's dome. The octagonal tambour was vaulted with a double-shell. The inner, stronger shell supports the lighter outer shell. Both consist of a combination of rows of stone laid in herringbone pattern and open ribs. What was particularly new about this structure was the way in which a self-supporting structure was created which did not require centring (a system which supports a dome during construction).

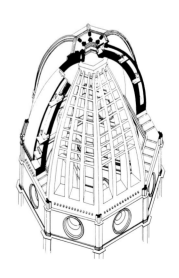

Filippo Brunelleschi: *Foundling Hospital*, Florence, begun in 1419

The Foundling Hospital is one of Brunelleschi's first buildings. Its clear articulation and strictly proportioned forms already include some of the essential features of the Renaissance style.

Leon Battista Alberti: *Palazzo Rucellai*, Florence, 1446–51

Palazzo Rucellai reintroduces the Classical column order: Doric, Ionic and Corinthian pilasters are stacked on the façade.

which would help them make a suitable statement about their status and achievements. For the first time, secular building was allowed a power of expression which went beyond pure functionality. Florence was also the forerunner when it came to the design and construction of the monumental private building, the palazzo. (This is derived from "palatium", the Latin name for the Palatin, the Roman hill on which Emperor Augustus and his successors lived.) The palazzo was modelled on the fortified houses found in Italian towns during the Middle Ages, which had been destroyed during the power struggles of the 13th and 14th centuries. Thus the exterior of Early Renaissance palaces was rather closed, defensive, raw and uninviting. This effect was achieved by the use of crude massive rough-textured blocks of stone with deep joints (rustication), and small rectangular windows on the ground floor. The upper floors were fitted with round arch windows (bifore) – the arch linking two windows completely surrounded by small rusticated masonry bands. Most of the buildings had three floors, which diminished in size as they moved upward and were separated by a string course along the window sills. The horizontal articulation of the rectangular, strictly symmetrical façades was further emphasised by the base cornice and powerful projecting eaves cornice based on the ancient Roman model. Early palaces were, however, open to their rectangular inner courtyards, which were enclosed by arcades and arcaded walks.

Although the early Palazzo Rucellai does not have an inner courtyard (it took a few centuries for this idea to take root), its architect, Leon Battista Alberti, is one of the artists whose work fully embodies the spirit of the new era and the widespread change it heralded. This is expressed in architectural terms, for example, by the façade of the Palazzo Rucellai. It is completely smooth, the rusticated masonry being merely ornament channelled into the wall. Moreover, the horizontal emphasis in this building is also accompanied by a vertical accent; pilasters with capitals from the ancient Classical orders were revived here again for the first time.

The Palazzo Rucellai was one of the first works by Alberti, who was the most important Early Renaissance architect after Brunelleschi. His marked awareness of himself as an artist meant that he saw the design of a building as the main priority and often left the actual job of construction to others. In this he betrayed an attitude emphasising the worth of the intellectual creation which was far in advance of his time. He also engaged in the theory of art and recorded the principles of his architecture in books, which played an important role in spreading the ideas behind Renaissance architecture, giving it a clearly formulated conceptual standard. Moreover, he was considered the first "universal man" (or "universal genius"). Like Bramante, Raphael, Michelangelo and Leonardo da Vinci, he excelled in a wide range of activities such as architecture, sculpture, painting, literature, mathematics, science and politics.

The circle as the most perfect form

As a result of their wide variety of interests and the linking of religious, philosophical and aesthetic ideas typical of the Renaissance, artists and intellectuals also began to show an interest in town planning and the proportions of the human body which had served as a basic unit for all design in (Greek) antiquity. Man was defined as the centre of the world and this idea was converted to a system for the measurement and representation of space – central perspective in spatial design. Brunelleschi is reputed to have used Euclid's mathematical system of optics in its development.

The rediscovery of ancient knowledge also played a role in the revival of the domed building. Both the ability and desire to build large domes like the

Florence cathedral dome were crucial here. Around the same time as he designed the cathedral dome, Brunelleschi also designed the Foundling Hospital, a building with arches supported by columns, and the Old Sacristy of San Lorenzo, the first centrally-planned Renaissance building. The circle symbolised perfect harmony and balance to an even greater extent than the square and the Greek cross – the other forms which featured regularly in the plans of this period. It was Alberti's belief that only the circle could express the essence of God and His creation. Studies of proportion also showed that the human body which was created "in God's image" fitted exactly into this form.

The circle or polygon was thus seen, not only by Alberti, as the ideal form for churches, and the only suitable crown for such a building was the dome, which also traditionally symbolised the universe. On the basis of this conception, the altar belonged in the centre of the church and the congregation assembled around it. Stasis is imposed rather than mobility. The view of the dome is the same from every point in the room. It climbs up towards heaven but does not get lost as in Gothic cathedrals; it is brought back to earth by the semi-circle.

The only Christian buildings hitherto based on a central plan were baptisteries, mortuary chapels and sometimes churches dedicated to the Virgin Mary – and the church was reluctant to abandon the standard axial plan. Therefore, the church of Sant' Andrea in Mantua, which was designed by Alberti in 1470 and embodied a compromise of the two styles, became a model for the new type of church. The single-aisle vaulted hall church with three vaulted side chapels (as abutments), a similarly structured transept, rectangular choir, semi-circular apse and crossing, with a dome resting on a tambour, was based on ancient models like the thermal baths and the Maxentius basilica. The façade combines the motifs of the triumphal arch and temple front, which show how the architect tried to achieve perfect unity and harmony in the building in the absence of a central plan.

HIGH AND LATE RENAISSANCE (MANNERISM) 1500–1600

Organic buildings

Humanism developed into an important movement in the mid-15th century. This development was helped by the conquest of Constantinople by the Ottomans in 1453, which led many Greek intellectuals to flee to Italy, and by the invention of printing by Johannes Gutenberg. The latter made it possible to rapidly disseminate information and theories to a wide audience. Many architects were now able to publish accounts of their experiences and approaches to design. Hence, "unrealised" architecture assumed greater importance and mere designs could influence developments for the first time.

Whilst the church bitterly opposed many of the Renaissance developments, above all in the area of natural sciences, at the same time it developed, like the princes, a considerable appetite for fame and prestige. As a result, by the end of the 15th century what had started out as healthy individualism had in some cases developed into unfettered self-glorification. The worldly attitudes of the Renaissance popes, and the humanists' criticism of the way in which the clergy lived, indicate the very real need for reformation which already existed. The focus in architectural development shifted from Florence to Rome, as if to indicate this change in spirit.

Architectural features also changed. Instead of being arranged in rows at equal distances, windows were now often arranged in groups, or alternating narrow and wide masonry strips followed on a wall axis. The stronger mobility which resulted from this development also corresponded to the way in which façade decoration became more sculptural. Windows were framed with socles, columns and pilasters, and crowned with "roofs" in the form of architraves, rounded arches or triangular gables. Portals were similarly accented or designed as rounded arches with keystones. Friezes were joined by medallions and triglyphs, and balustrades

Leon Battista Alberti: *Santa Andrea*, Mantua, from 1470.

Donato Bramante: *Tempietto San Pietro in Montorio*, Rome, 1502–03

Bramante's Tempietto (small temple) is acknowledged as the perfect High Renaissance building. Its symmetry is based on the consistent use of the circle as the purest geometrical form. The proportions of the individual architectural elements are so precisely related to each other that they exude a perfect balance. A ring of columns rises from a circular base consisting of three steps. The ring of columns supports an entablature above which there is a balustrade. The colonnaded ambulatory surrounds a slim domed masonry cylinder. The Roman Pantheon can be identified as a model for this completely harmonious centrally-planned structure. Bramante's plan to design the surrounding courtyard in such a way that the Tempietto would stand at the centre of a circular cloister was not executed.

Jacopo Sansovino: *Libreria Vecchia*, Venice, 1536–53

This architect, who came from Rome, was responsible for the introduction to Venice of the more strict orders of High Roman Renaissance style, as can be seen in his redesign of St. Mark's Square.

crowned the roof edges. Early Renaissance buildings showed a certain correspondence between the interior and exterior design. Now, however, the aim was to allow the building to develop steadily from its core and to show this organic structure in the exterior articulation.

The Tempietto in the courtyard in San Pietro in Montorio in Rome is seen as the ultimate example of this High Renaissance style. This small domed circular building rises steadily and harmoniously from the stepped base, demonstrating how the Renaissance used antique forms but adapted them to the spirit of the time. The circular colonnaded hall of the Tempietto has as little to do with the sequential arranged character of the Classical Greek temple as the inner structure which comes out of it. The Tempietto is the work of Donato Bramante, who soon went on to build large centrally-planned churches, including Santa Maria della Consolazione in Todi (from 1504 onwards) and Como cathedral (from 1519 onwards). His greatest work was to have been the reconstruction of St. Peter's in Rome (San Pietro in Vaticano), the main papal church.

The generous patronage of the arts by the Vatican began with Pope Sixtus IV (Pope from 1471 to 1484) and the commission for the Sistine Chapel which was named after him. It reached its culmination under Julius II (1503–13). Bramante's plan for St. Peter's, which literally overflowed with Greek crosses, circles, squares and interaction of these forms, was ultimately abandoned. The reconstruction of the church was mainly based on the ideas of Michelangelo, who had been responsible for the monumental ceiling design in the Sistine Chapel using an ever-increasing number of ingenious illusionist techniques. As the human observer is the measure of all things in the Renaissance, his/her powers of spatial perception also became the key measure for architecture. The observer was fooled when – for reasons of space – the architecture was unable to create an impressive spatial experience. Thus, for example, Bramante deceives the visitor to his church Santa Maria near San Satiro in Milan with an impressive choir space which is actually a "drawn shrine" with no actual depth. This phenomenon was perfected during the Baroque period to become the technique of illusionism.

Smooth transition to the Baroque

Such Baroque tendencies were even more prevalent in Venice. The bad quality of the building ground in the city had always necessitated the use of the lightest possible construction methods, such as the extensive piercing of the façade, in the Libreria Vecchia. The seemingly endless row of columned

MICHELANGELO

Michelangelo spent his crucial formative years in Florence, where he first studied painting under Ghirlandaio and later went on to study sculpture under Bertoldo di Giovanni. As his earliest sketches show, the young man had an exceptional talent for both disciplines. His paintings were modelled on those of Giotto and Masaccio and his sculpture was initially strongly influenced by Donatello. Lorenzo di Medici supported the fifteen-year-old artist, whose genius he quickly recognised, by taking him into the inspiring environment of his palace. However, despite this early and intensive contact with the great court of the Medicis, Michelangelo never became a man of court. Throughout his long life he remained something of a reserved loner, more of an individual than a sociable type, and very different from the urbane and courtly Leonardo da Vinci (1452–1519), who was already famous when Michelangelo was starting his career.

Michelangelo's first works – for example "The Battle of the Lapiths and Centaurs" – originate from his Florentine period. In 1496, at the age of 21, he went to Rome, where in 1498 he produced his Pietà for St. Peter's. With this magnificent group sculpture he brought marble to life and earned the justified admiration of his contemporaries. He twice left Rome to return to Florence for extended periods, and in 1501 sculpted his statue of David in Florence. In 1509 he started work on the frescos for the Sistine Chapel and worked on them at various intervals for almost thirty years.

Michelangelo came to architecture at a relatively late stage in his career. From 1516 – when he had reached the ripe old age of 40 – he worked on designs for the façade of S. Lorenzo in Florence which was never built. He finally saw the execution of his architectural designs with the Biblioteca Medicea Laurenziana and the Medici mausoleum, between 1520 and 1534. The division of the walls negates their boundaries, the interior and exterior become interchangeable, the separation of the floors is unclear, the architecture is treated like sculpture. However, Michelangelo

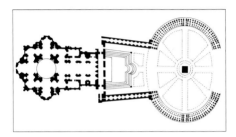

The Capitol, façade of the Palazzo dei Conservatori (above)

H. Cock: *View of the Capitoline Hill in Rome,* ca. 1544–45 (above left)

Etienne Duperac: *The Campidoglio as designed by Michelangelo,* 1569 (left)

Plan of St. Peter's church (Michelangelo) *and St. Peter's Square* (Bernini) (below left)

succeeded in creating a worthy setting for the books which were relatively valuable at the time. The almost sacred impression is perhaps created by the storage of the books in racks which resemble church benches, and are also arranged vertically along a central aisle. Like all his architecture, Michelangelo's Biblioteca Laurenziana is sober and solemn in its effect; not popular but serious, thought through to the last detail, full of strength and dignity.

Michelangelo spent the last thirty years of his life from 1534 in Rome where he worked on the fresco of the Last Judgement in the Sistine Chapel. In 1547, the aged artist took over the supervision of the construction of St. Peter's. This papal church in the Vatican city had existed in different forms since 324 A.D. The foundation stone for a completely new building was laid in 1506 by Pope Julius II. The size of the building was already dictated by Bramante's plans and the existing structures. However, Michelangelo succeeded in keeping the main idea – central plan of a Greek cross with central dome – but tightened up the plan and gave it a clear uniform shape. The church was given a main axis with the help of a columned portico and a flight of steps at

the front, plus a clear orientation towards the city, which Gian Lorenzo Bernini used fifty years later to great effect in the design of St. Peter's square (the plan on the left shows both church and square).

Michelangelo set his magnificent dome, a masterpiece of engineering and architectural harmony, on the crossing. Like the Pantheon dome, the dome of St. Peter's is 42 metres in diameter and attains a height of 132 metres from the marble floor of the church to the cross on top of the lantern. Like Brunelleschi's dome in Florence, Michelangelo's dome succeeds in dominating the entire city of Rome, which is not exactly short of domes. It exudes complete harmony, regardless of the perspective or distance from which it is observed.

During the last years of his life, Michelangelo designed the Palazzo dei Conservatori on the Capitoline hill, which he had been working on since 1536 when he designed the square on which it stands. This project was initiated after the *Sacco di Roma* (1529), the attack by the soldiers of Emperor Charles V, which was followed by comprehensive restructuring. By designing the first modern monumental square in the city, Michelangelo worked not only for the Head of the Church but also for the city authorities. The redesign of the square began with the erection by Michelangelo in 1538 of the equestrian statue of Marc Aurel which was intended to provide the central focus of the complex. The square was not completed until 120 years later, with the completion of the Capitol Museum in 1654. Michelangelo lived only to see the beginning of the construction of the Palazzo dei Conservatori, which was nevertheless built mainly in accordance with his design. The proportioning typical of Michelangelo, i.e. the vertical division of two floors with pilasters or semi-columns as the main façade articulation, gives the building a festive balance.

Michelangelo is without doubt one of the most important and multi-faceted artists in world history. As a painter, sculptor and architect he left much uncompleted work behind him. His universal genius exercised a lasting influence on all three disciplines for many centuries.

The powerful dome of St. Peter's in Rome

Juan Bautista de Toledo and Juan de Herrera: *El Escorial*, near Madrid, 1563–89

The strictly composed complex and sober façade of the monastery, commissioned by Philip II, is completely influenced by the High Italian Renaissance style. The monumental complex, which was mainly designed by Juan de Bautista de Toledo and built by Juan de Herrera, has an axial-symmetrical plan. Four extremely long (approximately 160 metres) wings surround the square complex, the corners of which are accented by towers. The monastery church and the royal palace lie along the main interior axis. The palace adjoins the choir and the altar can be seen from the king's bed. Buildings for the court and monastery are grouped around rectangular inner courtyards.

The Escorial is a typical building of the Counter-Reformation with its combined expression of religion and the divine right of kings. This combination of the castle and the monastery later exercised an important influence on the magnificent monastery buildings of the Baroque period.

arches was based directly on ancient models such as the Coliseum by the architect Andrea Sansovino. The prominent sculptural emphasis of the façade (which also creates a strong interaction of bright-dark features), the frieze with the medallions, putti and garlands, and the crowning of the building with a balustrade bearing statues and obelisks, creates an impression of festive excitement rather than imperial sobriety.

The first signs of Mannerism can easily be detected here. "Mannerism" (from Italian *manerismo*) is taken to mean the inauthentic imitation of a style and suggests that the style in question is being surpassed. Whilst the stylistic means are exploited with playful ease and virtuosity, the original idea behind them is diminished to the level of irrelevance. The intention is to ironically undermine order through the conscious juxtaposition of individual architectural elements and express in architectural terms how "out of sync" the world is.

Thus the Renaissance spirit initiated a development, the inherent dynamism of which led to the end of its own era. By observing the planets, Copernicus had come to the conclusion that the "geocentric" system, according to which the earth was centre of the universe and which was staunchly defended by the Church, had to be wrong ("Copernican system", 1543). The discovery of America and other great sea expeditions brought further proof that the earth was not a disc under a glass dome. Moreover, the excessive display of indulgent splendour by Renaissance popes led to the establishment of a new religion independent of Rome. The balanced world began to falter.

The response of the princes and clergy to this development was to suppress the urge for indi-

vidual freedom. In Spain, where the Inquisition had been particularly forceful in its efforts to deal with supposedly "unfaithful" members of the Church, the construction of the Escorial, a monumental building, clearly reflects the new way of thinking. A closed complex, with tower-like emphasis in the corners organically developed from the core of the central church, this structure was still rooted in the Renaissance. The combination of a monastery, castle and church, in which the King resided right next to the house of God and had direct access to it, demonstrates the monarch's claim to be the ruler "blessed by God" and to fulfil God's will on earth – entirely in the spirit of the Baroque.

THE RENAISSANCE NORTH OF THE ALPS 1520–1620

Renaissance decoration on Gothic buildings

The hold of the Gothic style remained so deep-rooted in its French and German strongholds that the emerging new style had difficulty in asserting itself. The fact that the churches had little or no role to play here can primarily be explained by practical concerns: large Gothic churches continued to satisfy all requirements in this area and many were still being constructed in the 15th and 16th centuries. The foundation stone for the Gothic cathedral in Berne (Switzerland belonged to the German Empire until 1648) was not laid until 1421, one year after Brunelleschi had started work on the dome of Florence cathedral.

Castles had already assumed greater significance in 16th-century centralised France. Kings François I and Henry II were responsible for the initiation of extensive architectural activity in and around Paris and in the hunting areas of the Loire valley. François I had seen the possibilities for self-promotion offered by Renaissance architecture during his expeditions to north Italy, and had brought Italian architects back to France.

In many cases, however, architects working north of the Alps had no first-hand experience of either Renaissance or ancient architecture, and based their ideas on copper engravings and the architectural textbooks of Vitruvius, Palladio, Vignola and others.

The late Gothic predilection for "picturesque" inter-connected complexes can be seen in the chateaux of Blois, Amoise, Fontainebleau and Saint Germain-en-Laye. In contrast, the chateaux in Encouen, Ancy-le-Franc and Charleval consisted of clearly grouped, mostly rectangular complexes built around inner courtyards.

ANDREA PALLADIO

With Andrea Palladio, Renaissance architecture reached a mature and happy synthesis in the Republic of Venice, its town of Vicenza and the Veneto countryside during the 16th century. Palladio succeeded in linking ancient tradition with the humanism of his time in a particularly harmonious way, and designed Classical buildings against the background of his writings. "Palladianism" was so popular that it strongly influenced the architecture of subsequent periods, for example, English Classicism.

Andrea di Pietro dalla Gondola was born on November 30th 1508 in Padua. At the age of thirteen he started work as a stone mason in the workshop of Bartolomeo Cavazza. Two years later

Villa Rotunda, Vicenza, 1566–69

he continued his education by studying architectural sculpture under Porlezza in Vicenza. He met his most important teacher in 1537 while working on the Villa Trissino in Cricoli. It was Trissino who inspired him to develop his own identity as a humanist architect from the roots of ancient tradition. It was presumably Trissino who gave him the name Palladio which is as elegant as his later work. As a humanist familiar with Neo-Platanism, Trissino also referred Palladio to ancient architectural theory, Vitruvius's Ten Books. Following Aristotle's dictum that knowledge must emerge from individual observation and experience, Palladio undertook not only theoretical studies but viewed and surveyed numerous ancient buildings, for example on his trips to Rome between 1545 and 1547. In 1570 he published his own four books on architecture which continue the great tradition of Vitruvius and Alberti. In these books, he discusses the contemporary views of proportion and

architectural beauty, explains what architects like Serlio and Vignola had made of the Classical column orders and, most importantly, presents his own work and its typology.

Palladio was already an expert in the field when he made his late breakthrough as an architect in his early forties. The focal urban building of Vicenza, the basilica, was converted in 1549. This marked the beginning of a new self-awareness for Palladio and an economic upturn in the town's fortunes. As the basilica was already an ancient style building, Palladio had a perfect opportunity to realise his ambitions while giving the Medieval façade a new urban face. He opened it onto the Piazza dei Signori with two-floored loggias behind arcades which, together with the column motif adopted from Serlio, gave the building a completely new rhythm. This marked the beginning of a long mutually beneficial relationship between Palladio and Vicenza which continued with the construction of some urban palaces. An example of these palaces is Palazzo Chiericati (1550–1609) where he succeeded in creating great urban charm by opening the façade and accentuating the central tract, an impression which contrasts strongly with the fortress-like rusticated and uniform façades of earlier Renaissance palaces.

However, the building in which Palladio's art can be seen at its most daring and original is the country house. He re-interpreted this genre for the discerning, educated affluent nobility in his area who wanted to combine agricultural activities on their estates with their social lives. Thus he adapted the Roman "villa rusticana" to that of a "villa suburbana", as can be seen in the villa Badoer in Frata Polesine, villa Emo in Fanzolo and the villa Barbaro in Maser, all of which were completed around 1560. The farming buildings and storerooms are located in wings behind the loggias, which are symmetrically aligned to a raised central structure. This provides a representative entrance to a banqueting hall with a tympanum on a Classical column order. This linking of the main building and garden with shady zones behind the columns and arcades is the

Il Rendentore, Venice, 1577–92

equivalent of his achievement in opening the basilica and palazzos of Vicenza to the square. The high point in Palladio's work is, however, the ideal architecture of the Villa Almerico-Capra in Vicenza. It is known as "La Rotunda" and is an exemplary centrally-planned building, having a circular domed room in the middle and identical sides with extended temple façades. Like the Pantheon and Bramante's Tempietto, it symbolises complete harmony between man and the cosmos. It was ideally suited to the humanists as a refined setting for the exchange of their ideas.

Palladio had reached the height of his career by 1571. Prominent and much in demand, he became Sansovino's successor as the leading architect in Venice, where he mainly designed churches. However, he was unable to recreate his ideal of the centrally-planned building in the rhythm of the Classical order without some element of compromise. The traditional plan of the religious building with its nave and side aisles, which were dictated by the hierarchy of religious ritual, made it impossible for him to use the preferred central plan. With the façade of San Francesco della Vigna (from 1562 onwards) and San Giorgio Maggiore (1565–75, façade after 1600), Palladio developed intermediary solutions to this problem, paving the way for the construction of his final church, Il Rendentore. The façade powerfully clamps the nave and side chapels with the help of interlocking columns and framed stacked tympana. The refined openness of former buildings is replaced here by a closed sculptural quality, an impression which is repeated in the later Palazzo Valmarana (1566–81) and the façade of the Loggia del Capitaniato (1566–71) in Vicenza, and which points towards the approaching Baroque.

In 1580, the year of his death, Palladio returned to Classical architecture once more with the Teatro Olimpico in Venice. He built a semi-circular arena for the audience for revivals of Classical theatre and an illusionistic *Gassenim* stage.

Teatro Olimpico, Vicenza, 1580–85

Domenico da Cortona (?) and Jacques and Denis Sourdeau: *Chambord Castle*, begun in 1519, staircase (below) ca. 1530

Chambord Castle, which was commissioned by François I, demonstrates individual interpretation of the Renaissance in France. A symmetrical rectangular complex, the building is based on a clear plan which was probably designed by Domenico da Cortona. The wide regular garden at the front of the complex is open, whereas the fortress-like central building resembles the donjon of a Medieval castle. The steep roofs and apparently randomly distributed chimneys, dormer windows and pinnacles are completely indebted to the late Gothic style.

The double-spiral staircase at the centre of the central building, which is possibly based on a design by Leonardo da Vinci, shows that the castle also has Mannerist characteristics. The spiral staircase with its cord-like intertwining flights of stairs is not an ideal serene Renaissance structure but a highly attractive confusing irrational space.

The Louvre in Paris, construction of which was started on the basis of plans by Lescot in 1546 but continued in a different form, is one of the most famous of these buildings. The Loire castle Chambord was the biggest of the French Renaissance castles but it was never completed. With its 365 towers, chimneys and architecturally accented dormer windows (lucarne), Chambord is the most extreme example of the Gothic tradition of steep roofs with richly decorated roof structures, which were also used on almost all French Renaissance castles. Other typical features included the accented corner towers adopted from the castles of the Middle Ages, which no longer had any defensive function to fulfil, and the stair turrets integrated into the façade. With their gardens relating to the castle building, the complexes in Verneuil and Charleval also point in the direction of the approaching Baroque.

Protestantism and its consequences

The situation in Germany was similar to that in France, the main difference being that large areas of the country had never been ruled by the Romans and there was no ancient architectural tradition to refer to. As in France, elements of the new architecture were adopted – rectangular windows, string courses between floors, gables crowned with obelisks, flanked with volutes and decreasing in size from one floor to the next, mainly as decorative details which had not changed very much since the late Gothic era. Examples include the Pied Piper's house in Hamlyn (1602–03), Heidelberg castle (from the mid-16th century) and Antwerp town hall (Cornelius de Vriendt, 1561–65), which became the model for all town halls in north central Europe. Buildings developed during the Renaissance period appeared later; for example Aschaffenburg castle (Georg Riedinger, 1605–14),

which was the first regular castle complex in Germany, and Augsburg town hall by Elias Holl, which is seen as an original example of middle-class architecture. Domed buildings were almost non-existent.

The consequences of Renaissance philosophy had a far greater impact on religion in Germany than on architecture. The resentment against the "over-secularised" church was particularly strong here. Renaissance popes made the situation worse with their pursuit of pomp and splendour, which led to serious financial problems in the Church. The Church tried to deal with these problems by, among other things, engaging in the sale of indulgences – through which the faithful could purchase atonement for their sins. As part of the Renaissance spirit, the entire behaviour of the Church was scrutinised by its critics to see if it still reflected its origins. Martin Luther translated the Bible into German (it was previously only available in Latin) and by doing this made it accessible to a far wider population.

The refusal of the Pope, clergy and Emperor to become involved in reformation eventually led to the Schism, which was initially the furthest thing from the intentions of Luther and the other reformers. The new religion, moreover, came from "below" and was strongly influenced by the Renaissance spirit. Man with his faith and conscience faces God as an equal. The Church is not authorised to forgive sins, mediation by the clerics is only conditional and is not possible through the Virgin Mary and the saints. Art should not be used to convey faith. Iconoclastic events involving the destruction of religious paintings and sculptures were held during the Reformation. However, the Lutherans eventually withdrew the ban on paintings and the strict separation of politics and religion and – precisely as a result of this renewed link between secular power and religion – ornamental Protestant churches were built. The religious building had lost its prominent position in the Protestant areas of central, west and northern Europe.

Palladianism comes to England

Gothic architecture remained popular for so long in England that the Renaissance had practically no influence on religious buildings and its influence did not affect secular buildings until the end of the 16th century. A key role was played by the architecture of Andrea Palladio. As a result of his influence, Classical European architecture from the late-16th to 18th century ultimately became known as Palladianism.

Wollaton Hall in Nottinghamshire (Robert Smithson, 1580–88) – like Burghley House near Stamford, Northampton (started in 1575), one of the most important Renaissance castles in the country – is a symmetrical complex developed from the central hall with volute gables and balustrade, string courses and pilasters. The large rectangular windows with their lattice tracery are reminiscent of the Perpendicular Style of the English Gothic era, whereas the stacked protrusion of the building to the corners points towards the Baroque.

This tendency can be observed even more prominently in the work of the most important English architect of the late Renaissance: Inigo Jones. Inigo Jones spent some time in Italy and studied the Classical formal language of Palladio intensively. In 1615, he was appointed General Buildings Inspector to the London Court.

With buildings such as the Banqueting House of Whitehall Palace in the centre of London – a perfect structure in the Renaissance spirit – he introduced Palladio's style to England. It was to remain a decisive influence there for the next two centuries.

Elias Holl: *Town Hall*, Augsburg, 1615–20

As town architect of Augsburg, Elias Holl designed a number of public buildings. Inspired by Palladio, whose architecture he encountered on a trip to Venice around 1600, Holl developed a balanced Classical style which is evident in the symmetrical emphasis of the façade of his town hall.

Inigo Jones: *Banqueting House Whitehall Palace*, London 1619–22

The Italian Renaissance made a very late appearance in England with the architecture of Inigo Jones. The Banqueting House is the first and most important work of English Palladianism. Jones studied the architecture of Palladio and ancient Rome during two study trips to Italy. The cubic building exudes Classical discipline and monumental dignity. The façade of the two-storey building is vertically divided by Ionic and Corinthian pilasters. The three central window axes are lightly accentuated by columns which protrude further than the pilasters. The entrance portal was located at the side of the building so as not to disturb the uniformity of the main elevation. The building has one single large hall in which the engagement of the Prince of Wales was to have been celebrated.

Jones's buildings inspired great enthusiasm for architecture and the theoretical writings of Palladio which lasted until the 18th century.

THE EMERGENCE OF THE BAROQUE IN ITALY 1600–1700

Life as a party

BAROQUE AND ROCOCO

1600–1780

Revising the Renaissance

The transition from one architectural era to the next generally takes the form of a gradual process which initially goes unnoticed. This is particularly true of the changeover from the Renaissance to the Baroque. The question arises, therefore, as to the specific point at which the desire for elaborate ornament, swirling movement, painted interiors and the clear articulation of Late Renaissance buildings was taken to such an extreme that it is possible to speak of the Baroque.

The way that the new style grew directly out of the Late Renaissance is demonstrated by the fact that the acknowledged model for all Baroque churches, the Jesuit church Il Gesù in Rome (1568–75), was designed in the mid-16th century by one of the most important (Late) Renaissance architects, Giacomo da Vignola. With this pier church, a modern version of the Early Christian basilica, Giacomo da Vignola created a church type which was to become the standard model for Catholic Baroque churches for the next two centuries. A basilical, barrel-vaulted nave leads to a central crossing capped by a high dome resting on a drum or tambour. The side aisles were replaced by a series of individual chapel niches, which opened off the nave and had a structural function as abutments. This plan is often described in terms of the interpenetration of two spaces, i.e. the nave

and central crossing. It would be more accurate, however, to describe it as the fusion of these spaces. Shortly after its completion, the main church of Catholic Christians, St. Peter's in Rome, was converted into a longitudinal scheme through the addition of a nave to the central scheme – by Carlo Maderna in 1607–26. Thus the Roman Catholic Church, which had always shown a certain reluctance in adopting the Renaissance idea that the central plan was the only suitable plan for a house of God, now reverted to the old style longitudinal plan. This reversion to a former model was not limited to architecture. On the contrary, developments in architecture were merely symptomatic of a general trend. The Renaissance had led to an enormous loss of power by the Roman Church in many areas. Large parts of Europe had converted to Protestantism and the emergence of the modern rational sciences had proved the fallacy on which many of the fundamentals of the Catholic faith were based, for example with regard to the shape of the earth and its place in the universe. The Church had lost its monopoly in education and the religious building had relinquished its position as the sole source of authority in architectural development.

Increasingly severe measures were gradually introduced to counteract this trend. The Counter Reformation, which began with the Council of Trent in 1545, marked the introduction of long overdue reforms within the Catholic church and the start of a fierce campaign against Protestantism. The Index of Forbidden Books was compiled in 1559 and from 1562 there was widespread religious struggle and

---

1602: The Dutch East Indian company is founded in Batavia as the first modern limited company with 6.5 million guilders.

Ca. 1610: Barter is replaced by money-based economy.

1622: Richelieu is appointed Cardinal and becomes a powerful influence in French politics.

1633: Gallileo is forced to retract his support of Copernican teachings.

1634: Dismissal and murder of Wallenstein for negotiating with the Protestants.

1638: Amsterdam theatre (first national theatre in Europe) is inaugurated.

1642: Obligatory school attendance is introduced in Saxony-Gotha.

1644: René Descartes publishes his "*Principia philosophiae*" (*Principles of Philosophy*).

1648: Peace of Westphalia ends the Thirty Years War, the Augsburg

Confession agreement (1555) is reiterated with inclusion of the Calvinists.

Ca. 1650: Urban postal service with post boxes in Paris; regular newspaper published in Berlin.

1651: Publication of *Leviathan* by Thomas Hobbes (philosophical defence of absolute monarchy).

1655: Rembrandt paints *Ecce Homo*.

1664: Molière writes the play *Tartuffe*.

1666: "Académie des Sciences" is founded in Paris.

1673: The Test Act is passed in England excluding Catholics from state office (until 1828). France is unified under Colbert le Droit.

1675: Greenwich observatory is founded.

1685: Louis XIV of France repeals the Edict of Nantes. Mass flight of the Huguenots.

"L'état c'est moi": Louis XIV, The Sun King, in a portrait by Hyacinthe Rigaud (1701).

1686: Sir Isaac Newton publishes his main work "*Philosophiae naturalis principia mathematica*" (*Mathematical Principles of Natural Philosophy*).

1689: Constitutional monarchy is established in England under the "Bill of Rights".

1701: Prince Frederick III of Brandenburg crowns himself Frederick I "King of Prussia".

1703: Peter the Great allows St Petersburg to be built on the Western model.

1710: The German Meissen porcelain works are founded.

1724: Official Parisian stock exchange is opened.

1742: Première of Georg Friedrich Handel's *Messiah* in Dublin.

---

the persecution of Protestants (Huguenots) in France.

There were few Protestant Baroque churches whose influence spread beyond their immediate surroundings. The churches of the Anglican faith in England are an exception. However, this new religious faith was not the product of a reformation "from below", as was the case with the movement in the German Empire, it resulted from a dispute between King Henry VIII and the Pope. The Frauenkirche in Dresden, designed by Georg Bähr (1726–38), is another exception to this rule: the city's Protestant middle class wanted to build something which could compete with the majestic buildings of the Catholic royal house. The Frauenkirche, which is acknowledged as the most important Protestant Baroque church, has a central plan. The sermon, which plays a central role in the spread of the Protestant faith, was given a central role in the midst of the richly pompous Baroque environment.

A sweeping appeal to the senses

It was the advent of the Counter Reformation, however, which was to exercise the main formative influence on the development of Baroque architecture. Like secular power, religious power was seen as absolute and its legitimisation a matter of divine right. Baroque architecture set out to tackle the task of representing both authorities on a suitable scale and with due ceremony, using similar methods in the representation of both. The idea was to dramatise the power and to appeal to the sensuous perceptions of the observer. The express aims of the new style were to confuse and overpower. For example, the advantages of the church nave in terms of Counter Reformation strategies are obvious: the visitor's eye is steered along the nave in the same way as it would be directed along a triumphal path, making it possible to stage numerous other productions along the way.

Like the names given to other artistic periods and styles, the word "Baroque" was initially used to define something which was seen as oddly shaped and tasteless: it derives from the Portuguese word "barroco", meaning a misshapen pearl. During the second half of the 18th century, it was specifically used as a term of abuse to describe the architecture of Borromini and Guarini, which was perceived as a crass aberration from the rules of Classical architecture. Today, it is generally used as an adjective in the sense of "sweeping, overflowing and ornate".

Most Baroque architects had, indeed, very fecund imaginations. Every attempt was made to blur clear

contours and to individualise, decorate and convert walls into the most pliable swirling and dynamic forms possible. The most varied parts of façades were given concave and convex forms, while windows and doors were capped with complex structures such as triangles and segments of circles, which in turn were often dispersed, moulded, bent, broken and even, as in the façade of Il Gesù, fused. Cornices were strongly gradated and roof versions were often interrupted by window heads. Other typical decorative details included garlands, vases, urns, putti, s-shaped volutes, oeil-de-boef (oval) windows and cartouches (oval scrollwork with numerous curled edges).

As in ancient Roman architecture, which shared a similar delight in rich ornament, composite capitals and other permutations of the ancient orders, pilasters (including downward tapering "herm pilasters" terminating in a human torso) and columns with no load-bearing function, were all very popular. Baroque design was multi-faceted but always monumental in its overall effect. The supporting elements were emphasised and massed. For example, columns and pilasters were paired or enlarged to form the colossal order. This rose uniformly from the ground through two floors and sometimes formed the entire ground floor as a – possibly rusticated – socle area.

This enormous variety of architectural possibilities did not, however, add up to mere chaotic heaping of ornament and embellishment; it was based on a rationally composed concept. This was often based on what later on became known as the "Gesamtkunstwerk" (total work of art). The desire to confuse, impress and overwhelm not only

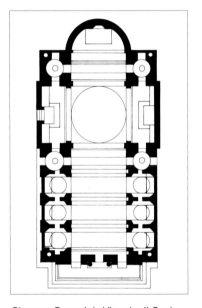

Giacomo Barozzi da Vignola: *Il Gesù*, Rome, 1568–75

The plan of Il Gesù provided a model for churches for the following two centuries, as it marked the introduction of the continuous Baroque spaces which replaced the additive spatial principle of the Renaissance. Il Gesù combines a central plan with a nave in one building. Transepts and nave chapels are condensed and all the energy is directed to the dome crossing. However, the vault formations do not yet intersect and the walls have no undulations – the main features behind the dynamism of High Baroque style. Architecture, sculpture and painting did not enter their illusionistic conspiracy until later buildings. The rich painting here is also distinguished from the architectural details. A strict rhythmical linking of the spatial elements, achieved by means of the channelled pilasters which also line the interior of the drum on which the dome rests, is also firmly rooted in the Renaissance.

Gian Lorenzo Bernini: *Sant' Andrea al Quirinale*, Rome, 1658–61

The original oval plan of the building is exquisitely visualised from the exterior by means of the concave stairway leading up to the entrance portal.

Francesco Borromini: *Palazzo Spada*, Rome, 1652–53

Borromini heightens perspective in the design of this illusionistic colonnade by moving the columns at the back closer together and shortening them. Reduction of the column height, which automatically draws the observer's eye forward, and the conscious choice of a statue which is smaller than usual, make the colonnade seem much longer than it actually is.

created a sense of splendour, dynamism and pomp. It also supported the absolute symmetry of almost every Baroque building and the strong emphasis on the central axis, to which the accentuation of the portal had an important contribution to make.

The fact that the "Baroque" evolved into an attitude pervading all aspects of life throughout Europe, can be observed not only in the unfolding of architectural ostentation. The whole of society developed a "Baroque lifestyle" which was proudly and actively demonstrated, not only in the arts – i.e. sculpture, painting and above all music – but also in magnificent celebrations of royal and church festivals, excessive piety, literary style (which could be either sentimental or coarse), fashion, hairdos, furniture, and even in the way people spoke.

There was, of course, a correlation between the aims of the Catholic Church and the changes which influenced the times. Following the "discovery of the world" during the Renaissance, the "splendour of the world" was now perceived as something painful and overshadowed by the idea of death ("memento mori!" = "remember your mortality!"). Typical Renaissance people were very much focused on themselves and this world, where they recognised and tried to explore the laws and harmony of God. The Baroque period, however, was characterised by a strong sense of self and a passionate preoccupation with the fate of man in the next world. Its art therefore focused on two areas: the representation of the visible universe and the invisible which was known to lie behind it, i.e. transcendence. The extended, imbalanced dynamic form of the oval (ellipse) became the symbol of the Baroque, featuring repeatedly in the plans of buildings and replacing the perfect, tranquil circle, which had symbolised the philosophy and emotion of the Renaissance. At the same time, however, all Baroque architecture continued to adhere strictly to the principle of unconditional symmetry.

This suffices to demonstrate the contradictory nature of the Baroque spirit. Whereas Gothic pointed arches soared speedily and powerfully upwards, the Baroque ellipse displays an irregular, swinging dynamic. The Gothic era was characterised by the search for a way of overcoming the misery of earthly existence, whilst the Baroque period was pervaded by a melancholy attitude to the transitory nature of this life. Unlike their Gothic counterparts, Baroque churches do not engage in an ecstatic and almost desperate reach to heaven. Instead – as in Sant' Andrea al Quirinale – the perspective swings in a festive and happy manner along the naves, which almost overflow with ornament and allegorical representations, and finally

moves up towards heaven in the dome area. To maintain consistency, the choir area is usually as weakly defined as the transept arms, which have been reduced to little more than deep niches. This means that the altar borders almost directly on the dome area, so that the eye carefully guided along the nave "collides" with it and immediately swings up towards heaven.

Illusion, confusion, drama

It follows, therefore, that enormous emphasis was placed on the design of domes. These no longer embodied a tranquil centre, as in the centrally-planned buildings of the Renaissance, but were the destination towards which all movement was aimed (a further reason for the return to the longitudinal plan). They bestowed the desired air of splendour and monumentality on the church exterior and, as in ancient and Byzantine architecture, provided a symbol of heaven in the interior. This symbolism, which had not suffered from the insights uncovered by the natural sciences, was usually emphasised by means of a suitable illustration, showing the actual sky and the religious heaven with exultant angels swaying in the clouds. A favourite trick, based on the clever use of perspective, was to make flat ceilings look as though they were vaulted and to make actual vaults and domes look higher than they were. Thus the space was raised to eternity. However, unlike the Gothic cathedrals which pursued height with equal if not greater energy, Baroque spaces did not disappear into an uncertain darkness.

The Baroque used more than graphical tricks to create confusion and illusion. The illusionism typical of this period consciously blurred the boundaries between architecture, sculpture and painting until they were no longer recognisable. It continued structural or decorative elements on painted surfaces and integrated sculptures into murals. Façades were also highly sculptural. It comes as no surprise to learn, therefore, that many artists like Gian Lorenzo Bernini and Andreas Schlüter were both architects and sculptors. Distorted perspectives were another popular ruse as can be seen in Borromini's Palazzo Spada.

The strict control exercised over the movement in Baroque architecture is equally matched by precise calculation of the overall effect and mood of the buildings. In addition to optical illusions, light was cleverly manipulated to achieve this effect. The principles applied to the design of interior walls were also applied to the design of façades. However, the possibilities offered by the effect of light and shadow, for example by letting daylight in

Bernini's St. Peter's Square is a dramatic production which focuses on the central building of the Catholic Church. St. Peter's church, designed by Maderna, Michelangelo and Bernini himself, is the main work of art representing sacred power. To the present day, the faithful assemble at its feet to receive the papal blessing – "urbi et orbi" – from the benediction loggia above the central portal. The square is conceived as an open-air theatre for staging the spectacle of the religious service. The scene is set by a slightly upward-sloping area in front of the church, which encloses the façade like a curtain – not in the form of a rectangular picture-frame stage, but with rows of columns which extend slightly further apart to the rear. From the square, the view opens to an imperceptibly raised and widening perspective, which makes the church look even more powerful and lighter than it actually is. This trick involves inversion of the central perspective model from the observer's eye, and the Renaissance spatial concept whereby the building generally surrounds an inner courtyard. The three-aisle colonnades surrounding the oval in front of the church were seen by Bernini as the motherly arms of the Church extending to embrace its followers. The obelisk in the middle is flanked by two fountains. Entrances are integrated into the colonnades like the Greek temple with its naos, and thus refer to the continuation of ancient architectural tradition, to which the entire square subscribes with its motif of the ancient arena or theatre.

through side chapel niches or directing it through the dome area, were obviously greater in the interior than on the outside. The concealed manipulation of light can also be used to make a wall appear to move forward or backward. This effect could be easily achieved in the central areas, with the result that this space no longer evoked a strong sense of tranquillity as it did in the Renaissance context. Thus, for example, the elliptical plan of Borromini's Catholic church San Carlo alle quattro fontane is "indented" by corner chapels (also elliptical in shape), on the four corners where the long and the narrow sides meet, filling the room with swaying rhythms.

The Baroque delight in drama included the inter-action of architecture and open space in urban design. An excellent example of this is St. Peter's Square in Rome, which was designed by Gian Lorenzo Bernini. His design of an axis leading to St. Peter's church is based on the interaction of open spaces (which increase in size) and tapering spaces. A small square was salvaged from the area between the slightly convex streets approaching the square. A gate opens onto another square which borders on a large colonnaded elliptical square – a very popular feature in Baroque architecture. This in turn leads into a smaller square which opens like a trapezium and rises gently to the church, making the already overpowering dimen-sions seem even larger with the help of a few optical illusions.

The Baroque "delight in the world" was not concerned with the natural "God-created" world, nor with the world refined by man in the Renaissance sense. It focused exclusively on an entirely man-made world. Thoughts of the next world did not inspire humility but the decision to give a particularly beautiful form to a transitory existence. The most important aim was to create a rich and splendid impression consisting more of appearance than reality, and no effort was spared to achieve this. Plaster was gilded, wood was painted to look like expensive marble. Buildings are wide but not particularly deep; the entire building is not particularly accentuated, merely the façade. The nobility wore wigs, wide crinolines, high heels – an uncomfortable and impractical "get-up" which clearly distinguished them from the lower (and middle) classes. Feudal society mustered all its splendour for the last time.

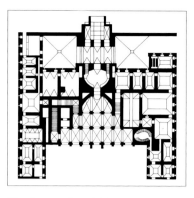

Gian Lorenzo Bernini: *Palazzo Barberini*, Rome, plan; designed and begun by Carlo Maderno in 1625. Bernini took over project supervision from 1629; Borromini helped both architects.

The façade of the palazzo does not reveal anything about the interior Baroque concept. Deviation from the closed Renaissance block with the wings extending to the city was new. The key innovation, however, consists in the suggestion of a monumental villa suburbana within the horseshoe-shaped plan in an urban setting.
The Baroque dynamic arises from the way in which the entrance portal, with its seven-bay projection right at the front, gradually tapers inwards. It leads to an oval hall which opens out to the garden via a long ramp. The central axis is, thus, strongly emphasised. Another innovative feature is the way in which the façade is open on all floors.

Pierre-Antoine Delamair: *Hôtel de Rohan-Soubise*, Paris, 1735

Delamair succeeded in outdoing his rival Hardouin-Mansart by gaining the commission for the conversion of the old Hôtel de Guise as a palace for the Prince of Rohan-Soubise. The distinctive image of this building is defined, in particular, by its size (which exceeds that of all other contemporary complexes) and the cour d'honneur which is surrounded by colonnades.

PALACES AND GARDENS IN FRANCE 1630–1750

The inclusion of outdoor spaces

Just as the idea of the transitory nature of existence failed to lead to humility and modesty, and the world moulded by any hand other than that of man failed to inspire any kind of appreciation, the princes failed even more spectacularly to show restraint in their desire for pomp and self-glorification. The religious dimension increasingly deteriorated to the level of mere lip service. The ruler may have declared himself as being "blessed by God", but in doing this he practically declared himself God's representative on earth who did not gladly suffer the presence of the Church at his side, not to mention above him. Equally, he strove to free himself from the often rather weak opportunities for co-determination available to the nobility or upper classes. According to the theory of Jean Bodin, which was essential to this form of "absolutism", the king embodied the slowly emerging nation which consisted of a uniform state. He therefore already possessed the sovereignty, absolute and indivisible power which he was supposed to use in serving the common good.

Absolutism reached its peak under the French King Louis XIV, who uttered the famous phrase "L'état c'est moi". Other Baroque princes may have had as much power, but none succeeded in surrounding himself with greater pomp and splendour than the "Sun King". Already a leading European power, France now also achieved cultural hegemony and an image as a centre of elegance, taste and manners which persists to the present day.

In accordance with their excessive sense of self-importance, Baroque princes expressed their self-glorification through their palaces. When it came to sheer splendour and size, these put all secular buildings since antiquity in the shade, and even managed to exceed church buildings in some instances. Whereas the Renaissance palace was a closed introverted structure built around an inner courtyard, the Baroque palace opened to the realm of the outdoors, which it integrated into its spatial effects and tried to influence. Although France was to become the leading influence in the emerging style of the Baroque secular building, one of the first such buildings with a Baroque plan is to be found in Italy, concealed behind a Renaissance façade. In Bernini's Palazzo Barberini in Rome, begun in 1629, two wings extend to form a courtyard in front of the building, facing the city. There is no inner courtyard. This innovation gave rise to the development in France of the "cour d'honneur" (court of honour),

the wings of which extended even further and were emphasised by corner projections. These protruding wings not only "framed" the approach to the building in great style, they also captivated the eye of the observer. To reinforce this effect, the central part of the building was also accentuated by a projection, a greater number of floors and sometimes also a particularly high roof. Whereas the Renaissance favoured low roofs which were barely perceptible behind the balustrades or cornices, mansard roofs (named after the architect Jules Hardouin-Mansart), which were often as high as two floors, were preferred during the Baroque. Their interrupted lines and volume made the entire building seem more powerful, and were completely in keeping with Baroque taste.

In the case of hôtels, the small city palaces of the French nobility, the opening of the building to the city remained incomplete. These buildings were usually located behind a closed courtyard, surrounded on the other three sides by lower ancillary structures. The Hôtel de Rohan-Soubise in Paris is a typical example of this type of building and also of the Baroque delight in pretty appearances: due to the physical dictates of the site, the courtyard here is located in front of the narrow side of the main wing, the façade of which is designed using the illusionistic architectural decoration usually reserved for the longer elevation.

Rays of power over the city and nature

Baroque palaces did not only open out to the city, they were poised between the city and nature. The Baroque concept of nature was, however, based on a form involving extensive human intervention ("the French garden"). Flowers were planted in the form of geometrical figures or arranged to form bizarre undulating surfaces. Hedges and shrubs were reinforced to form cubic shapes. Avenues were particularly important: they proceeded from the palaces in straight lines like rays of power penetrating the garden and, where possible, the town or city. Like the town or city, nature was visibly subjugated to the absolute will of the ruler; the same process was applied to the people and the state in a less visible form. In most cases, completely new palace complexes were built. Their size was based both on the desire to impress and the fact that they represented the seat of highest officialdom, which was in charge of the running of the increasingly bureaucratised state. Thus these new palaces were not only residential and representative structures but were also administrative buildings. Moreover, in some cases entire new residential towns were built – particularly when, as

VERSAILLES

No other palace, town and garden complex was as exemplary in character during the Baroque as that of Versailles, a suburb located south-west of Paris. In 1623, King Louis XIII commissioned the construction of a small moated castle. This was still firmly rooted in the Renaissance tradition and took the form of a four-winged complex surrounding a square courtyard. The fourth wing was replaced by a low arcade, later demolished when work on the extension of the castle commenced in 1661.

This was also the year that Louis XIV, later known as the "Sun King", assumed power; he remained in office until 1715. This long period of rule represents the pinnacle of royal power in Europe – with Paris as its political and social centre – and also the beginning of the Enlightenment, which eventually replaced absolutism at the end of the 18th century.

Vaux-le-Vicomte castle had been built near Paris by Nicolas Fouquet, the Minister of Finance, and was completed the year the new king came to power. It provided him with a source of inspiration for his own palace. The architect Louis Levau, the interior designer Le Brun and the landscape architect André Le Nôtre, all of whom had worked on Vaux-le-Vicomte, were commissioned to work in Versailles, where Louis XIV had chosen to locate his new residence. This project was not merely of immense spatial proportions. Above all, the brief was to create a symbol of national unity – a matter of extreme political delicacy – which would convey the greatness of the royal power far beyond France.

Encasing of the old castle was started on the basis of Levau's plans in 1661. The cour d'honneur was extended between 1668 and 1671 by the addition of two outwardly gradating wings, the ends of which were given large temple façades. The extensive garden elevation was created at the same time, its width emerging from the connection with the courtyard wings, which Levau tried to articulate with two corner pavilions (containing the war and peace salons). These were linked by a terrace above the ground floor, giving even greater emphasis to the first floor as the main floor of the palace and which housed the King's suite.

Jules Hardouin-Mansart, who in 1678 replaced Levau, converted the first-floor terrace into the famous Hall of Mirrors ("Galerie des Glaces"). The

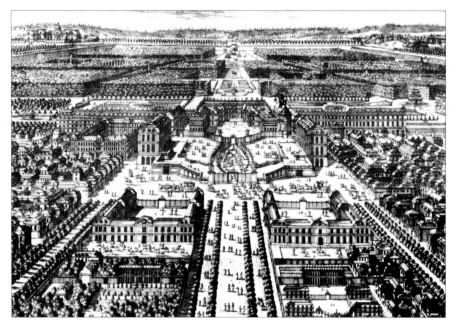

Bird's eye view of the town, palace and garden complexes, a copper engraving from 1700

lining of the walls with mirrors created both an extraordinary abundance of light and also, as a result of the constantly changing reflections, an optical confusion and apparent extension of the space into eternity, which was typical of Baroque illusionism. This room must be imagined as the backdrop for magnificent Baroque parties lit by hundreds of candles. It later assumed historical importance: the Paris Peace Conference, which ended with the signing of the Treaty of Versailles, started here on January 18th 1919 and ended on June 18th of the same year.

The conversion of the terrace to the Hall of Mirrors resulted in the transformation of the façade from a protruding and retracting structure to a uniform surface, which was barely enlivened by the light central projection. Including the two wings, the garden façade was extended even further to a total length of 576 metres. Thus for the most part the typical dynamism of Baroque buildings yielded to an unrelenting, intimidating splendour. In keeping with Louis XIV's self-conception as the embodiment of the state and unrestricted ruler, the design focused exclusively on the desire for representation and relinquished any concessions

to human dimensions. This attitude is also evident in the enormous courtyard in front of the palace and the large cour d'honneur, later extended by the addition of two further wings (one designed by Ange-Jacques Gabriel and the other an exact copy built in the 19th century). The entire palace complex reached a depth of 407 metres, the aim being that it could not be outclassed anywhere else in Europe.

Le Nôtre started on the design of the gardens in 1667. Between the Neptune Basin in the north and the Orangerie in the south, to which two twenty-metre-wide "Great Staircases of 100 Steps" descend, there was a wide surface with regular low hedges. These were clipped in patterns known as the "broderieparterre" (from the French "broder" = to embroider – nature was formed into a decoration in the form of embroidery patterns). The Latona Basin and Tapis Vert (64 × 335 metres) are located along the main axis which leads away from the palace at a right angle, as is the Apollo Basin (82 × 116 metres) further down the axis. Lined with topiary and clipped hedges, the Apollo Basin surrounds the statue of the Sun God, with whom the King identified, in his chariot pulled by horses and Tritons (sea gods). This basin is the centre of the radial, axial and star system which pervades the entire garden. It is difficult to appreciate this system fully today as the trees are now much thicker and higher than originally planned.

The powerful dimensions of the open complex are highlighted by the 1560-metre-long canal which also lies along the main axis. It is intersected by a short transverse canal to the north of which two pleasure palaces were constructed – the Grand Trianon built by Hardouin-Mansart and Robert de Cotte in 1687–88, and the Petit Trianon built in 1764–68 by J.-A. Gabriel. After the death of Louis XIV, the court favoured these palaces as residences over the enormous main palace.

The Hall of Mirrors in the Royal Palace

terms of representation were on the longitudinal axis, i.e. the centre, from which – entirely in keeping with the Renaissance concept of organically grown "buildings" – the entire complex developed. This included the vestibule (entrance hall on the cour d'honneur), the staircase (which hitherto merely housed insignificant interior stairs and now occupied its own often elaborately designed space at the centre of the building) and the festival or banqueting hall on the first floor. This often extended up to the height of two floors and opened out onto the garden. The latter either sloped gently up to the palace or was reached from a terrace with an open staircase. The fact that the banqueting hall was located at the centre of the palace is self-evident and can be explained not only on the basis of its size and the desire to maintain symmetry. Glorious parties, processions and social events were very popular during the Baroque. Following some initial stirrings during the Late Renaissance, for the first time since antiquity a large number of permanent theatre buildings were constructed, and were often integrated into the large palace complexes.

in Karlsruhe in Germany, the town authority opposed the prince's plans. In the case of Karlsruhe, a new complex was promptly built based on one of the most impressive Baroque urban design concepts. The main model for this and numerous other complexes was Versailles near Paris, the residence of Louis XIV where secular Baroque architecture reached its apotheosis.

In addition to city or town complexes with roads radiating from the palace (or from the opposite perspective leading up to its cour d'honneur), others like that in Mannheim, Germany, were designed in chessboard style. The position of the palace as the "head of the town" remained the same, as did the use of visual axes, arbitrary forms and unconditional symmetry. The application of these principles led to structural mass being conceived in terms of its perspective effect; churches were "built into" house façades, and different buildings were masked with the same façade to create uniform squares. These principles were also applied to the interior of secular Baroque buildings, particularly palaces. The central axis emphasised the "inclusion" of the urban realm within the building, which was then abandoned at the back in the natural realm of the garden. Ideally, the longitudinal axis was counteracted by a horizontal axis, the enfilade: rooms in the wide extended buildings were arranged in a sequence so that it was possible to look through all the rooms from a single point. The most important rooms in

THE BAROQUE IN GERMANY AND THE ROCOCO 1710–80

Late blossoming

Staircases in the new palaces of the German empire were particularly large and ornate. They were an expression of the late but powerful blossoming of the Baroque in the country which had finally come through the greatest national catastrophe in its history, the Thirty Years War. This war was primarily a struggle between Catholics and Protestants, and many of the European powers fought out their conflicts on German soil. Following the Treaty of Westphalia of 1648, the country, which was still divided on a religious basis, was split into almost three hundred territories. The Emperor resided in Vienna and, with the exception of a few years, had always been appointed by the Habsburgs. He remained the formal ruler of the "Holy Roman Empire of the German Nation". In actual fact he was virtually powerless outside the Habsburg states.

This situation proved advantageous to the spread of the Baroque. When the devastating consequences of the war had finally been overcome by around 1680 and the "Turkish threat" (the threatened expansion of the Ottoman Empire beyond the Balkans to central Europe which had been a threat for several centuries) had finally subsided, many

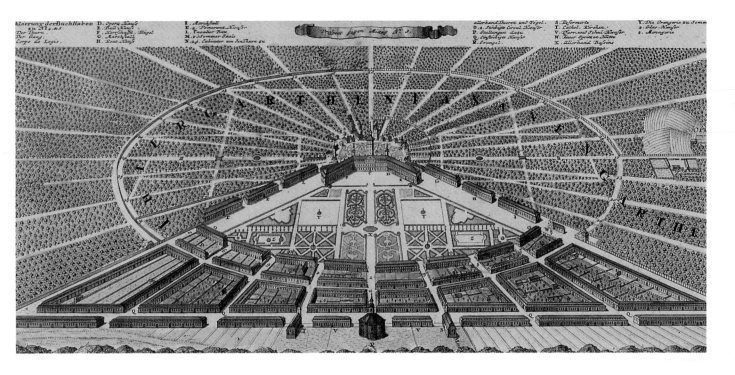

KARLSRUHE: THE RADIAL TOWN PLAN

The idealised plan of Versailles – the palace, garden and town which conformed to a strict symmetrical order – was the source of inspiration behind the town complex of Karlsruhe in Germany. Margrave Karl Wilhelm von Baden-Durlach originally planned to pursue his passion for hunting in the Hardtwald forest and decided to build a free-standing, octagonal tower surrounded by thirty two radial paths. The number corresponded to his thirty one knights of the "order of loyalty" and himself as master of the order. However, the complex extended to the original town, which was founded in 1715, with the free-standing tower watching over the entire complex at the centre of a circle 850 metres in diameter.

The southern quarter of the circle was given a central axis and subdivided by nine radial paths. The existing town centre, which with its market square and Concordian church lay outside the circle, was integrated into the symmetrical complex by the alignment of a road leading to it. The quarter circle was enclosed by the palace and adjoining houses for noble officers of the administration. It also contained parterres and ornamental shrubbery. The middle-classes, traders and

craftsmen settled in the segment along the radial road. Construction workers, servants and labourers had to find accommodation outside the circle.

The complex reflects the feudal hierarchy both in its plan and in the decreasing quality of the architecture. The central axis was named after the Margrave and the other radial paths after the knights. The tower is the highest symbol of the prince, who is identified with the state, and his task of watching over the feudal society with the help of knights whose radial paths spread into the surrounding countryside. As in Versailles, settlers were lured by means of special privileges and favours. They were given religious freedom, a plot on which to build and basic building materials. They were obliged, however, to build their houses on the basis of the Dutch model prescribed by the Margrave, which consisted of structures of up to two floors in height and red-plastered timber-framed mansard roofs. The buildings were destroyed in a bomb attack in 1944. However, the basic form of the town complex can be seen to the present day as the exteriors of many of the buildings have been reconstructed.

princes wanted to assert their self-image by building splendid palace and garden complexes. The most important of these new palaces include Schönbrunn near Vienna, which was designed by Fischer von Erlach, Andreas Schlüter's City Palace in Berlin, and Ludwigsburg palace near Stuttgart. Balthasar Neumann was advised and inspired by a wide variety of architects from all over Europe for his excellent design of the Würzburg Residenz. The prominence of the central and side wings had already given rise to the division of the entire complex into pavilion-like structures linked by galleries. This principle was applied on an enormous scale in Nymphenburg palace in Munich, with its six hundred-metre-long façade. A smaller and more graceful version of this style can be found in the Dresden Zwinger, a hall building designed by Daniel Pöppelmann, regional architect under Prince August the Strong. However, only a small part of the considerably larger planned complex was actually built.

It was rare for the large-scale "ideal projects" conceived as monasteries to reach completion. This

is the case with the monastery of Melk, the biggest of the Austrian Baroque monasteries. The church in this complex is largely based on the model of Il Gesù, which had already been adopted in Germany for the Jesuit church of St. Michael in Munich. Its powerful tunnel-vaulted piered hall marked the introduction of the Baroque to south Germany and served as an exemplary model of this style for over a hundred other buildings.

The extent and speed at which the Baroque developed in Germany reflects the way in which the inspiration of the Italian architect Guarino Guarini, who developed buildings with mathematical precision conveying a sense of lively movement and imagination bordering on the ludicrous, was adopted during the 18th century. Bohemian and south German architects were particularly influenced by his widely disseminated theoretical work. Thus, not only were the Dientzenhofer brothers inspired by him for the church of St Nicholas on the Kleinseite, but Johann Balthasar Neumann, the architect from Würzburg, was also strongly influenced. His pilgrimage church of Vierzehnheiligen

Jakob Prandtauer: *Benedictine monastery of Melk*, on the Danube, 1702–46.

Dominicus Zimmermann: *pilgrim church "Zum gegeisselten Heiland"* (Wies church), Wies near Steingaden, Upper Bavaria, 1745–57

The faithful of the Late Baroque era no longer went on pilgrimage to Rome but to the south German pilgrim churches which were situated in villages and in the open countryside.
Dominicus Zimmermann's Wies church has a joyous interior evoked by the generous flood of daylight and the white oval nave. This is further intensified by the shining colour tones in the choir.
The upper loggia of the two-floor choir ambulatory is enclosed by decorative blue marbled columns. These contrast with the red marble of the high altar, above which sways a blue baldachin (canopy). A miraculous image of the scourged Christ stands in the lower part of the two-floor high altar and dominates the visual impression right up to the ceiling painting which depicts angels displaying the torture instruments to God the Father.

completed Guarini's notion of spatial penetration: the oscillations which mobilise the entire interior are reinforced by a creative interaction of colour and an abundance of ornament. Dominicus Zimmermann, the architect of the pilgrim church of Die Wies, also adopted this concept and carried it even further by playing a trick on the pilgrim approaching the church: the bare white simplicity of the exterior gives no clue as to the fairy-tale splendour of the interior.

Rococo and withdrawal to the private sphere

A certain weariness of pomp and monumentality set in following the death of Louis XIV in 1715. A new style emerged in Paris which was called "Louis quinze" after King Louis XV. The more common name "Rococo" is derived from the French word "rocaille", meaning loose water-worn stones and shells which were one of the basic motifs of the style. Seashells, gnarled symmetrical shapes, flowers and vines crawled up architectural elements in naturalistic and also bizarre stylised forms, sometimes loose and asymmetrical and sometimes overpowering.

It was not only the decor which became more delicate, smaller and more intricate. Greater significance was given to intimate and personal areas and more emphasis placed on the design of the interior. Gallant pastoral games were very popular, as were delicate porcelain figures. Small garden palaces were built which were often given romantic-sounding names like "Monbijou" in Berlin and "Solitude" in Stuttgart.

Johann Balthasar Neumann: *pilgrim church "Zu den 14 Nothelfern"* (Vierzehnheiligen), north Franconia, 1743–72

With its unrestricted spatial system, this church presents a complete synthesis of Baroque plasticity and Rococo lightness, whereby the tension between the nave and the centrally planned building are resolved in a very original manner.
The delicate altar of the fourteen helpers is not located in the choir but stands freely at the centre of the nave under a baldachin, the pillars of which are surrounded by an oval.
The large dome resting on a tambour above the crossing, which gave Italian churches their great sense of height, is replaced here by opposing oval and circular forms, which make the vaults disappear and dissolve all sense of mass. In this way, Neumann heightens Christoph Dietzenhofer's method of syncopated penetration of the vault. Stark monumentality is no longer relied on to create an impression, but the joy of a well-lit space makes the atmosphere of this church particularly attractive.

Experts are fond of arguing whether Rococo should be seen as an independent style or as a Late Baroque variant. Even taking into account the boundaries of style, it is ultimately a question of interpretation as to whether a decoration seems delicate and fine enough, and a building light and fragile enough, to warrant its classification as Rococo. Soon after the mid-18th century, the Rococo was replaced by a more linear, positively strict and economical form of decoration. In France this became known as "Louis seize" after Louis XVI who ruled from 1774. It was later mockingly known in Germany as "Zopfstil", i.e. an old-fashioned, traditional style.

Sir Christopher Wren: *St. Paul's Cathedral*, London 1675–1710

When Wren was given the opportunity to build a monumental church following the Great Fire of London in 1666, he was strongly influenced by the Italian Baroque. His cathedral has a standardised variant of the dome of St. Peter's. However, this is counteracted by a portal with antique characteristics, consisting of two-floor rows of columns and a tympanum. Due to the compromise arising from the Anglican requirement for a basilical nave and Wren's own notion of a centrally-planned building, the dome was shifted to the centre of the nave.

Moderate Baroque towers are integrated into a building which summarises various stylistic elements and is rather sober in character. Instead of heightening it with theatrical gestures, Wren clearly delineates the square. This points to a Palladian-style Classicism which is well suited to the reserved spirit of the Anglican Church.

ENGLAND AND THE TREND TOWARDS CLASSICISM 1700–70

Reduction and severity

Along with the rise of the Rococo and Late Baroque in Germany, the mid-18th century also saw the development of an increasingly obvious trend towards greater severity. This was particularly true of France where the Baroque had tended to be more muted than in Italy. However, a schematic arrangement familiar from the Late Renaissance became more and more apparent: harmony and beauty should be created by applying mandatory, specifically mathematical, rules of construction. Thus in the church of the Invalides in Paris, which was designed by Jules Hardouin-Mansart, all horizontal and vertical proportions were based on the radius of the central circular room. This triple-shelled dome is another typical example of Baroque dramatic production and illusionism. The first dome is flatter and provides a view into the second, more strongly vaulted, dome. This shines more brightly than the first – an effect which is inexplicable to the observer as it is lit by concealed lower windows. The third shell is based solely on its effect from the outside.

The dome of St. Paul's Cathedral in London, the most important work of the British Baroque architect Christopher Wren, who was appointed General Director of the reconstruction of the city following the Great Fire of 1666, is similar in structure. The exterior of St. Paul's is, however, very different from that of the Invalides. Nothing swings dynamically from one level to the next; individual elements are clearly distinguished from each other and severely juxtaposed. The colonnade does not encircle the structure in a rhythmical fashion but is almost regular and endless. The dome cap which opens into the lantern is no longer emphasised by wide coloured bands but only by narrow lines. The way in which the entire dome resting on a drum is set on the church is almost Classical. Conversely, the use of a porticus (as also in the church of St. Martin in the Fields by James Gibbs), the severity of the exterior walls and their schematic pilasters correspond to the continuous reproduction of Palladio's architecture, which had been in vogue in England since the early 17th century.

While France was heading towards the heights of absolutism, England had already experienced its bourgeois revolution including civil war, execution of the monarch, abolition of the monarchy between 1642 and 1649, and the introduction of a written constitution in 1653. The republic did not last very long, and following further conflict the country finally became a constitutional monarchy in 1689, with a king appointed by parliament. The lower nobility and their closely associated middle-class counterparts (title was only handed down from father to son, the others mainly earned their living by trade) had fought for the right of co-determination and the promotion of their economic interests.

To a great extent they had stripped the estates of their powers. Vain attempts were made in other countries to deal with the growing economic problems and social tension without introducing fundamental change. Evil premonitions of the approaching demise of the feudal world, from which the endless party of the Baroque tried to deflect attention, were finally fulfilled at the end of the 18th century.

James Gibbs: *St. Martin-in-the-Fields*, London, 1721–26

This late masterpiece by James Gibbs betrays the influence of Wren's churches. The tower sits on a Classical temple and reflects the sober attitude of English Rationalism and Empiricism. The large Roman porticus sets a particularly powerful accent and points to the influence of ancient architecture, which spread in England via the architecture of Palladio and went on to embody a Classicism independent of the Baroque. This building was often copied in the British colonies and even managed to reach Australia.

The architecture of reason

CLASSICISM

1750–1840

ENLIGHTENMENT AND REVOLUTION ARCHITECTURE

Democracy replaces absolutism

The intellectual movement of the Enlightenment developed within the rigid system of rule known as Absolutism. The new movement aimed to liberate not just philosophy but every aspect of life from its traditional shackles, and provide a new strictly reasonable, "ratio"-based orientation (Rationalism). For the philosopher Immanuel Kant, the aim of the Enlightenment was "the exit (= liberation) of man from self-induced nonage". "Reason, and the critical spirit arising from it, should form the basis on which the correctness of every insight is decided, and also provide the basis for all decisions concerning the norms of ethical, political, and social behaviour" (Friedrich Schiller "Have faith only in your own reason!").

The Enlightenment, which attracted increasing numbers of followers during the 18th century, also demanded political change, especially as it was mainly supported by the middle classes. As a result of their activities as intellectuals and traders in money or goods, rational thought and action played an important role in the daily lives of the middle classes. In economic terms, they were growing increasingly important. However, when it came to participation in political rule, they were totally excluded in countries like Germany and France.

Even monarchs like Friedrich II of Prussia and Joseph II of Austria, who practised "enlightened absolutism", were unable to solve social problems through the introduction of reforms such as relative freedom of religion, abolition of torture and the establishment of a regulated system of justice. On the contrary, continued survival of the existing feudal order and the imperative need for fundamental change became even more widespread.

The alternative model was devised by philosophers like John Locke, Jean-Jacques Rousseau and the state theorist Monesquieu, with their ideas of the people's state and the separation of powers. The people themselves and not the king should represent the nation. State power should therefore emanate directly or indirectly from them (through elected representatives), although control and limitation of the power of monarchy by parliament and constitution were initially given some consideration. In order to prevent abuse and decisions based on the aims of self-glorification, power previously held by the absolute ruling monarch was to be divided among three "powers" (legislative, executive, judicial). Moreover, all state activity should be based on known defined rules (constitution, laws) and after a specific period, rulers should be given a renewed mandate by the sovereign, i.e. the people. It should also be subject to control by the other powers and, above all, to public criticism, in terms of which, according to the Enlightenment, all action and thought had to prove itself. Behind this was the conviction that a conflict

"Boston Tea Party" as protest against English import taxes and tea monopoly on December 16th 1773, coloured lithographic print from 1846.

1750: Johann Sebastian Bach, the composer, dies.

1759: The British Museum in London is opened (exhibits from private collections).

1762: Jean-Jacques Rousseau's theory of state "Du contrat social" (The Social Contract) provides an ideal image of democracy.

1764: Johann Joachim Winckelmann's book "Geschichte der Kunst des Altertums" (History of the Art of Antiquity) is published.

1765: James Watt invents the steam engine (patented in 1769). The potato is used for human consumption in Europe.

1768: James Cook explores

Australia, New Zealand, the South Seas and Alaska during three expeditions.

1773: Middle-class citizens disguised as Indians destroy a cargo of tea from the East India Company in Boston Harbour, intensifying the conflict with the English mother country.

1776: The American Congress declares the independence of the 13 colonies of the British Crown. Declaration of Human Rights.

1781: Immanuel Kant publishes his philosophical treatise "Kritik der reinen Vernunft" (Critique of Pure Reason). Johann Heinrich Voss translates Homer's Odyssey.

1789: Beginning of the French Revolution with the storming of the Bastille.

1796: English doctor Edward Jenner administers the first vaccine against small pox.

1797: Senefelder develops lithography (offset printing).

1804: Napoleon Bonaparte crowns

himself French Emperor in Paris. Formulation of the Napoleonic Code.

1808: Goethe's Faust (Part 1) is published. Collection of folk songs Des Knaben Wunderhorn (The Boy's Magic Horn) is published by Achim von Arnim and Clemens von Brentano.

1813: Massacre near Leipzig; victory of Prussia, Austria and Russia over Napoleon I.

1814: Napoleon abdicates and is exiled to Elba. Allied Congress of Vienna is called to remake Europe after the downfall of Napoleon I.

1824: Ludwig van Beethoven completes his 9th symphony.

1832: Hambach Festival of German Democrats.

1838: Samuel Morse develops a code for the transmission of messages by telegraph.

Ca. 1840: Frédéric François Chopin composes his most important piano works (nocturnes).

of views (pluralism) would ultimately – with the help of reason – lead to the right decisions and make it possible to avoid serious errors of judgement. The creators of this system actually wanted the democratic decision-making processes to be long and complicated. The correctness of this view is demonstrated by the fact that although this system never works perfectly, it is the only one which actually works at all on a permanent basis. This can be seen in the way that all dictatorships end sooner or later, at the very least in economic ruin.

However, this system of Enlightenment was based on a rather visionary (impassioned) image of man. Rousseau considered man as fundamentally good "by nature" and ruined by civilisation. He saw the solution to this problem as a return to the "most natural" form of state, a society consisting of individuals with equal rights who should enter a "social contract" based on (and justified by) the rules of reason. John Locke had already identified freedom, equality and inviolability of persons and property as the most important legal possessions. These human rights, and the rules governing the structure of the democratic state described above, were defined for the first time in the constitutions which the North American States drew up for themselves in 1776–80. They were ultimately adopted in the constitution of the USA in 1787/ 1788 and in the French constitution of 1791.

Architecture based on moral criteria

The belief that human reason would ultimately prevail and bring about good did not merely have serious political consequences. It also resulted in the marked secularisation of society which has lasted to the present day. The person who is guided solely by reason can accept a God as creator, but not as a guide. From now on architecture no longer served religion and even less so the feudal ruler. It was believed that the built environment could be used to have a positive influence on the spirit of the

people, and inspire them to behave in a manner based on reason and morality. To achieve this, however, architecture itself had to fulfil ethical-moral criteria. Carlo Lodoli developed the theory as early as the 1740's that architecture should be true to its purpose and materials – and therefore "true" in itself. Similarly, in his "Essai sur l'Architecture", the French Abbot Laugier demanded an "honest architecture", in which structure and ornament would again constitute a unity. Hence architecture must itself "speak" and express the ideas of the Enlightenment.

Representatives of the French "revolution architecture" implemented these ideas so clearly that they are often referred to as "expressive". Their designs are classified as "architecture parlante", i.e. architecture which speaks for itself. According to their utopia, the democratisation of art could take place through the emotions and was not necessarily based on intellect and education.

Etienne-Louis Boullée wrote the following comments to accompany his design of a cenotaph in honour of Newton, which he completed in 1784: "Oh Newton, you have defined the form of the earth through the greatness of your wisdom and the magnificence of your genius. It was my idea to surround you in your discovery". The physicist's shrine was to have been placed at the base of a 150-metre-high sphere. A planetarium was to have been built in the sphere above the shrine.

Around the same time, Claude-Nicolas Ledoux, the other main proponent of this architectural style, designed a house for the surveyor of the river Loue. The structure consists of a horizontal cylinder through which a stream is directed, which then flows into the river as a waterfall, symbolising the mastery of the river by rational technical means. Other excellent schemes by Ledoux include the Royal Salt Mines in Arc-et-Senans and the accompanying "ideal city" of Chaux, the theatre at Besançon and the Paris toll houses ("barrières", 1785–89).

Etienne-Louis Boullée: *Design of the Newton Cenotaph*, 1784, view and interior view/section

Boullée's project for the Newton cenotaph (Greek for empty grave), which is reminiscent of a planetarium and refers to Newton's contribution to the sciences, is an excellent example of the two most important features of revolution architecture: the stacking of mass and the use of simple, geometric forms.

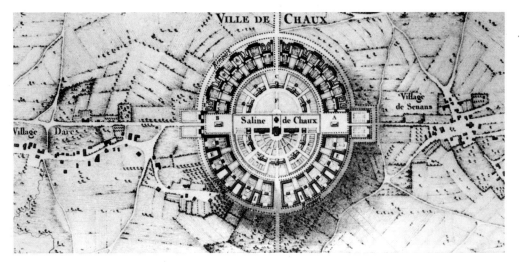

Claude-Nicolas Ledoux: *Project for the ideal city of Chaux near Arc-et-Senans*, published as a Folio edition in 1806

The idea of an ideal town or city, which has been around since ancient times, is based on the idea of fulfilling all the material and aesthetic requirements of a city. The main feature of this design is the use of simple geometric forms and the regularity of the complex. Ledoux's plan is not, however, abstract; it is expressive or "parlant". The text published to accompany the scheme is full of ideas for social reform. For example, it was Ledoux's aim to construct a building for the "cult of moral values". The principle of the ideal city was continued in the early 20th century by Bruno Taut and Le Corbusier.

Jacques-Germain Soufflot: *Sainte-Geneviève*, Paris, 1764–90, renamed *Panthéon* after the French Revolution

The main building of its time, the Panthéon marks the beginning of the Romantic period of French Classicism which was based on the splendour of ancient Rome. Soufflot's contemporaries referred to the Panthéon as "the first example of perfect architecture". The gigantic domed building, which competed in size with St. Peter's in Rome, St. Paul's in London and the Dome of the Invalides in Paris, was intended to dominate its surroundings and mark the place where the city patron was buried. It was Soufflot's aim to achieve a synthesis of Gothic lightness with ancient form. The plan, based on the Greek cross, follows the Renaissance ideal. The wall is no longer the structural element but the column. The use of reinforced concrete on the portico, with its 22 columns, set a trend for modern architecture. Soufflot's refusal to use a complicated system of pillars, columns and wall mass, along with the rationality and purity of form, make this a very impressive building.

As the dates indicate, this style is not known as "revolution architecture" because it originates from the French Revolution of 1789. (Ledoux was at his most productive when he was appointed court architect during the 1770's, and the subsequent political changes actually marked the end of his career.) The new social models, such as the utopias supported by Boullée and Ledoux, were always expressed in "revolutionary" building projects. What was revolutionary about this architecture was the fact that it broke with tradition, in that the ability to be built was no longer an essential criterion in its design. Many schemes, for example Ledoux's park-keepers' houses consisting of spheres with thin smooth exterior walls poised on a minuscule surface, could never have been built at the time. Hardly any of Boullée's schemes were built, not least because his designs, like the Newton cenotaph, were often monstrous in their proportions.

In stylistic terms, as part of the Classical movement revolution architecture embodies a reaction to the excessive formal language of the Baroque and Rococo, with clear elegant purity of line within compact, usually stereometric structures, the prototype of which was the ancient temple.

CLASSICISM AS STATE ARCHITECTURE 1780–1840

Tranquillity, severity, sublimity

In his "*Sammlung architektonischer Entwürfe*" (*Collection of Architectural Designs*) of 1830, Leo von Klenze makes the following comments: "There is, was and will be one architecture, that is the architecture which reached its culmination in the period of Greek history and education". Von Klenze sees the architecture of Classical Greece as "the architecture of the world for all time and there is no climate, material or cultural difference which stands in the way of its general application". This renewed focus on ancient architecture is logical in view of the fact that the Enlightenment continued the intellectual approaches of the Renaissance and Humanism. However, the idea of ancient civilisations containing the origins of an architecture which embodies the eternal laws of harmony and beauty was even more popular in the 18th century than it was in the 15th and 16th centuries.

By the mid-18th century a strong dispute had arisen as to whether Greek or Roman antiquity should be given historical and architectural-historical priority, whether Rome had refined or falsified Greek culture, or had been far more strongly influenced by the Etruscans. Both camps could substantiate their arguments with archaeological insights to a far greater extent than was possible during the Renaissance, when the only available references consisted of ancient buildings and ruins in their country of origin, i.e. Italy, and the writings of Vitruvius, and hence concentrated mainly on Roman antiquity.

Conversely, from the 18th century Western Europeans started to go on pilgrimages to Greece, which at the time was an insignificant province of the Ottoman Empire. From 1751 to 1753, the young Englishmen James Stuart and Nicholas Revett produced detailed drawings of ancient buildings which they published in 1762 (*Antiquities of Athens*).

The excavations of the ancient cities of Herculaneum and Pompeii, which had been destroyed and "preserved" when Vesuvius erupted in 79 A.D., were started in 1738 and 1748. The excavations and their findings were described by Johann Joachim Winckelmann, who with the 1764 publication of his book "*Geschichte der Kunst des Altertums*" (*History of the Art of Antiquity*) founded the modern theory of art. His analysis of the spirit of Greek art as "noble simplicity and quiet grandeur" would later exercise a key influence on German Classicism.

In France and Britain, where the tradition of "Classical" architecture had been carried on since the Renaissance, particularly in the form of Palladianism, the new style became known as neo-Classicism. The same term was used in Germany, initially for the revival in Classical tendencies around 1900, which became increasingly coarse and monumental.

Just how early the (neo-)Classical trend started in France can be seen in the church of Sainte-Geneviève in Paris, which was designed from 1757 onwards by Jacques-Germain Soufflot, and built between 1764 and 1790. Its plan is reminiscent of a Renaissance church: a dome resting on a drum rises above a circle at the centre of a Greek cross. Individual architectural elements are, however, starkly juxtaposed; for example, in the way in which the dome crowns the church without any form of transition. In 1791, the building was re-dedicated as a tomb and memorial for important French citizens and renamed the Panthéon. This reference to one of the most important remaining buildings of Roman antiquity was not the only contemporary gesture incorporated into this project: the unity of the gods, to which this building was dedicated and from which it took its name, was replaced in revolutionary Paris by the unity of genius.

Classical design principles dominated architecture throughout the last decades of the 18th and first decades of the 19th centuries. These consisted of clarity and reduction of the exterior elevation and plan, the dominance of right angles and straight lines, stereometric structures, starkly juxtaposed elements, tranquillity, severity, sublimity appropriate to the "grandeur" of the ideas embodied by the building, or the task it had to fulfil, and a spirit of ethics and morality in place of pomp and representation. Buildings were still strictly symmetrical, but porticoes were often used on façades and the emphasis of the central axis was omitted, e.g. when a colonnaded hall was built in front of the building. In the case of the British Museum in London, it was originally planned to completely surround the building with columns. As the building itself is an elongated cube, like the Greek peripteral temple, this would have given extensive uniformity to the external elevations and denied the building a clearly defined façade. Columns were once again used mainly for structural rather than decorative purposes. The form of the columns was intended to reflect the nature of the structure more clearly, which is why Doric and Ionic orders were preferred to the more decorative Corinthinan and composite capitals.

Thomas Jefferson and United States architecture

Thomas Jefferson, the multi-talented architect and statesman, also used Rome's Pantheon as a model for the design of his Monticello country house outside the gates of Charlottesville. The house with outstretching wings stands on the crown of a hill, the curve of which is mirrored by the dome. Despite the use of exposed brick, the building exudes a sense of self-confidence as opposed to reticence and modesty. Jefferson had Palladio's Villa Rotunda in mind when designing the house. Therefore, the link to the Late Renaissance, and through it to Roman antiquity, is no coincidence. This is also evident in his design for the first US state university

Sir Robert Smirke: *British Museum*, London, 1823–47

The early 19th century in England is characterised by the "Greek revival", the exploration of Classical Greek architecture which was quickly adopted as a model for the new Classical architecture. The external formal language of a building was intended to express its function and history. Public buildings could now not only compete with religious or royal buildings, but actually outdo them in terms of architectural excellence. The British Museum represents one of the great achievements of European Classicism. The south side of the building is based on the style of Greek temple architecture. It has a powerful colonnade with 48 Ionic columns. The severe monumentality of the museum design contrasts with the Baroque idea of the *Gesamtkunstwerk*. The playful integrative principle of the Baroque is replaced here by the block-based additive organisation of the building.

The United States' Capitol, Washington D.C., design by **William Thornton**, begun in 1793, project management 1803–17 **Benjamin Latrobe**, to 1824 **Charles Bulfinch**; extension and dome by **Thomas Walter** (1851–65)

The construction of the State Capitol aroused great feeling in America. The model was the ancient Capitol in Rome as the original site of democratic activity. The architectural form is clearly based on Palladio's Classicism and his theory of proportion.
Thomas Walter's powerful dome is the symbol of the city of Washington. It embodies the American dream of freedom and unlimited possibilities. It was, however, also a daring technical achievement. Walter used cast iron here for the first time. To counteract the expansion forces of this material, he constructed two complex shells which were belted and bolted to each other. The Capitol dome can compete with Michelangelo's Baroque dome of St. Peter's in Rome and Brunelleschi's dome of Florence cathedral.

campus in Charlottesville, which was built between 1817 and 1826. Once again, a structure based on the Pantheon can be found; this time the library at the top of a slightly inclining avenue which is surrounded by columned pavilions housing the individual faculties. The different Roman orders, or variants of them, are used in these buildings – including Ledoux's style. Jefferson had encountered the work of Ledoux during his time as ambassador in pre-Revolution Paris.
For Jefferson, Republican Rome was the social and architectural model which he saw as re-emerging in the USA. This went as far as the names given to the

parliamentary representative body, the Senate, which met on Capitol Hill. As Governor of Virginia, Secretary of State and, finally, President of the USA, Jefferson promoted an architecture which was independent of that of the defeated mother country, Great Britain. This was at a time when buildings were urgently needed, not only for administration and government, but when large numbers of big buildings were also being constructed in the country for the first time.

American Classicism reached its most monumental expression in the Capitol, the biggest and most magnificent building in the new state, which was based on ideas from the Enlightenment and put them into practice to a significant extent. Its impressive dome, in particular, resulted in many other parliament buildings in the individual states of the Union, and in most Central and Southern American states, being based on the Capitol.

The Rise of Classicism in Restoration Germany

The situation in Europe was rather different. Like some other revolutionary movements, the French Revolution of 1789 quickly went far beyond its initial aims. The monarchy was abolished, Christian chronology was replaced by a new system based on the decimal system, churches and monasteries were closed as "places of superstition" and, like Sainte-Geneviève, re-dedicated as temples of hero worship or even demolished. (This was the fate, for example, of Cluny Abbey, the most important religious building to be demolished, which was subsequently leased as a quarry.) The culmination of this reversion was reached when, after years of

Thomas Jefferson: *Monticello*, Charlottesville, Virginia, USA, designed in 1769

Based on the ancient concept of democracy, Jefferson recognised a basic rule-based principle of order in ancient architecture. In a society based on universal equality, architecture must not be overpowering and diffuse but simple and comprehensible. The President demonstrates this in the architecture of his house. Inspired by Palladio, he modelled his house on the ideal villa. The architectural realisation captivates through the horizontal accent and symmetrical composition, with the accentuation of the two porticoes at the front and back of the building. Jefferson combines the straight lines of Palladio, demonstrated in the porticoes and ancient window jambs, with the French elegance of the high cornice and balustrade.
The use of red brick, from which the white architectural elements protrude, follows the American tradition.

Leo von Klenze: *Glyptothek*, Munich, Königsplatz, 1816–34

As King Ludwig I of Bavaria's court architect, Klenze was commissioned to design the new city of Munich. In addition to the Odeonsplatz square and Ludwigstrasse street, the Königsplatz square represented the largest coherent ensemble of buildings. Along with the Glyptothek (which housed a collection of ancient sculpture), it was surrounded by the State Antiquities collection and the Propylaeum.
Klenze, who had been to Greece in 1823 to study ancient buildings, used the elements of the cube and Greek temple in his architecture. The "temple" of the Glyptothek uses the Ionic order, which the architect deemed more suitable for a museum building than the Doric. The only decoration on the stereometric windowless cube consists of niches for statues. It is otherwise uninviting and cold.
The exhibition room in the interior of the museum was designed by Klenze completely independently of its external appearance, as though the Greek repertoire of styles was only suitable for the façade and form.

power struggles and terror, Napoleon Bonaparte assumed power and crowned himself Emperor in 1804. However, his dreams of creating a world empire finally collapsed when he had conquered half of Europe. In 1814–15, the major European powers met to reorganise the continent at the Congress of Vienna. Promises of reform elicited from the oppressed kings were broken and a rigid policy of restoration introduced, particularly in Central Europe, under the leadership of the Austrian Foreign Affairs minister Metternich, who later became Chancellor of Austria. However, the old conditions, which had been abolished during Napoleon's campaigns or replaced by his reforms, could only be re-established with difficulty and for a limited period. The ideas of the Enlightenment lived on and Classicism also thrived in Restoration Germany.

Its centres were Baden, Bavaria, Prussia and their capitals: Karlsruhe, where Friedrich Weinbrenner filled the Baroque city plan with Classical buildings; Munich, where Leo von Klenze, a pupil of Gilly and Durand, was active as court architect from 1816 onwards; and Berlin, where Carl Gotthard Langhans's Brandenburg Gate, the building which represented the foundation of German Classicism, was built. The Brandenburg Gate was built as a triumphal gate at the beginning of the prestigious thoroughfare, Unter den Linden. The fact that this building type, actually Roman in origin, was designed in a form based on Greek inspiration typified the stronger influence of Greek antiquity on the Classical architecture of Bavaria and Prussia. This went as far as the imitation of individual buildings and the use of ancient Greek names.

Examples include the Propylaeum in Munich and the Walhalla, a copy of the Parthenon which was built high above the Danube near Regensburg as a hall of fame for "great Germans", and which was also designed by Klenze. The King of Bavaria, Ludwig I, had a building designed for the same purpose as that for which the church of Sainte-Geneviève had been re-dedicated by the French revolutionaries. This also demonstrates the extent to which the ideas of the Enlightenment spread throughout Europe.

Churches and palaces of high architectural quality were now very rare. In accordance with the educational ideals of the enlightened middle classes, museums, libraries and theatres were built everywhere – not just in Germany. These secular buildings often had a portico, i.e. an element originating from religious buildings. This was actually consistent with the philosophy of the time: by replacing the house of God in terms of its significance, the place of education had actually become a "temple of art" or "temple of education". In keeping with Enlightenment thinking, knowledge – not faith – was the key issue. Thus, for example, banks and stock exchanges had antique-style temple fronts. Universities were also established in greater numbers; large numbers of schools, government and administration buildings were constructed. Functions which had previously been carried out in the palace or monastery now had their own buildings. Modern society demanded a greater degree of architectural specialisation.

All of these buildings could not, however, be financed through unashamed exploitation of the

Friedrich Gilly: *Design for the Berlin Schauspielhaus* theatre, 1798 (not built)

The theatre was one of the architectural tasks which became a focal topic of interest in the late 18th century, with the emergence of a middle-class public. The middle classes saw the theatre as a "moral institution" and educational institution where its emancipation from the nobility was completed. The planning and building of theatres was hence accompanied by lively public discussion. In contrast to the court theatre with its boxes, some architects worked on arenas inspired by the ancient amphitheatres which emphasised the equal status of all spectators.

Gilly designed a theatre for Berlin which was based on the architecture of the French Revolution and consisted of clearly delineated, strictly geometrical spaces. The façade was accentuated by a monumental columned portico. Gilly planned the auditorium as an open semi-circle which is focused mainly on the stage, in keeping with the new role of the drama. It does not, as was the case in the court theatres, allow the audience itself to become the most important spectacle.

population, as was the case in feudal society. Thus Durand, a pupil of Boullée, introduced the issue of cost as part of the general aesthetic considerations in his "*Abriss der Vorlesungen über Baukunst*" (*Outline of Lectures on Architecture*) in the early 19th century. As the most expensive of the arts, architecture could "only be based on private and public functionality, the well-being of the individual, the family and society". Thus "functionality and thrift [are] criteria which are naturally applied in architecture and are the resources from which it must create its principles, the only principles which can be of use to us as a guide in the study and execution of this art".

Two possibilities for development

As in France, certain future-oriented trends emerged in Germany alongside the rather conventional imitation of ancient models. Friedrich Gilly, who died in 1800 at the age of 28, was an important influence in this respect, almost exclusively through his designs – particularly that for a memorial to Friedrich II in Berlin. Earlier statues were dedicated to rulers or other excellent personalities; in this case, however, the monarch was the contemporary idea. The sarcophagus would have been accommodated in the base of the monument, above which rose a Greek peripteral temple, the symbol of the spirit of the king. Visitors could have enjoyed a view from the memorial right across Berlin and its surroundings – the area where Friedrich had been active and, in a sense, creative. Stylistically, Gilly combined Greek and Egyptian features in his design with those of the French revolution architecture. Gilly was to have an important influence on Karl Friedrich Schinkel, who perfected his approach of fusing ancient formal language with the new functionality.

However, architecture first took a different path which was also rooted in Classicism: the emotionally charged, dreamy Romantic style was actually a reaction to the rational, unsentimental Enlightenment. However, Rousseau's love of nature had already incorporated a similar spirit.

Just how well Romanticism and Classicism combined in post-Napoleonic Germany, where the prospect of escape from politically oppressive reality was particularly attractive, is demonstrated by the popularity of the "English garden". Here the Baroque palace would have seemed completely out of place but it worked well with Classical buildings. Landscape architects like Herman Fürst von Pückler-Muskau and Peter Joseph Lenné created marvellous complexes based on the English model. In English gardens, houses were placed right in the garden and not separated from it by a terrace, emphasising the collision of the severe man-made structure with the unrestrained natural environment, with its lakes and hilly lawns, irregular paths and waterways, rampant hedges and free-standing trees. Everything in nature should be arbitrary and harmonious, not – as in the French garden – forced into an artificial form but allowed to reach perfection.

Whereas the visual axes in the Baroque aimed to impress in their sheer monumentality and constantly remind the observer where the centre was located by steering and manipulating the view, it now became important to refine nature with the help of surprising and stimulating views and vistas. What is viewed is distinctly Romantic: ancient temples, stone bridges, small palaces and artificial ruins. Gothic forms were also a popular feature in the design of these structures.

KARL FRIEDRICH SCHINKEL

The small town of Neuruppin north of Berlin was the birthplace of two great men of the Prussian Kingdom: the writer Theodor Fontane (1819–98) and the architect Karl Friedrich Schinkel (1781–1841). Schinkel learned about Classical architecture, which had been in fashion since the end of the 18th century, at the Berlin Academy of Architecture, where he studied mainly under David Gilly (1748–1808).

The Greek temple and its character had been (re)discovered as an architectural model just a few years earlier. For example, the Doric temple in Paestum was hitherto unknown and its baseless columns attracted considerable attention. By acknowledging the way in which ancient Greek architecture had elevated consummate beauty to an ideal, while at the same time embodying absolute truth in its functionality, the architecture of the 18th century radically rejected the preceding Renaissance and Baroque eras and began to incorporate these new ideals into teaching. The aim was to replace the organic and corporeal approach to building with the clear cubic forms of classical antiquity. Schinkel was a student at the precise moment when this revolution was taking place in architectural history, which for the first time was actually honouring its entire tradition. Another famous contemporary of Schinkel's at the Berlin Academy was Leo von Klenze (1784–1864), whose importance in Bavaria is comparable to that of Schinkel in Prussia.

On completing his studies, Schinkel travelled in Italy from 1803 to 1805. In addition to designing buildings, not only in the Classical but also in the Gothic style, he also painted Romantic pictures. He designed stage sets for operas like the *Magic Flute* and a range of functional structures including memorials, bridges and weirs. Like most architects of his time, Schinkel's talents were multi-disciplinary.

Schinkel's great period began after the wars of liberation when building recommenced in Prussia, whose territory had been considerably extended following the Congress of Vienna. Schinkel was soon appointed court architect, a member of the influential architectural division of the Prussian Public Works Department, and was finally appointed head of the department. His seminal influence on Prussian architecture led to the establishment of a kind of "Schinkel school", the followers of which included Persius, Stüler and Strack.

The Schauspielhaus theatre on the Gendarmenplatz square in Berlin, 1818–24

Schinkel worked in at least three styles simultaneously – the Classical, neo-Gothic and Romantic. It was, however, his Classical buildings – among the most beautiful built in this style in Germany – which brought him most fame. They combine optimum serviceable functionality with harmonic clarity, and are consequently viewed as the purest expression of classical antiquity.

Of Schinkel's churches, the Nicolai Church in Potsdam, which was originally next to the Palace, is still the most impressive. Its powerful dome evokes the former beauty of Potsdam. The impressive Berlin Cathedral, which was renovated by Schinkel, was replaced in 1890 by Raschdorff's ostentatious edifice. The Friedrichswerder church in Berlin is still extant and today houses the Schinkel Museum. Other churches, such as the church in the Moabit neighbourhood of Berlin, are built in the Florentine-Romantic style.

A large number of Schinkel's palace designs have survived. The project for the Acropolis in Athens, which also involved Klenze and other reputable Classicists, is particularly worthy of mention. To be able to build a palace at the original site of the Classical tradition was an enormous challenge for individual disciples of the tradition. The small Charlottenhof Palace in the grounds of Sanssouci in Potsdam is particularly attractive, as is the small Liegnitz Palace beside the Charlottenburg Palace in Berlin. Schinkel's neo-Gothic Kamenz Palace in Silesia is rather sombre by contrast.

The most distinctive features of Schinkel's Altes Museum (Old Museum) beside the Berlin Lustgarten (Pleasure Garden) (begun in 1822) are the open staircase, from which the former City Palace could be viewed, and the central rotunda – an excellent example of classical use of space.

The Neue Wache (New Guard House) on the Forum Fridicianum (1817), which was originally built for the stay of a company of guards and is now a memorial to the victims of the Second World War and the genocide of that period, is also one of Schinkel's masterpieces.

The Academy of Architecture (begun in 1825), which has unfortunately been demolished, was a prototype of brick architecture. This building reflects the processing by Schinkel of impressions gathered during a trip to England where he saw factory buildings and weaving shops. In Schinkel's opinion, these were nothing more than monstrous masses, which had nothing to do with architecture which strove to reach the level of art. With his designs for the Berlin goods depot of 1829–32, which included offices for customs and administration and warehouses built along the Kupfergraben quay in central Berlin, Schinkel showed just how functional buildings should be designed. This row of buildings had a sombre cubic aesthetic, similar to that of the Academy of Architecture.

The Schauspielhaus theatre situated on the Gendarmenmarkt square in Berlin, one of Schinkel's most important buildings, is framed by the steep domes of the German and French Cathedrals. The Greek temple façade, which like all the columns, entablature, and gables is taken directly from the antique box of tricks, conceals a building designed on the basis of strictly functionalistic criteria, the individual stereometric units of which consist of several independent parts.

Mozart's *Magic Flute*, with sets designed by the architect, was staged to mark the opening of the theatre. It is indeed fortunate for Berlin that this valuable building survived the War unscathed.

Academy of Architecture, begun in 1825

The technical revolution

HISTORICISM AND INDUSTRIAL ARCHITECTURE

1840–1900

Borrowed styles

Whilst basing itself on antiquity and adopting some of its architectural features, Classicism also initiated the introduction of new elements to the architectural repertoire, pointing the way to future developments. Stereometric structures, tectonic clarity, straight lines and reticent decoration all contained the seeds of subsequent modern approaches. Historicism, which could be interpreted as Classicism's final mannerist chorus, does not deny the existence of these approaches. On the contrary, it makes use of them in both its structural and spatial concepts. However, instead of making them consistently visible, the tendency was to introduce other past styles – not only from Western architecture – into the design of the façade. In a spirit of playfulness, or perhaps out of fear of technical progress, the new technical possibilities were disguised behind familiar but more deceptive forms.

The beginning of this new trend was marked by a Gothic revival. This style had been developed in England in a particularly individual way, and had remained a decisive influence there far beyond the Middle Ages. Repeated moves were made to revive the Gothic style from the mid-18th century, particularly in country residences, and elsewhere from the turn of the century. The situation in Germany was similar; the sense of national identity had been boosted following victory over Napoleonic France, but had not yet reached its culmination in the foundation of a nation state. The Gothic, which had been widely despised since the Renaissance –

the word "gothic" was a term of abuse used to describe a style perceived as barbaric – was now seen as something specifically German. It was not until the second half of the 19th century that art theorists revealed that the severe and sublime Gothic cathedral architecture, of which Cologne cathedral was a prime example, had actually originated in France, i.e. the very country which Germans saw as the "arch enemy".

The clear retreat from pure Classicism to Historicist architecture started in 1840, with the construction of the new parliament building in London. This was an enormous complex consisting of approximately 1,100 rooms and a façade stretching 275 metres along the River Thames. The box-like building was framed with a lattice-like decoration echoing the Perpendicular Style of the Late English Gothic. The architect, Charles Barry, whose allegiances were completely Classical, refused to comply with the requirements of the competition brief for a "Gothic" building. He employed Augustus Welby Pugin, a passionate disciple of the Gothic, to design the façade details. Pugin articulated the long walls optically. However, just as it was impossible to pretend that the façade concealed an interior characterised by Gothic spatial uniformity, the absence of a powerful vertical thrust was equally obvious. In fact, string courses gave the façade a strong horizontal accent. The decorative details are small but schematic – as dictated by the dimensions of the building. The same traditional forms of decoration were repeated until the building was completely covered.

The design for the Houses of Parliament combined the main features of Historicism: elements are

---

1842: China cedes Hong Kong to England and opens its ports to the West European powers and the British opium trade.

1843: Felix Mendelssohn-Bartholdy composes his overture to Shakespeare's *A Midsummer Night's Dream*.

1845: Latin is abolished as the language of lectures and examinations at Berlin University.

1847: Introduction of the legal 10-hour working day in Great Britain.

1848: Karl Marx publishes his *Communist Manifesto*. Discovery of gold deposits in California results in the gold rush.

1861: Abraham Lincoln is elected President of the USA and abolishes slavery.

1863: The International Red Cross is founded.

1864: Jules Verne writes *A Journey to the Centre of the Earth*, the first science-fiction novel.

1865: Lewis Carroll writes *Alice In Wonderland*. Georg Johann Mendel publishes his theories of genetics (ignored until 1900).

1869: The Suez Canal is opened and shortens the sea route to Asia. Publication of Alfred E. Brehms' *Tierleben*.

1871: Foundation of the German Empire following the end of the Franco-Prussian war in Versailles. Bismarck becomes the first Reich Chancellor.

1874: First group exhibition by the Impressionists in Paris.

1876: Alexander Bell patents his speech apparatus, the precursor of the first telephone.

1877: Leo Tolstoy publishes *Anna Karenina*.

Since 1880: By continuing to pursue the colonial policy of the 16th to 18th centuries, the major powers fight for economic and political division of the world (Imperialism).

The embodiment of the cultural and international politics of an entire epoch – Victoria, Queen of Great Britain and Ireland, portrait photograph ca. 1890.

1882: Premier of Wagner's *Parsifal* in Bayreuth.

1885: Gottlieb Daimler and Carl Benz build the first automobile. The first successful submarine is built by Nordenfeldt.

1886: Ludwig II King of Bavaria (since 1884) certified insane and commits suicide.

1892: Gerhard Hauptmann publishes *The Weavers*, a drama of mass social revolution.

1894: The Jewish-French officer Alfred Dreyfus is condemned and deported for alleged treason.

1895: Wilhelm Conrad Röntgen discovers the X-ray. Sigmund Freud founds psychoanalysis. First film presentation by the Skladanowsky brothers in Berlin and the Lumière brothers in Paris.

1899: The First Hague Peace Conference is held to discuss the peaceful resolution of international conflict and the laws of war.

adopted from a past style which has long since completed its development (this is known as "eclecticism"), and applied in a completely new type of architectural task, such as the construction of an enormous parliament building. Moreover, the rules of the style are applied with "academic" severity and precision, in a way which would never have entered the minds of architects of the past era in question – because it was creative use of the forms making up the style which afforded them the opportunity to create something significant. Unlike the Renaissance or Classical eras, the adoption of old styles did not represent the starting point for independent creative innovation, but rather for schematic and soulless imitation. The partly involuntary combination of stylistic elements from one or more eras culminated in corresponding inauthenticity and chaos. For example, the Houses of Parliament have projections in the façade which would never have been seen in the Gothic era. According to Gottfried Semper, one of the few Historicist architects who managed to create something positive – by working on the basis that the function of a building should be expressed in its plan, exterior and decoration – the stylistic forms were "borrowed and stolen, they do not belong to us at all".

Whatever the forms used, it was above all the proportions which were inappropriate in most instances. The new buildings – like the London Parliament – had completely different dimensions from those for which the styles were originally developed. The application, for example, of decorative details from a bourgeois Renaissance palace to the two-hundred-metre-long, four-storey high façade of an administration building inevitably resulted in enlarging, coarsening and repetition of the forms in question. Moreover, it was not only the dimensions of individual buildings which reached hitherto almost unknown proportions. The number of buildings constructed from the mid-19th century onwards reached a level which put even the fervent architectural activity of the Baroque princes in the shade.

Something new in familiar packaging

The taste of the time was determined by two major factors: clients no longer tended to be highly-educated individuals, i.e. princes, bishops or affluent middle-class citizens, but for the most part anonymous groups and committees. They generally negotiated on behalf of abstract bodies such as administrative institutions and companies, a situation which did not foster and encourage innovation and risk-taking. Moreover, as a result of the development of an industrialised society based on the division of labour, in many cases the

Charles Barry and A. W. Pugin: *Houses of Parliament*, 1840–88, London, seat of the English Parliament with the Victoria Tower (1858, 102 metres high) and Big Ben (1859, 97 metres high)

The new parliament building – which was built on the site of the old Palace of Westminster destroyed by fire in 1834 – is a testimony to the Gothic Revival, the renewed enthusiasm shown by the English for the Gothic style which emerged in the mid-18th century. The rectangular complex is divided into numerous sequentially aligned asymmetrical units. The west front on the Thames is defined by the Victoria Tower, the north side by Big Ben. Decorative cladding is inspired by Pugin's Gothicism. In a reference to the Perpendicular Style (the specifically English form of the Late Gothic), vertical decorative details are emphasised and the surfaces are framed by a lattice. It appears as though a veneer has been superimposed on the basic structure. It also shows how the formal vocabulary, previously exclusive to religious buildings, could become the equally exclusive preserve of a secular context: "*Heavenly Jerusalem*" is replaced by an "Earthly Jerusalem".

Charles Garnier: *Opéra*, main staircase, interior view, 1871–74, Paris

To see and be seen! This was the motto behind the opera house as the symbol of the *Seconde Empire*, the "cathedral" of 19th century Parisian bourgeoisie and the epitome of the "style Napoléon III". The ensemble of the grand escalier and grand foyer represent the architectural high point of the entire scheme. There is more than enough space for visitors to stroll around and present themselves. The eclectic use of decorative and formal vocabulary clearly demonstrates the move away from a normative to a more descriptive aesthetic: the aim is no longer to evaluate but describe. Historical styles are seen as pure forms which can be combined in new ways as desired. They are no longer vehicles of expression – their value is defined by fashionable, social perspectives.

administrative and political elite no longer coincided with the intellectual elite. This inevitably led to an increased dominance of mass taste. The familiar and well recognised became the basis for orientation.

Mass taste was, however, characterised by fundamental insecurity – the second major factor. The triumphant victory of the machine and equally precipitous developments in the natural sciences had brought greater change to all areas of life than had been experienced in any previous era. For example, when the first railways were opened, a German doctor had expressed the belief that the enormous speed of the trains would inevitably lead to serious brain damage among passengers – the average speed of the first trains was approximately thirty kilometres per hour. People were torn between a sense of euphoria at the progress and a romantic blurring of the past. Thus, Paul Wallot's Berlin Reichstag building may strike some chords

from the Late Renaissance, but instead of reflecting the heady and noble magnificence of this period, it makes a rather bulky and weighty impression. The dome on this building is a light iron-glass structure, a daring aesthetic gesture for a building with such an elevated function, even in the 1880's.

Conversely, it was not unusual to present steam-operated pumps and view their powerful movements with enthusiasm, whilst concealing the pumping station behind the exterior of an imitation Norman castle. This was the most typical feature of Historicism: something new was packaged as something "familiar". Examples include an enormous parliament building presented in the form of a Gothic cathedral (as in London where even the high crossing tower typical of the English Gothic was not forgotten); factories, power and water stations disguised as castles, town halls or churches (the chimney was concealed in the tower); and shopping arcades, which marked the start of the transfer of retail trade from the open market to indoor venues, being made to look like a Renaissance palace.

In the face of the onset of a seemingly chaotic future, the Middle Ages were reproduced in a romantic and nostalgic form in many places. Italy, which had traditionally viewed the chapter between the demise of the Roman Empire and the Renaissance as one of the "dark" parts of its history, now finally forfeited the inspiration and power it had exercised over Western cultural development since the Renaissance.

Numerous historical buildings and entire castle complexes were restored, above all in those countries which had played a prominent cultural role during the Middle Ages, i.e. France, Germany and England. The information needed for such projects was provided by art history, which was developing very rapidly in response to the surge in interest in the past. However, restoration projects were often approached so rigidly and strictly that they actually did more harm than good: architectural history was often "corrected", inconsistencies of style and later alterations were obliterated and incomplete work "finished". Thus, unfinished buildings like Cologne, Ulm and Bern cathedrals were completed. In those places which had nothing available for restoration, new buildings were erected which loosely imitated past styles, e.g. Neuschwanstein castle in Bavaria, which combines Romanesque features with a large dose of imagination.

These architectural forgeries not only provided an excellent way of escaping from the present, but also helped counteract any sense of cultural inferiority and made it possible to pretend that

Paul Wallot: *The Reichstag*, Berlin, Platz
der Republik, 1884–94

With the rapid development of Berlin into
a world metropolis, architecture was
quickly forced to express a national and
representative self-image. The
architectural implementation of this aim in
this "Reichstag worthy of the German
people" is based on heightened
monumentalisation – emphasised by the
exposed and free-standing site – with the
simultaneous use of Baroque elements
and forms from the Italian Renaissance.
The three-storey, (horizontal) rectangular
building is introspective and symmetrical
on the central axis. The centre consists of
the assembly room, above which rises a
dome consisting of an iron-glass
structure. In the very complex façade,
Wallot used antique-style columns and a
very sculptural projection, in front of
which stands a portico and projecting
architrave.

history had taken a different course. Cities and
towns which had enjoyed minimal status and
importance in the 18th or 19th centuries were
adorned with neo-Gothic town halls. Neo-Gothic
cathedrals were built in the USA, and large neo-
Romanesque buildings were constructed in areas
of Prussia east of the River Elbe, where Germans
had not actually settled until the late Romanesque
period. Now that they had finally achieved a position
of power, the middle classes, which had once
demanded social change and been responsible for
new impulses in architecture, aimed to appropriate
the glory of the fallen feudal orders. This desire was
reinforced by the fact that the potential social
explosion and discontent of the working class was
becoming an increasingly real threat, and because
the political situation still harboured some feudal
elements, e.g. the German Empire founded in
1871 and the French Empire under Napoleon III
(which collapsed the same year). The Paris
Opera, built between 1861 and 1874, provides
perhaps the most outstanding architectural
testimony to this development. Of many opera
houses built at the time, it was the most grandiose.
It is also a particularly good example of the
influence of the Paris École des Beaux Arts on
Historicist architecture, which later spread as far as
America.

In order to satisfy the Parisian opera-going public's
taste and desire for representation, the architect
Charles Garnier opted for a mix of Baroque and
Renaissance in his design. More than one third of
the entire house is allocated to the social sphere.
Thus there is an enormous entrance hall, a large
foyer and a staircase which stretches right up to the
roof. However, the staircase does not form a closed
autonomous space as was customary in the
Baroque, but is part of other interacting spaces, i.e.
it is a spatial sequence in itself. Therefore, for all the
revelling in inherited forms, the Paris Opera still
betrays some modern tendencies.

Machines imitate handicrafts

In the course of time a fateful correlation emerged:
those machines which were behind the refuge in
past forms also became the means by which this
could be achieved. In the past it would have taken a
great deal of time and skill to produce a richly
decorated elaborate piece of cut glass, which would
have come with a correspondingly high price tag.
However, no matter how skilled and experienced
the glass blowers and cutters, one piece was never
exactly the same as another down to the last detail.
The invention of pressed glass brought about the
transformation of a luxury into a cheap consumer
item. Faced with competition from faster and
cheaper mechanical production, many craftsmen
were forced to close their workshops, move to the
towns and cities, and take jobs in factories.
Knowledge and skills which they would have
passed on to the next generation were lost. Instead
of producing their own individual work, they were
now involved in the mass production of goods at
machines which made tens of thousands of copies
of hand-made goods.

This development was repeated in all areas.
Complex metal structures could now be produced
in cast iron. Mechanically produced decorative
fittings replaced laborious sculpture and, like goods
in a catalogue, could be selected from pictures and
merely stuck on the walls. The situation is best
illustrated by the following question which a master
mason put to his client: "The house is finished now,
what style do you want it in?"

Neuschwanstein castle, built in 1869–86 for King Ludwig II, near Schwangau in the Allgäu

Neuschwanstein documents the transcendental image of the Middle Ages, which became popular from the Romantic period onwards, in a way which no other castle succeeds in doing. It was built in the middle of a wild romantic landscape on a site containing the ruins of a former Medieval castle. Inspired by the illusory world of the theatre, the monarch had his "Wartburg" built high on top of a rock as a temple to Richard Wagner. This building is a testimony to King Ludwig's late Romantic introversion. In a reference to the Romanesque period, the castle represents the attempt to unite art, nature and architect in a *Gesamtkunstwerk*.

The craft movement tried to counteract this development by encouraging designers and consumers to study exemplary crafts in the newly-founded museums. However, this ultimately led to a heightening of the crisis, because the idea spread that the most perfect design forms had long since been developed and it was now only a question of copying them. Museum collections were used as rich treasuries of style from which individual pieces could be adopted at random.

Technology and the natural sciences demolished one apparently unshakeable certainty and permanent boundary of knowledge after the other: why shouldn't the limits of time and space also be removed from culture? Thus elements from Western architectural history were enthusiastically complemented by those from other cultures, which the European colonial powers encountered in the course of their conquests and were keen to copy. The Palace of Justice in Brussels, built by Joseph Poelaert between 1866 and 1883, was the biggest administrative building of its time in Europe and was actually an interconnected stereometric structure. However, in keeping with the fear of empty unadorned spaces prevalent at that time, it was filled to the brim with Baroque, Roman, Greek, Assyrian and Renaissance ornamental forms. Indian and Chinese elements also began to appear – more often than not in the form of neo-styles and eclectic mixtures which originated for the most part from the imagination of the architects. The extent to which elements from the past were imitated was

matched only by the scant attention paid to historical stylistic references. These were repeatedly plucked from their originally pure contexts.

As a result of the strong growth in population and the migration to the cities of rural populations, who saw no future for themselves in agriculture and village crafts, and instead found employment in the urban factories, the population of the cities multiplied very quickly. This gave rise to continued spatial expansion of the cities and the increasing density of their populations.

During the second half of the 19th century, town planning still consisted mainly of the definition of building lines, eaves heights and some fire safety regulations. A famous example of the latter is the regulation in Berlin whereby the minimum size of back yards of residential buildings had to be able to accommodate the turning circle of fire engines – all of 28.52 m². Everything else was left open to the forces of competition. Concepts involving public health concerns, like that established by Peter Joseph Lenné in the 1840s for parks in Berlin, played no part. Even the boulevards which Baron Haussmann had laid in Paris from 1853 to 1870 showed little concern for such matters: the main aim was to give the increasingly formless flowing mass of the city wider, straighter roads. This 137-kilometre-long system accelerated the flow of traffic and gave the capital city a suitably representative appearance. The idea that the boulevards would make the building of barricades more difficult was also taken into account – a cautionary political measure following the revolutions of 1848. The historical structure of the city and its buildings were swept away without consideration – Haussmann later boasted of having been responsible for demolishing 20,000 houses in the extended city area, of which 4,300 were located in the old centre of Paris.

The opportunity to use the removal of ring ramparts, which had long since become outdated and were an obstacle to the expansion of cities, to provide more space for parks, was only exploited in a few places. The additional space surrounding the old city area was more often used for constructing large ring roads, the most impressive example of which can be found in Vienna.

INDUSTRIAL ARCHITECTURE

Fragile iron and glass structures

The modern age had thus begun. But where was modern architecture? The fact that one path leading out of the dead-end of Historicism had long since been discovered was overlooked. The price of crude (pig) iron began to decrease from around 1750. The steam engine was so well developed by the end of the 18th century that it could be used to produce increasing volumes of pig, cast and wrought iron. A cast iron arched bridge over the River Severn near Coalbrookdale, the first of its kind, had been built between 1775 and 1779: five parallel girders spanned a distance of approximately thirty metres. Their semi-circular form represented a complete departure from the structure and appearance of timber bridges. The lightness and transparency of this fragile-looking structure also distinguished it clearly from a masonry arch. This difference was further emphasised by the fact that it was spanned between two masonry abutments.

Lightness, transparency, the impression of tension and fragility – these are the main aesthetic features of metal structures. However, it took more than half a century before a wider public became familiar with them. Between 1836 and 1840, Joseph Paxton, the Duke of Devonshire's estate manager, had a glasshouse built which was 100 metres long, 38 metres wide and 20 metres high. It used cast iron columns, through which rainwater drained, and standard glass panes. Paxton perfected this technique for his Crystal Palace, built for the first World Exhibition which was staged in London in 1851. The Crystal Palace was an extremely wide, five-aisle hall; 600 metres long, 120 metres wide and up to 34 metres in height. The structure enclosed an enormous space separated from the outside world merely by a thin glass and iron membrane. What was so revolutionary about the Crystal Palace was not only the new spatial experience it offered. It was also the first building to be constructed using pre-fabricated and standardised elements exclusively. Thus it represented a pioneering achievement in the development of rationalised construction. Only this level of standardisation made it possible for the Crystal Palace to be erected, mainly by labourers, in a mere seventeen weeks: eighty men fitted 18,392 panes of glass per week, one man alone up to 108 per day. It made it possible to have parts (including 3,300 columns and 2,300 girders) manufactured simultaneously by different companies. The Crystal Palace consumed one third of the annual glass production in England for that year! Standardisation alone made it possible to dismantle the structure at the end of the exhibition and re-assemble it in a slightly modified form in Sydenham in London, where it was destroyed by fire in 1936.

During the second half of the 19th century, world exhibitions became prestigious high-publicity showcases for increasingly impressive technical and scientific achievements. Gustave Eiffel constructed a tower for the World Exhibition of 1889 in Paris which reached a height inconceivable for its time: the tower of Ulm cathedral was planned to reach 162 metres but had to be abandoned at seventy. The Eiffel Tower was 300 metres high and remained the highest structure ever built for forty years.

It was accompanied by the equally impressive achievement of the wide-spanned Galérie des machines. This structure was 442 metres long and 47 metres high, with steel girders spanning a width of 114 metres.

In comparison, the highest Gothic arch which did not collapse – that of Amiens cathedral – is 145 metres long, 14.6 metres wide and 42.3 metres high. Furthermore, whereas a similar degree of transparency in the walls could only be achieved

Joseph Paxton: *Crystal Palace*, London, 1851, destroyed by fire in 1936

Building in iron and glass is closely associated with the typical construction tasks of the 19th century: market arcades and passages, bridges, railway stations and exhibition buildings. Thus the Crystal Palace is seen as a product of the industrial and commercial boom which coincided with the Industrial Revolution in England.
Paxton presented his design uninvited for the first World Exhibition in London. The engineers, Fox and Henderson, succeeded in building the hall – which is 8.4 hectares in size – in Hyde Park in less than five months. This represents a phenomenal achievement, not merely with respect to the clear and rational structure of the design. The puddling process for iron, which had been patented in 1748, made it possible to prefabricate iron parts in large volumes. Paxton's exhibition hall is acknowledged as the first example of prefabrication in building.

Gustave Eiffel: *The Eiffel Tower*, Paris, opened for the World Exhibition in 1889

Charles Dutert (architect) and Victor Contamin (engineer): *Galérie des machines*, Paris, World Exhibition 1889, 422 metres long, 47 metres high, 117 metres wide.

during the Gothic era by constructing a system of abutments on the outside of the building, the twenty three hinged arches of the Galérie des machines tapered to the ground, culminating in a single point. Although the structure exerted a pressure of 412 tonnes and a shear stress of 115 tonnes, it was literally poised on points which rested on rollers.

Due to its use of the standard structural system of perpendicular supports, on which cross members rested, the Crystal Palace gave the impression of being a very rigid static structure. By contrast, in the Galérie des machines there was a constant interaction between support and load, which created the impression of an enormous tent.

Artistic expression in iron and steel

The structure of the Galérie des machines, which was demolished in 1910, impressively demonstrated the enormous technical possibilities made available by steel structures. It therefore represented one of the prime monuments of the industrial age. This structure was directly based on

the functional requirements of the building. For example, it was possible to counteract the effects of expansion due to changes in temperature by balancing the hall on rollers. Gustave Eiffel wrote of his own creation: "I firmly believe that my tower will have its own unique beauty. Do not the correct calculations of stability always coincide with those of harmony?"

In the 19th century all these structures, which are today described under the heading of industrial architecture, were not seen as architecture at all. Factories, department stores, exhibition halls and railway sheds, bridges spanning wide distances, i.e. architectural tasks extremely typical of the time, were classified as "functional buildings". They were seen as having nothing to do with architecture. Iron and steel were "false" materials not worthy of use in artistic design. For this reason they should not be openly flaunted when used. The Eiffel Tower consequently became known as the "shame of Paris" and was originally to have been demolished immediately after the World Exhibition. Meanwhile architecture was reduced to the level of mere façade design. For example, the station hall of St. Pancras railway station in London, which at a width of 75 metres was the widest building in the world until the Galérie des machines was built, and also housed the Midland Grand Hotel, was made to look like a pseudo-Gothic castle. This approach became typical of the construction of large railway stations. The starting points of this revolutionary means of transport, which remained the main means of long-distance travel up to the mid-20th century, were treated almost everywhere as "*mi-usine, mi-palais*" (half factory, half palace). Grandiose train sheds, the "cathedrals of the industrial age" (which due to the smoke from the locomotives had to be so high) were concealed from the city behind historicised stone façades. Station sheds as naked and sober in appearance as that of King's Cross station, which stands directly beside St. Pancras, remained the exception.

However, the new materials were also increasingly used for non-industrial structures. Even cast iron, an essentially brittle material, is approximately four times as resistant to compression as stone. Wrought iron, which is forty times as resistant to tension and bending as stone, is only four times heavier. Moreover, it can be formed and moulded into any shape. Cast iron columns were decorated with Classical capitals to disguise their alien nature. Structures consisting of metal columns and girders no longer needed walls for their statics. This marked the onset of the most significant technical revolution in architectural history. Solid structures

could be replaced by skeleton structures, making it possible to erect buildings of almost unrestricted height and width very quickly, using prefabricated elements.

As early as 1801, James Watt, who had made considerable progress in the development of the steam engine, built the first cast-iron skeleton for a seven-storey spinning mill. This created the model for factories and warehouses of the 19th century. It also created a precedent, however, by putting a massive external wall in front of the building. Henri Labrouste used a similar principle in his design for the Bibliothèque Sainte-Geneviève in Paris. Labrouste's achievement consists not only in the fact that he was the first to apply this method in a public building, but also in the way in which he inserted a line of bare iron columns along the centre of the room. This predicted the principle of reinforced concrete construction by building the "vaulted" ceiling as a rendered iron frame. Labrouste took his innovative approach to design one step further in the reading room of the Paris National Library, where the central columns were extremely refined and delicate, despite being historical in form.

Another new building material – concrete

The invention of iron and steel constructions was important. However, the revolution in building technology was not complete until metal was combined with concrete. This material consists of cheap raw materials such as lime, clay, marl, gypsum and water, which are available all over the world and can be made into prefabricated elements or produced on site relatively quickly and easily. It can be used in a large number of applications and is extremely tough, with the same linear extension as iron or steel when exposed to heat. The development of modern versions was greatly helped by the invention of Portland cement during the first half of the 19th century. Concrete is extremely resistant to compression, but has little tensile strength and thus cracks under the least strain. It is possible to counteract this effect by the addition of (usually round) steel, or iron reinforcements which absorb the tensile forces.

François Hennebique played an important role in the development of reinforced concrete construction. In particular, he found a way of overcoming the weakness which existed in previous reinforced concrete structures – the point at which the ceiling connects with the beam and the beam connects with the supporting member – known as the ceiling joist. He deflected the iron reinforcements laterally

and combined them with supporting members made of reinforced concrete, which replaced the cast-iron columns previously used. This gave rise to a cohesive reinforced concrete skeleton, a "monolithic" composite method of construction. The thickness of individual elements can be reduced if the degree to which the concrete is reinforced and the strength of the concrete and iron are increased. In order to reduce the weight of the skeleton structure, already significantly lower than that of a massive masonry structure, it is possible to pile more and more floors on top of each other without having to widen the load-bearing elements to the foundations. Therefore it became possible to create more and more usable space on the basis of the same floor space.

THE CHICAGO SCHOOL 1880–1900

Building up to the sky

The rule of optimising the use of available floor space was also applied in the construction of residential and administrative buildings. Sites available for construction became increasingly rare and more expensive. This is particularly true of the economic and administrative centres in the USA and, in particular, Chicago. In 1850 the city had only 30,000 inhabitants. By 1870 this number had increased tenfold; it reached half a million by 1880 and finally exceeded one million by 1890. Chicago had by this time become the main city of the American Mid-West. It was the main junction for railway and shipping traffic, the transhipment centre for grain and timber, the site of major metal processing works and the biggest slaughterhouses in the world.

In 1871, the harshest possible lesson demonstrated that iron was not as fire-resistant as had originally been believed: the city's iron structures melted like butter in a great fire which destroyed almost the entire city. In view of the economic boom, ways of building increasingly higher buildings were constantly being sought. However, the Monadnock Building by Burnham and Root, the highest brick building in the city, constructed between 1884 and 1892, required two-metre-thick walls at ground floor level. This was in order to support the fifteen floors and at the cost of valuable shop-window space on the ground floor. The design of the building as an unadorned red-brick slab, solely articulated by flat, house-high bays and the deep insertion of the windows into the wall, was indicative of future developments.

Henri Labrouste: *Bibliothèque National*, Paris, 1858–68, interior view

Labrouste uses iron in the columns and vaults, and emphasises the slim elegant forms made possible by the use of this material. The library is the first monumental public building in which iron was used on such a consistent basis.

George Gilbert Scott: *St. Pancras Station*, London (façade is Midland Grand Hotel), from 1861 onwards.

Form follows function

Chicago, the metropolis which revelled in euphoria for the future, showed greater openness to simple and more economical design than, for example, New York. Here the skyscrapers were adorned with heavy, historicised exteriors. In Chicago there was no desire to imitate motifs from European architectural history, but a strong impulse to develop a self-confident individual style. As early as 1879, William le Baron Jenney merely covered the supports and cross girders on the façades of his First Leiter Buildings, which were supported by cast-iron columns, and filled in the resulting grid with enormous windows. This architect, who designed the Home Insurance Building of 1883–85, the first ten-storey skyscraper with an exclusively steel skeleton, used the same principle for the Second Leiter Building. A stone-faced exterior was almost completely plain and was articulated solely by horizontal and vertical masonry bands; only the suggested capitals at the heads of the wide

Daniel Hudson Burnham: *Flatiron* (Fuller building), New York, 1902

This skyscraper on New York's Broadway stands on an extremely angular site and is shaped like a domestic iron (hence its name). It is acknowledged as an extreme example of the optimal use of a restricted site.

D. Adler and L. H. Sullivan: *Guaranty Building*, Buffalo, New York, 1894–95 (left); D. H. Burnham and J. W. Root: *Reliance Building* with so-called "Chicago windows" in bay form, Chicago, 1890–95 (centre); L. H. Sullivan: *Carson Pirie Scott*, Chicago 1899–1906 (right)

SKYSCRAPERS

When the old "village" of Chicago was destroyed by fire in 1871, it took several years to overcome the fear of further catastrophe and start on the construction of a modern business centre with office blocks, department stores and hotels, aided by extensive funding from the urban authorities. The first designs were by engineers and very similar, mainly because several technical inventions created the necessary framework conditions: i.e. the steel skeleton structure and new systems for stone foundations. The new Chicago grew up in regular blocks – buildings with eight or nine floors were described as skyscrapers – which always complied with the crucial condition of fire resistance. To this were added the pioneering inventions of the electric lift, the telephone and tubular post. For the first time it seemed possible to build to an unlimited height – the upper floors which were previously cheaper and less desirable now became sought-after and expensive addresses.

The Chicago architectural partnership of Adler and Sullivan represented an optimum combination of talents; Adler was an expert on finance and technology whereas Sullivan was more the visionary. Sullivan would ultimately make a key contribution to the renewal of international architecture in the 1890s. He gave his buildings a radical modern appearance, with their reticent decoration and large glazed surfaces. In theoretical treatises, he divided the building into the base, shaft and capital, using the Classical column as his model. The base or socle was reserved for rows of shops, the business or residential floors were accommodated in the shaft, and the capital, which was given particular emphasis, contained the building technology. Theorist Emilio Cecchi describes the cool undecorated façade articulation as follows: "The skyscraper is no symphony of lines and mass, surfaces and openings, power and resistance, it is much more an arithmetical operation, a multiplication." The architecture of the Chicago School was the harbinger of the "new world".

masonry bands at intervals of four windows were vaguely reminiscent of pilasters. Fire resistance was guaranteed by encasing its metal frame with cavity blocks. Bessemer steel, later to play an important role in the development of construction technology, was used for the first time in this metal frame.

By inserting a projecting perpendicular strip of masonry between the windows on the Wainright building in St. Louis, 1890–91, and the even more famous Guaranty building in Buffalo, 1894–95, Dankmar Adler and Louis H. Sullivan emphasised the vertical thrust of rectangular buildings. Sullivan had the following comment to make on the design of a skyscraper: "It must be proud and impressive to the last inch, rise up in joy so that it forms a unit from the ground to the roof without a single deviating line." He repeated his motto "form follows function" until it became the guiding principle of all of modern architecture. Thus the functions of different floors can be distinguished on the basis of the differentiation of the façade design into socle, shaft and capital. The ground and first floors are fitted with large windows and hence are suitable for retail trade. Above these lies the regular grid of the main floors which are used as offices. Finally, beneath the

projecting flat roof, there is an almost sealed surface with bulls'-eye windows which contains the technical equipment. There is some Art Nouveau decoration but this contributes little to the overall impression of the building's exterior. Sullivan's department store Carson Pirie Scott in Chicago is similar. Here, however, he emphasised only the rounded corners of the building with perpendicular masonry strips. The main floors, which were for retail use, are fitted with wide "Chicago windows". If one ignores the decoration added in the socle zone, this building already looks like something built in the 1920's or 50's. Such buildings, whose consistently simple design was derived from constructive conditions and functional requirements, gave Chicago the most modern architecture in the world at the turn of the century. This was most evident in the "Loop", the business quarter of the city. This approach to the construction of skyscrapers became known as the "Chicago School". However, it did not set a trend. On the contrary, one of its main representatives – Daniel H. Burnham – "betrayed" its aggressive modernity by turning back to a more communicable neo-Classicism, as can be seen in his historical façade design for the Flatiron building in New York.

New man and new building

THE FIRST HALF OF THE 20TH CENTURY

1900–45

THE SEARCH FOR A NEW FORM 1890–1925

Back to nature

Industrialisation brought with it a hitherto unknown level of economic, technical and social change. People in the highly-developed countries no longer lived in the country and worked in agriculture, but moved to big cities where they worked in industrial production and made do with inadequate living conditions. Many people had to live in extremely densely built tenement blocks which, due to the greed of their owners, were overfilled and often poorly maintained. Inadequate lighting and ventilation in these flats was usually matched by paltry sanitary conditions (insufficient running water and toilets, no bathrooms). Illnesses associated with poverty, such as rickets and tuberculosis, were very common and were an unavoidable outcome of the enormous disadvantages endured by many of the population. Areas in which the endless streets were devoid of trees or any form of natural life, and which had been built not on the basis of social or public health but solely with a view to maximising profits for land owners and property developers, were only populated by people who could not afford better, i.e. the workers.

The backlash against these inhuman and unnatural conditions in the early 20th century was initially known as the "back to nature" movement. Hostility towards the modern metropolis which had emerged with industrialisation was not restricted to the working classes. Many members of the upper classes also felt themselves unduly challenged by the speed of technological and social development, and alienated from nature. Due to continuing expansion of the cities, open spaces and countryside had become a vast distance away from many people, and could only be reached on Sundays. The "reform of lifestyle" became a popular topic for discussion. A characteristic expression of this mood is embodied, for example, in the founding of movements such as the German *Wandervogel* (rolling stone) youth movement and Rudolf Steiner's anthroposophy, which aimed to bring human development into harmony with that of the universe.

This focus on nature represented a promising development for architects and other artists seeking a way out of the rigidity of Historicism. They used plant forms and flowing lines, while motifs such as tendrils, streams and long, wavy women's hair also became popular. In Germany, this style of decoration became known as "Jugendstil". Its name derived from a publication entitled "Jugend" (youth), which was first published in 1896 and referred to the youthful and innovative nature of the new philosophy. In Austria, the style was referred to as the "Sezzessionsstil" (secession style) as it referred to a "secession" or departure from the

1900: World Exhibition and Olympic Games in Paris. Imperialistic powers quell the anti-European revolution of the "Boxer" secret society in China.

1901: Theodore Roosevelt is elected President of the USA. Thomas Mann publishes his novel *Buddenbrooks*.

1902: The Russian socialist Leon Trotsky flees from East Siberian exile to London.

1903: First flight by the Wright brothers in a biplane. Margarethe Steiff exhibits her "Teddy bear" at the Leipzig trade fair.

1905: Erich Heckel, Ernst Ludwig Kirchner and Karl Schmidt-Rottluff found the Expressionist artistic group, the "Bridge"

1910: Igor Stravinsky composes the ballet *The Firebird*.

1912: The Titanic sinks.

1913: The Indian poet and philosopher, Rabindranath Tagore, receives the Nobel Prize for Literature.

1914: Assassination of the Archduke Franz Ferdinand of Austria in Sarajevo leads to the outbreak of the First World War (until 1918). Henry

Ford starts mass production of the Model T.

1917: October Revolution in Russia overturns the Tsars. Lenin, Trotsky and Stalin found the Soviet Union.

1919: The Weimar Republic is declared in Germany. Beginning of prohibition in the USA.

1920: Mary Wigman opens her school of dance in Dresden and founds modern expressive dance.

1921: Discovery of insulin as cure for diabetes. Arturo Toscanini appointed director of La Scala opera house in Milan.

1926: Première of Fritz Lang's film *Metropolis*. Television successfully presented for the first time in London.

1927: Charles Lindbergh flies non-stop across the Atlantic. Hermann Hesse publishes his novel *Steppenwolf*, Marcel Proust publishes the last (7th) volume of *Remembrance of Things Past*.

1928: China is unified under Chiang Kai-Shek. Penicillin is discovered by the English bacteriologist, Alexander Fleming.

1929: The New York stock exchange crashes – "Black Friday".

1935: Nuremberg Racial Laws passed against the Jews in Germany.

1937: Picasso paints his monumental work Guernica as a reaction to the bombarding of the city by the Fascists.

1939: German troops invade Poland on September 1st. Beginning of the Second World War.

1940: Discovery of the Stone Age cave paintings in Lascaux. Charlie Chaplin plays the title role in the film *The Great Dictator*.

1941: Japan enters the War with the attack on Pearl Harbour.

1945: Germany surrenders. Americans drop the atomic bomb on Hiroshima and Nagasaki. The first electronic digital computer is built at the University of Pennsylvania.

Ford Model T, production in Detroit, photograph from 1913.

previously dominant artistic style and formal language. In Italy, it became known as the "stile Liberty" (Liberty style) after the London department store, which with its imported textiles acted as an ambassador for the new style. In England itself, there was talk of the "modern style" and in Belgium and France of "Art Nouveau". What specifically characterises "Art Nouveau" is the strongly individual art and craft dimension, which is entirely dependent on the personality of the artist in question. Its restricted focus on the purely decorative is reminiscent of Historicism. However, it also harboured the modern desire for a form which is derived from material and function.

Catalan architect Antonio Gaudí, the outstanding architect of the "Modernismo" in Spain, as the movement was known there, occupies a unique position in this movement, which differed significantly from region to region and country to country. Instead of being satisfied with the mere decoration of surfaces, Gaudí interpreted the entire house or building as a sculpture and approached its design from a purely plastic perspective. His façades became porous fluid surfaces which resembled tendril-covered or coarse rock surfaces, windows were transformed into the entrances to caves, and roofs made to look like coral reefs covered with abstract ceramic and glass mosaics. In 1883 the architect was commissioned to take over the design of the church of La Sagrada Familia in Barcelona, which had begun as a conventional neo-Gothic building. Gaudí did this by applying a highly individual interpretation and adaptation of the Gothic, which he mixed with Moorish elements. However, he failed to complete this project before his death in 1926. Gaudí's credo was based on an all-embracing concept of architecture which was, however, at the same time highly individual. The way he turned away from traditional notions of interior and exterior space, decomposing them both and using an ingenious structural system to achieve his effect, was highly progressive. The same cannot be said, however, of the way in which he concealed the steel structure behind thick stone facings. The over-abundant craftwork on his buildings, in which he decided every last detail, and the complete absence of straight walls and right angles in the luxury apartments of the Casa Battló or Casa Milá, could not be described as pointing the way towards a solution to the urgent need for accommodation, one of the main tasks of 20th century architecture.

Quality, suitability and effect of materials

More important than the actual forms developed by the Art Nouveau movement were the attitudes and

theoretical approaches behind it. In many countries, these transformed it into the beginning of a modern design movement. The accentuated linearity marked the re-introduction to architecture of dynamism, which had last appeared to such a widespread extent in the upward-striving forms of the Gothic. Historicist architecture was massive, heavy and static. The trend now favoured more flowing, dynamic, graceful and ethereal forms. These were far more appropriate to a period which witnessed an enormous increase in the means of transport (railway, automobile, aeroplane), access to information (telephone, wireless telegraphing) and of images (cinema). Even more significant was the emphasis which proponents of the style placed on the quality and suitability of materials: the materials used in construction should no longer be brutally exploited and concealed, but treated in a way which suited their nature and allowed their true effects to show. Thus the aesthetic decorative effect should be created equally by the material, the structure and the function of a building. As the important Art Nouveau artist Henry van de Velde (painter, graphic designer, designer and architect) wrote in 1902: "The role of decoration in architecture is in my opinion a dual one. It consists partly in supporting the structure and suggesting its methods, and partly in bringing life into an otherwise too evenly lit space through the interaction of light and shadow. I

Antonio Gaudí y Cornet: *Casa Battló*, Barcelona, conversion 1905–07

Even the plan of Casa Battló, which was converted by Gaudí, is reminiscent of a network of plant cells. The movement which gently bends the corners and curves the walls is continued in the door knobs, lamps and picture frames, as Gaudí also designed the furnishings and fittings. The coloured ceramic crust of the façade glistens magnificently in the sunlight. The roof resembles the scales of a dragon. With the balcony balustrades shaped like eye masks, the house, which stands on the Passeig de Gràcia, the prestigious boulevard of the rich Catalonian middle classes, gives the impression of looking down. This building marks the beginning of the development of sculptural architecture.

Victor Horta: *Musée Horta*, staircase, Brussels, 1899

Victor Horta exercised a considerable influence on Belgian architecture shortly before the turn of the century. With his villa for the industrialist Tassel in 1893, he created a building which was seen as one of the first ostensibly Art Nouveau residential buildings in Europe.
This house on the Rue Américaine in Brussels, which is now used as a museum, is another example of the virtuosity of the architect. He succeeded in converting the strictures imposed by the typically narrow restricted sites in the city of Brussels into the virtues of transparency and lightness. He designed each structural detail on the basis of its aesthetic, as dictated by the material. The stair balustrade demonstrates the development of ornamental forms from new structural solutions.

Hector Guimard: *Entrance to a Métro station*, Paris, 1900

Due to the effects of industrialisation and the migration of people from the country, the volume of traffic in cities increased significantly around 1900. With his entrances to the Paris Metro, Hector Guimard, who referred to himself as "*L'architect d'art*" succeeded in creating a symbol for the new mobility. The dynamism of the traffic underground was reflected in its railings and glass roofs. The floral forms of the leek-green lamps growing out of the street paving reconciled the world of technology, which was beginning to control daily life, with the longing for nature which they evoked. Sensuous and almost exotic, swelling cast-iron forms surged up against rigid stone façades. The integration of script into the iron frame also predicted the appearance of advertising in the public realm.

believe that by applying such principles it is possible to create a totally new kind of architectural decoration which follows the intentions of the building, its individual structural aspects and organisation, step by step."

Iron was particularly suited to the creation of flowing lines, and the bending, clustering and edging of rods also represented a suitable use of the material. Famous examples include Hector Guimard's entrance to the Paris metro which was opened in 1900. Iron had been a common building material for some time. However, like concrete, the use of which was gradually becoming more widespread, it had hitherto been hidden behind stone, plaster or timber. It was now used for the first time in the design of interiors, as can be seen in the aesthetically revolutionary staircase designed by Victor Horta in 1893 for the Tassel house in Brussels. Instead of concealing the structural form of buildings, this was now made visible and the decoration was derived from it. Iron or steel structural frames even began to appear in the façades of more progressive buildings; they were, however, usually integrated into the grid pattern produced by the supports and intermediate floors, and filled in with large panes of glass.

Apart from the Chicago School, which had had little or no influence in Europe, this approach had previously only been used in bridges, glasshouses, libraries, train sheds, factories and exhibition halls – so-called "industrial" buildings which were not considered as part of the architect's brief but the concern of the engineer. This was not the only attitude undergoing a radical change: the traditional divide between arts and crafts and the "liberal" arts was also disappearing. The Jugendstil architect Otto Wagner, whose Postal Savings Bank in Vienna

was one of the most modern buildings of its time, declared "nothing which is not useful can be beautiful". Architects were now concerned with all areas of life. Nothing was too banal for a designer to work on, be it a lamp, an armchair or a salt cellar. The aim which would later pervade all modern architecture was expressed here for the first time: the key issue was not reform of the concept of decoration or the conception of a building, it was re-design of the entire world, which was in the course of being rebuilt both literally and metaphorically. It was believed that the technical requirements to achieve this were now available. The focus on the suitability and effect of materials represented a link with the 19th century Arts and Crafts movement. However, unlike William Morris, the greatest proponent of this movement who died in 1896, progressive architects and designers of the early 20th century were no longer anti-machine. They realised that it was wrong to dream of the Middle Ages, to see the machine as the root of all evil and want to base production on purely traditional manual methods. If the aim was to re-design the world, it must be achieved in a way which would be compatible with the machine, so that goods could be produced in large volumes and made available to the masses at low prices.

It was against this background that in 1907 a group of like-minded German artists, craftsmen, experts and progressive entrepreneurs, who wanted to convert an assumption (that well designed high-quality products valued by specialists would be more marketable) into economic gain, joined forces to found the Deutscher Werkbund. This association promoted the application of "good form" in furniture, domestic appliances and even entire buildings. The belief was that anything manufactured or constructed using high-quality suitable and functional materials is real and good and, hence, beautiful. The Werkbund staged exhibitions to spread its ideas and products. The most important – mainly due to their buildings – were held in 1914 in Cologne and 1927 in Stuttgart. The latter took the form of the famous Weissenhof Estate, which was planned and supervised by Ludwig Mies van der Rohe.

Is ornament a crime?

The formal language of the Art Nouveau style quickly degenerated to a level of mere trifle. Its popularity faded as quickly as that of any passing fashion. The style was subject to mockery and disdain in both artistic and wider public circles, even prior to the First World War, and this attitude remained unchanged until the early 1970's, which saw the beginning of a wave of nostalgic revival.

In a controversial article written in 1908, Austrian architect Adolf Loos, a precursor of Modernism, pronounced ornamentation in general as "a crime" – on the basis that decorated products were more difficult to produce than simple ones but could not be sold at higher prices, and therefore forced craftsmen to work for subsistence incomes. Furthermore, due to the fickle nature of taste and fashion, such objects became unacceptable before they had actually worn out. "Ornament is criminal in that it causes severe damage to people in terms of their health, national treasures and cultural development." Moreover, "We have overcome ornament, we have reached a state which is devoid of ornament. Look, the time is nigh, fulfilment awaits us. The city streets will soon shine like white walls!" This prediction proved completely correct and his own buildings, such as the Goldman & Salatsch house in Vienna, with their smooth bare façades and simple forms, were a provocation. These bare surfaces alone represented a considerable gain when compared with the addiction to decoration expressed in excessively ornamented walls and overfilled rooms.

Garden cities

Hellerau Garden City near Dresden, the ambitious housing estate built after 1909 on the basis of an overall plan by Richard Riemerschmid, was associated with the Werkbund. The idea of garden cities originated in Great Britain, the first and for a long time most industrialised country in the world, which also suffered from the social consequences of economic progress. Ebenezer Howard published the agenda of the garden city movement in his book "Tomorrow – A peaceful way to urban reform", which was published in 1898. The ideas were first implemented in 1903–04 in the English town of Letchworth, under the architectural direction of Barry Parker and Raymond Unwin. Howard's concept involved the acquisition of a site which would accommodate approximately 30,000 people, by an association which would remain the owner of the land and thereby eliminate any opportunity for speculation. One and two storey houses would be built around a central park and along small tree-lined streets. The advantages of urban and rural living would be combined through the provision of shopping facilities and work opportunities. Surrounding farms would supply the garden city with fresh food. However, it proved impossible to sustain the independence of garden cities from the big cities. Garden cities, which in subsequent years continued to be built in a romantic, small-town and village architectural style, soon degenerated into purely residential estates located on the outskirts of large cities. The increased popularity and availability of the car made it possible to extend these suburbs without taking into account the previous condition that they be located within walking distance of the nearest railway station. The "breaking up", "greening" and "segregation" of the city later promoted by modern planners originates in the concept of the garden city.

The aim in Germany was to achieve something more than the mere improvement of living conditions. A progressive entrepreneur backed the Hellerau project, and the furniture factory "Deutsche Werkstätten" (German workshops) became the economic heart of the estate. The desire to create reform and social harmony, and an existence in harmony with nature, was even more pronounced there than in the aims formulated by Howard. It is no coincidence that the controversial cultural centre of the estate, designed by Heinrich Tessenow and also known as the festival theatre, was used as a training centre for rhythmic gymnastics.

Adolf Loos: *Goldman & Salatsch residential and commercial building,* Vienna, 1909–11

The radical rejection of ornament in Adolf Loos's polemical essays was consistently reflected in the simplicity of his buildings. The Goldman & Salatsch corner building is defined by its clear structure. The two lower retail floors are differentiated from the rest of the building by a marbled cladding of the façade and a variation in floor height. At this level, simple columns continue the rhythm of the window axes, the openings of which are simply cut into the white walls of the upper elevations. This extreme reduction of design originates in an instinct for social responsibility: Loos, who had travelled in the USA for three years, was opposed to the wasting of space which was a very scarce resource in modern cities. His idea of town planning was based on the movements and requirements of people. These anthropomorphic values paved the way for the later emergence of the Rationalist movement.

Peter Behrens: AEG Turbine Factory,
Berlin, 1908–09

Peter Behrens built his high and bright
AEG Turbine Factory in the middle of the
Berlin working-class neighbourhood of
Wedding, which is renowned for its dark
and narrow tenement buildings. Whereas
previous factories were surrounded by
reinforced walls, with the construction of
the turbine factory Behrens marked the
outbreak of an epoch flooded with light, to
which AEG's products had an important
contribution to make.
The reduction of the mass and the clear
visibility of the structural framework not
only emphasised the technical structure
but also raised it to a more elevated level.
From a distance, the pillar-shaped
supports projecting from the glazed
façade, and the gable which is decorated
with the company logo, clearly refer to the
form of an ancient temple. There was no
contradiction between art and industry as
far as Behrens was concerned. He strove
to bring them together in his design for
the factory building and also in his design
of industrial products.

Expressionism and the seeds of Rationalism

While Hellerau represented the social concept
associated with the Werkbund, its founding
member Peter Behrens embodied the idea of the
universal artist, at least in the early years of the
movement. Behrens started out as an artist and
then devoted his energies to applied art. In 1900 he
was appointed to Darmstadt, where he became
involved in the Mathildenhöhe artists' colony, the
centre of Art Nouveau architecture in Germany. In
1907 he was appointed artistic advisor to the
electronics concern AEG. It was in this position that
Behrens advanced to become the pioneering
proponent of what is known today as "corporate
identity". He was responsible for every design
aspect of AEG's public image – from the company
letterhead and logo to the lamps and household
appliances produced by the company, and even its
production sites. His Turbine Factory in Berlin
became a milestone of modern architecture as a
structure which totally rejects any form of alienating
Historicist disguise. Its monumental form is solely
derived from the structural frame which protrudes
pillar-like from the façades, giving a broken gable
line on the street elevation and creating a high,
column-free light-filled hall in the interior.

Behrens also made an important contribution to
architectural history in a different context: around
1910, Ludwig Mies van der Rohe and Charles-Édouard
Jeanneret, alias Le Corbusier, met and worked in
his office. Neither had completed architecture
studies but they were to become two of the most
important architects of the 20th century.

As early as 1911, Walter Gropius, another important
Behrens pupil, went on to develop what his teacher
had achieved in the AEG Turbine Factory. A certain
fondness for monumentality and neo-Classicism,
which repeatedly came to the fore in Behrens's
designs, had made the turbine factory into a temple
of work. By contrast, the Fagus Factory designed by
Gropius and Adolf Meyer was completely devoid of
symbolism and celebration. It had no gable,
accentuated pillars or even massive corners (which
were actually of no structural significance in
Behrens's building). The Fagus Factory was an
expression of pure objectivity, a light transparent
cube which seemed to consist entirely of glass.
Whereas the large window surfaces of the turbine
factory seemed to be spanned between supports,
in the Fagus Factory, the glass and massive
elements seem to blend to form a single uniform
surface. With this dematerialisation, the extreme
reduction of the structure to a stereometric form,
and the balance of horizontal and vertical lines,
Gropius and Meyer predicted the formal language
of Rationalism.

However, Expressionism was the next movement
to occupy the focal point in architectural interest. In
Expressionism the emphasis on structure, material
and function took second place to the artist's
personal will to express. The architect's thoughts,
desires, emotions and world view were seen as the
primary force in giving the building its form.
Expressionist buildings were mainly built in North
Germany, the Netherlands and Scandinavia, where
there was a long tradition of façade design based on

FUTURISM AND CONSTRUCTIVISM

When the 20th century began it was greeted with a sense of hope, not only by the majority of intellectuals: it was believed that further progress of technical, intellectual and social changes would lead to a completely new era with completely "new" people. Particularly noteworthy achievements in architecture bore witness to this enthusiasm in two countries whose political and industrial development had hitherto been somewhat retarded: Italy and Russia.

In Italy, a style and philosophy known as "Futurism" emerged, named after the Latin and Italian words for future. The "Manifesto of

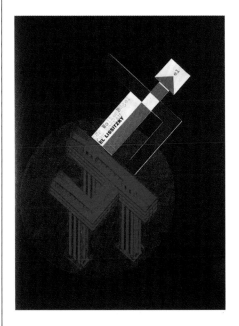

El Lissitzky: *Wolkenbügel design at the Nikitskije Gate*, Moscow, 1923–26

Futurism", published in 1909 by Filippo Tommaso Marinetti, focused on the speed, danger and violence of the industrial age. It bemoaned the omniscient presence of the ancient cultural legacy, which was seen as a burden, and called for the destruction of the traditional world – a reason for glorifying the War, "this sole cleansing of the world" and "the beautiful ideas, for which one dies". A famous sentence from the manifesto states that "a racing car whose body is decorated with big wheels like snakes with explosive breath (...), a shrieking car which seems to run on grapeshot, is more beautiful than the *Nike of Samothrace*".

In architecture the Futurists, particularly Antonio Sant'Elia and Virgilio Marchi, mainly worked on buildings used in the service of technology and transport, i.e. new tasks created as a result of the industrial revolution and which could also be used to celebrate it. Power stations, railway stations, airports and, of course, entire cities consisting of powerful collections of skyscrapers and multi-storey transport systems, were the focus of the Futurists' designs. They showed greater enthusiasm for the urban chaos of the metropolis than the majority of the architectural avant-garde in other countries. Of the innumerable dynamic, upward-striving and gigantic designs, few projects were actually realised. They were too aesthetically and financially advanced for the resources available at the time .

Despite realising so few projects, the Futurists were prolific publishers of manifestos. Their dramatic words and Utopian plans penetrated as far as Russia, where Constructivism was soon to become the leading style. Among other things, it shared with Futurism an enthusiasm for the apparently unlimited possibilities which new building technologies offered the architect. Other important influences included Cubism and Suprematism, which was founded by Kasimir Malevich. He was concerned with overcoming flat surface thinking in favour of three-dimensional spatial thinking in painting, and the development of an "art of spatial, constructive design".

El Lissitzky, the multi-faceted artist who had worked in Germany, was a key figure in the spread of Constructivism in the area of architecture. In 1922 he co-organised the first Russian art exhibition in Berlin, and made an important contribution to the influence of Constructivism on De Stijl and the Bauhaus. When applied to architecture, the principles of Constructivism mean that spatial design is understood as a form of design which thoroughly embraces space. Buildings consist of harshly juxtaposed elements reduced to basic forms and colours, reaching obliquely or directly to the sky, their design directly derived from the structure, which is exposed by generous glazing. Famous Constructivist projects include Tatlin's Monument for the Third International of 1919, a dynamic sculptural structure which was to have provided an office and conference building for the communist world organisation, El Lissitzky's Lenin Tribune, a steel framework which was to have projected at an oblique angle above the masses assembled for inspiration, and his "Wolkenbügel" skyscrapers which he designed around 1925. El Lissitzky also provided important inspiration for modern architecture with his graphical pages which he called "proun" (Proun = "For the new art"), and which contained playfully free combinations of geometrical bodies and surfaces in a wide variety of structures and colours. The few Constructivist projects to be realised include the Leningradskaja Prawda house in Moscow (1923, Wesnin brothers) and the Lenin Mausoleum on Red Square in Moscow, which was designed in 1924 by A. Sstuschussew but was not built until 1930.

It is not surprising that the aesthetic Utopians with their radical design ideas were particularly strongly attracted to radical political ideologies. The attraction of Russian Constructivists to comm-unism ultimately proved far more disastrous than the links between many Italian Futurists and the emergence of Fascism in Italy. Initially sharing the

Vladimir Tatlin: *Sketch of the Monument for the Third International*, 1919

philosophy of the Bolshevists who seized power, they were increasingly alienated by the political paralysis which occurred with the rise of Stalin in the mid-1920's, and were finally completely outlawed. The ideas of Constructivism were, however, to exert an influence on the future: Golosov's Club of Communal Workers (1927–29) in Moscow, with its contrasting glass and wall surfaces of round and clear rectangular forms, looks like something built in the 1990's.

Alexander, Leonid and Viktor Wesnin: *Competition scheme for the Soviet Palace*, Moscow, 1933 (not built)

Fritz Höger: *Chile Haus*, Hamburg, 1922–23

The corner of the Chile Haus rises up powerfully in front of the observer. The pointed arches in the ground-floor façade, the network of vaulted ribs above the entrance, and the brick ornamentation, are a play on North German backstein Gothic architecture. The enormous complex is built surrounding three courtyards and contains one working cell situated next to another in conveyor-belt style. Its expressive pathos suppresses the individual and integrates him/her into the mass of industrious workers.

unrendered red brick. The zigzag ornamentation, protruding cornices, pilaster strips and pilasters favoured by the Expressionists were easily integrated with this tradition. Wide white window frames, which were often adorned with numerous astragals, formed a stark contrast with the red brick surfaces.

The most monumental example of this style is probably Fritz Höger's Chile Haus in Hamburg, an enormous office complex which not only has 2,800 identical windows but other details repeated on the same scale. Höger used bricks for the elevations which had been rejected due to damage caused during the manufacturing process. By doing this, he achieved a lively detailed raw finish without the complex involvement of craftwork, which would not have been feasible in financial terms. According to Höger, his Chile Haus represented "a turning point in German architectural culture, the very opposite of eclecticism and Classicism, and above all victory over the 'Neue Sachlichkeit' ('new objectivity'). Its intellectual value is Gothic-dynamic in nature. Its appearance is free of earthly weight. Yes, the building is Gothic although it does not have one single pointed arch. Physically, its main dimension is horizontal and spreading in width; however its spirit is upright and victorious over the dreadful times."

This pathos was typical of the times. Due to the First World War and its consequences, architecture and construction had largely come to a standstill. It was only possible to start work on the Chile Haus

during a period of inflation because the client was a dollar-rich foreigner whose prosperity originated in Chile – hence the name of the complex.

Meanwhile the underemployed avant-garde architects let their imaginations run wild on paper and designed the most daring of projects for a future society. They joined forces in groups and associations such as the "Arbeitsrat für Kunst" ("working council for art"), the "Glass Chain" and the "Ring". Behrens, Gropius and Mies van der Rohe were not completely immune to the attraction of Expressionist ideas.

When the Expressionist approach to decoration became more reticent, it was clear how flexible the division between it and Rationalistic architecture was, in view of the widespread preference for stereometric architecture. This was the case, for example, with the work of Erich Mendelsohn. His Einstein Tower in Potsdam was conceived as a built sculpture, but due to the inadequacies of the available construction technology was built as a rendered brick building. Soon after this, Mendelsohn found more direct ways of deriving his preferred dynamic forms from the functional design of his buildings. The dynamism of his buildings was not archaic and heavy like those of Gaudí. Neither did it originate from applied decoration like the Jugendstil buildings. It was created through the audacious and expressive layering of parts, streamlined window bands, projecting staircases and curves derived from the shape of the site.

Walter Gropius and Adolf Meyer: *Fagus Factory*, Alfeld-an-der-Leine, 1910–14

The commission from the Fagus shoe factory represented a great opportunity for the young architects Gropius and Meyer to open new functional areas to the modern materials of glass and steel. Using these materials, which were seen as "insubstantial" (Gropius) and immaterial, they sheathed the main building of the Fagus Factory in a compact but transparent materiality. The extensive dissolution of the wall into a large glazed surface had previously only been tried out in the construction of large halls. These two architects were the first to transfer the transparent structure of a glass curtain façade to a masonry multi-storey building. The omission of piers at the corners of the transparent building, which gives an unrestricted view of the unsupported landings, contradicted the received idea of stability. An impression of the fragility and lightness of the staircase is emphasised by the wall of the adjacent entrance, which is articulated by means of narrow joints. Gropius's reputation was founded on his achievements in the Fagus Factory and a model factory for the Cologne Werkbund exhibition of 1914.

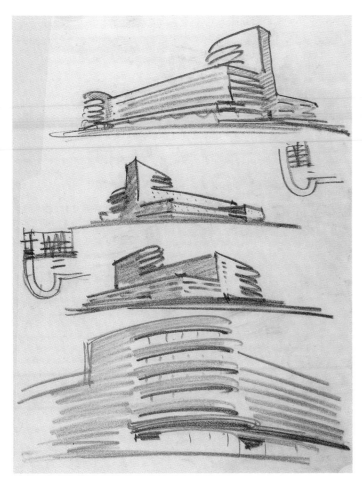

Erich Mendelsohn: *Schocken department store in Stuttgart*, design sketches, built from 1926 to 28; *Einstein Tower on the Telegraph Hill*, Potsdam, 1920–21

ERICH MENDELSOHN

The Einstein Tower rises from the ground like a submarine periscope from the waves. The observatory mirrors also steer sunlight into the underground laboratories like the periscope guides the image of the sea surface into the body of the ship. Its entrance is like a cave opening its arms wide to embrace the visitor. The windows are carved deeply into curved hollows. The Potsdam tower was quickly acknowledged as the epitome of built expressionism. Although its soft contours are based on masonry covered with cement, it stood like an exclamation mark for the "building material of our new will for form", as Mendelsohn described reinforced concrete.

Mendelsohn had begun to give form to an image of the future, which would finally begin after the War, in small sketches he produced in a trench on the Russian front. He developed designs of daring dynamism which seemed to approach the observer from a void. Industrial building tasks were a particularly interesting challenge – silos, furnaces, aviation hangars. He described the relationship between function and aesthetics in the following sober terms: "Economics, industry, transport put tasks in front of the architect in which the real moment represents 99 per cent of the design. But it is only the addition of one per cent intuition which makes the "material" into a work."

The constructive mood of his programmatic sketches also pervaded Mendelsohn's lectures: "Seize, build, convert the earth! – But form the world which awaits you. – Form the functions, their reality with the dynamism of your blood, brighten their functions to a supra-sensuous level. – Simple and sure like the machine, clear and daring like the construction." The architect saw himself as the creator of a new order.

INTERNATIONAL STYLE OR RATIONALISM 1920–45

A radical break with the past

According to their manifesto, the aim of the Dutch group "de Stijl" (the style), which was founded in 1917, was to "abolish natural form" and "eliminate that which stands in the way of pure artistic expression, the ultimate consequence of every concept of art". The aim to create a "pure reality", which is hostile to nature and cannot be reduced any further, gave rise to compositions such as those of Piet Mondrian. These consisted of red, yellow, blue and white rectangles separated by black lines. Of the few buildings realised in this style, the most important is probably the Schröder House in Utrecht which was designed by Gerrit Thomas Rietveld. Rietveld started out as a carpenter and furniture maker, and in 1917 built a controversial armchair consisting of standardised timber elements. His Schröder House was quite close to Rationalistic architecture, which had emerged and spread within a very short period. This represented a radical break with the past. The modern age demanded completely new aesthetic forms stripped of all picturesque, associative or Historicist tendencies. Consequently it was referred to as the "new architecture" and also "functionalism", and in Germany as "Neue Sachlichkeit" (new objectivity). Around 1930, the term "International Style" was also coined in connection with Rationalism, as it had spread through large parts of the world within a few years. The global uniformity of architecture, and culture in general, is thoroughly in keeping with the nature of modern, increasingly rapid methods of transport and communication.

Gerrit Th. Rietveld: *Schröder house*,
Utrecht, 1924

Gerrit Rietveld, carpenter and architect, had become famous for his "rood-blauwe stoel" (red-blue chair). The distribution of coloured surfaces, made of rectangular pieces of timber and boards laid above and below each other, made the chair look like a sculptural version of one of Piet Mondrian's abstract studies. In his theories, Mondrian hoped for a development in which the design of the "tangible reality of our environment" would be able to "replace the work of art". The dismantling of the visible into a geometrical abstract vocabulary, which enabled the search for a balance between the elements, was seen as ensuring this process. With this building, which he designed with the interior designer Truus Schröder, Rietveld also comes closer to realising the dream of "living in an art which has become reality" (Mondrian). The wall surfaces look like dynamic fields set into a swaying dance, like a mobile of balconies, canopies and balcony railings. However, the Schröder house remained an exception because the visual impression of a flexible modular system did not fulfil either the production technology requirements or economic constraints of the day.

The Bauhaus

The Bauhaus, a completely new kind of art college, was founded in Weimar in 1919 on the basis of a concept developed by Walter Gropius, who was also its director. It became the most influential educational institution for architecture, design and art in the 20th century. Its name was a play on the "Bauhütten", i.e. the associations of builders and artisans of the Middle Ages, and many of the most important modern artists taught there. The aim of the institution was to bring together art and crafts, theory and practice. The crowning achievement of these was the *Gesamtkunstwerk*, the building. This involved using contemporary technology and applying the old virtues of the arts and crafts to the conditions of the industrial age. Indebted to ideas of material and functional suitability, similar to those on which the Werkbund was based, the functionality of products was the main concern. Industrial production was seen as the ultimate aim of the design process. An "industrial art" was to be produced.

J. J. P. Oud, co-founder of the de Stijl movement, as city architect of Rotterdam provided excellent examples of Rationalistic buildings with his Kiefhoek estate and community housing in the Hook of Holland. As early as 1921 he promoted architecture as follows, "the tension as it is aesthetically realised in the great rhythm, in the balanced complex of mutually referential and influencing parts, whereby one supports the aesthetic intention of the other, where nothing can either be added or removed, whereby each part in its position and measurement relates so completely to the other parts, in itself and as a whole that any – even the smallest – change results in a complete destruction of the balance. What today's architecture lacks in terms of this balance achieved with own resources, it corrects by applying ornament. An ornament-free architecture demands the maximum purity of the architectural composition". It will be objective without disintegrating into "barren Rationalism" but in that "will immediately experience something more elevated", "to unfold the attraction of the cultivated material, the clarity of the glass, the flashing and rounding of the surface, the shining and brilliance of the colour, the glistening of the steel etc." and hence "be able to exceed Classical purity through the absence of all superfluity".

In German, Dutch and Czech architecture "Neue Sachlichkeit" means clarity of form and purity of surface, i.e. straight lines, right angles, strict, smooth elementary forms which should look as if they could have been produced by machines. Another major feature of the style is the flat roof, which when introduced gave rise to an outbreak of cultural strife in some places – as if the existence of Western culture hinged on the shape of the roof! Buildings were usually parallelepiped in shape and plastered in white. Architects such as Bruno Taut and Le Corbusier also developed a distinctive use of colour in their designs, whereby colours changed from one part of the building to the next with, for example, balconies or staircases in different colours from the façade. This made it possible to emphasise the exciting play of the distribution of mass, the "balanced asymmetry". This had replaced the reign of symmetry which had lasted for centuries as a defining force in architecture. Window bands which articulated the entire width of the façade also became typical, as did glazed curtain façades or supports on which the houses seemed to sway above the ground. The steel and reinforced concrete skeleton was exploited in every case, reducing the structural frame of buildings to columns and cross beams, and clearly displaying the technology from the outside of the building. Function and structure formed a single unit.

The Bauhaus complex in Dessau, which was designed by Gropius, is a good example of what is meant. The complex consists of three interconnecting main buildings in which the main functions of the school were accommodated. The workshop section, which requires a lot of light, has a glazed curtain façade and window bands can be found on the lecture building. Conversely, the balconies and individual windows emphasise individuality and the division into many individual

units of the students' residence. The administrative wing, which is accommodated in a section bridging these buildings across a street, forms the connection between these two buildings.

It would, however, be incorrect to assume that the form of a functional building emerges virtually from itself. The ordering, organising hand of the artist and his/her creative spirit remain essential to the discovery of an obvious, simple, functional and, thus, "good" form. Or as the art historian Fritz Baumgart put it: "The innumerable repetitions of a gridded office block box based on a once proven plan does not involve any art."

Mechanised residential building and large estates

Despite this, however, Rationalism contained from the outset the danger of excessive repetition of its external forms. This was partly desired and it was, in particular, rationalist architects themselves who showed great enthusiasm for the much debated rationalisation of the 1920s. The general belief was that ultimately efficient and widespread mechanical production could create happiness and prosperity for all. Also, it became clear during this decade that the only way in which the acute housing shortage could be overcome was by the application of a strongly rationalised approach to building. This shortage had been exacerbated by the cessation of building activity during the War, the post-war economic crisis, and the flood of refugees from the new border regions.

The use of pre-fabricated parts and serial production, i.e. standardisation of building elements, was therefore an important priority. More to the point, entire buildings and entire estates were to be produced on a serial basis. Le Corbusier, undoubtedly the most influential Modernist

Bruno Taut and Martin Wagner:
Horseshoe estate, Berlin Britz, 1925–31
(photograph from 1931 when the outer
site had not yet been developed

The initial inspiration for the Britz
Horseshoe estate came from the small
lake in the middle. It was intended that
the natural landscape would be a strong
presence in the estate on the edge of the
city. As Taut wrote "the way in which this
room is situated, with regard to the sun,
wind and its proportions, has a significant
influence on the feelings of comfort,
attractiveness, tranquillity, harmonious
calm, cosiness, etc." The rows of family
houses and narrow gardens which radiate
from the centre are terminated by a multi-
storey structure. With the closed
structure, Taut, who sought to unite
functionality, organic flow and symbolical
form, set a symbol for the community
within the co-operative estate.

Bruno Taut and Martin Wagner:
Horseshoe estate

Exterior view of a house with typical
façade colours.

architect and town planner, designed his "Dom-ino"
system around 1914; the client, architect or user
could put together a standardised skeleton with
parts (walls, windows, doors) from a catalogue. Up
to 1922, he developed the "Citrohan" house, the
name of which was a play on the rationalised car
manufacturing system used by Citroën.

Ernst May, who was city building consultant in
Frankfurt from 1924 to 1930, probably took the
"mechanisation of residential building" to its
furthest limits. From 1926 onwards a factory in
Frankfurt produced large building parts, from which
entire estates, e.g. the Römerstadt estate of 1928–
30, were built. The aim was to solve the city's
housing crisis within ten years. In Berlin, smaller
experiments with in-situ cast slabs the size of entire
walls had been carried out, but the Frankfurt
"standard slab" was three metres long, 1.10
metres high and twenty centimetres thick. A further
revolutionary innovation in this area was the
"Frankfurt Kitchen" developed by Grete Schütte-
Lihotzky. For the first time, new flats came with
fitted kitchens. The necessity for this arose when
for reasons of cost the kitchens had been reduced
to a size which would no longer accommodate old
bulky kitchen furniture. Also, the furniture and its
arrangement were designed not only for optimal
use of available space, but also on the basis of
rationalistic perspectives. Moreover, it was
assumed that housework would continue to be the
sole task of women: the rationalisation of work in
the kitchen was intended to give them more free
time or make it possible for them to work outside
the home.

However, despite all the savings, the new flats
were still beyond the means of most workers in

Germany. Furthermore, due to the continuing
exodus to the cities, the number of new homes
was never sufficient. In Berlin alone, which after
Frankfurt am Main was the second largest centre
for housing estates in the Weimar Republic,
between 1924 and 1931, when flat-building
programmes were almost completely abandoned,
100,000 publicly-funded flats were built. As in
Frankfurt am Main, ribbon development was the
most popular. Instead of blocks along the street
which restricted the space of the latter, parallel rows
of houses were now built at right angles to the
street. The position of buildings was based on the
maximum exploitation of sunlight, and sufficient
space was left between the rows of houses to plant
trees and grass. Despite this dominance of ribbon
development, other ambitious attempts at original
arrangement of the exterior spaces through the
manipulation of mass also existed. This can be
seen, for example, in the Horseshoe estate in Berlin
designed by Bruno Taut and Martin Wagner, the city
of Berlin's building consultant.

In Austria, and particularly Vienna, a different path
was pursued. Enormous blocks were built here, such
as the Karl-Marx-Hof, which is over one kilometre in
length and had semi-private interior courtyards, instead
of the narrow dark back yards of previous developments. This arrangement was intended to reinforce
the sense of community in the "super blocks", which
later became known as "red fortresses" because of
the political orientation of many inhabitants.

Planned happiness

Mass residential developments of these proportions represented a new task for the architects
as well as clients. In Germany and Austria, it was
generally local or urban authorities which awarded
the commissions, either directly or indirectly
through urban or trade-union house-building
associations, which were subsidised by public
funding.

The estates were only intended, however, to give a
foretaste of future developments in urban planning.
Unlike in former times, the architects were no
longer satisfied with designing representative urban
complexes. They believed that, like consumer
objects, cities themselves should be designed on
the basis of rational, scientific principles. It is no
coincidence, therefore, that many modern
architects who saw themselves as artists with
social responsibilities were closely connected with
the political Left. There was an unshakeable belief in
the ability to plan happiness, in maximum state
intervention, from which – given the correct
scientific basis – a brave new world would emerge.

Salvation was sought in a radical new beginning, but
there was failure.

Le Corbusier became the spokesman for
Modernism through the publication of *L'Esprit
Nouveau*, his book *Vers une architecture* and
various urban design concepts. He was able to base
the latter in particular on the concept of a "*cité
industrielle*" which was published in 1917. Tony
Garnier, the author of this concept, had presented a
detailed plan for an industrial town with 35,000
inhabitants. It incorporated ideas for everything
from the use of space and economic independence
to the design of individual buildings, which were to
have been built mainly in industrialised form.

Le Corbusier had significant influence on the
"*Congrès Internationaux de l'Architecture Moderne*"
(CIAM) which he co-founded in 1928, and which
met eleven times until 1959. The Charter of Athens,
which remained a binding influence for most
architects right up to the 1970s, was passed at the
second CIAM congress in 1933. This concept
favoured the division of the city – which had long
since ceased to be a cohesive organism
concentrated around the market square, church and
town hall. In the course of continued growth and
physical expansion, the great metropolises had
disintegrated into individual agglomerations;
systems of units connected to each other by
transport links. The new idea was to divide the city
into areas based on its individual functions –
residential, administrative, production, consumption
and leisure. The implementation of this concept
after the Second World War demonstrated,
however, that the dismantling of the original chaotic
confusion would actually lead to the wholesale
disintegration of large parts of the cities, while
others even suffered complete physical destruction.

Open plans for open societies

The open plan was a characteristic feature of the
buildings of Rationalism. Closed square and
rectangular rooms were replaced by open spaces
which led from one to the other, giving a flowing
series of rooms. These could be subdivided as
required, because skeleton structures only needed
supports and did not require load-bearing walls. This
concept of the "flowing" space was applied to a
city which had been reduced to rows of houses and
free-standing buildings, giving an "open city plan",
which in the course of time had little more to do
with the layout of streets. The Charter of Athens
had stipulated that the construction of rows of
residential buildings along the streets should be
prohibited.

This corresponded to the search for "light, air and
sun", as a well-known motto put it. Thus in 1926 Le
Corbusier proposed that houses be elevated onto
thin supports ("*pilotis*"): "This means that rooms
will be removed from the dampness of the earth,
they have light and air, the building terrain remains
in the garden which consequently continues
underneath the house." The use of flat roofs as
gardens meant "the winning back of all built space
for a city".

Rationalism built on the radically innovative and cool
elegance was perfected by Mies van der Rohe in
his German Pavilion for the World Exhibition in
Barcelona in 1929. Shortly afterwards the architect,
who became director of the Bauhaus in 1930,
applied this design to the Tugendhat house in
Brünn, which is also a residential building.

The open plan of the interior and exterior
corresponds to the position of man in the modern
world. There is no fixed world view any more, no
model for society in which each individual has a

Grete Schütte-Lihotzky: *Frankfurt
Kitchen*, around 1925

All functions reduced to 6.5 m² – the
prototype of modern kitchens.

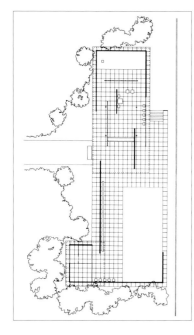

Ludwig Mies van der Rohe: *German Pavilion for the World Exhibition in Barcelona*, 1929

Like a poem about the possibilities of architecture, Ludwig Mies van der Rohe presented the necessary vocabulary in the Barcelona Pavilion. Wall surfaces made of reddish marble and shimmering onyx, slotted in under the freely spanned roofs, become abstract expressive surfaces. Chromed-steel pillars are free-standing. The play of reflecting light on the polished stones and materials falls onto two pools of water. The interior and exterior interpenetrate harmoniously. Merely built as a temporary structure for the world exhibition, the Pavilion soon became a legend representing the pure clarity of Rationalism. Since its reconstruction, the generous rhythm of the spaces seduces the observer to a meditation on pure architecture liberated from function.

defined place. Not even the perspective on buildings is fixed any longer. Gropius's Bauhaus complex has a clearly defined front and "show" side, whereas this building presents a new image from its different sides. This is nothing less than an architectural expression of pluralism.

Counter-movements

Historicism had produced stifling, asphyxiating, overcrowded interiors with a predominance of dark colours, and excessive decoration of furniture and façades. Art Nouveau had had a certain playful romantic note. In a time of political and social insecurity, like the 1920s and 30s, many people yearned for a familiar "cosiness" at home. They definitely rejected the idea of "machines for living in". Thus, in the 1920s people continued to build using the traditional methods, or gave buildings constructed using modern technology historical exteriors. The "*Heimatstil*" (homely style) which was based on forms taken from folk art, rural architecture and regional features, played an important role. It was particularly predominant in garden cities and rural areas, where the aim was to preserve the architectural image and develop it with particular care and attention.

In Germany, aesthetic issues escalated to a war. In 1925 the political right forced the Bauhaus to move from Weimar to Dessau, where it was finally closed down in 1932. An attempt to continue its work and tradition in Berlin failed in 1933, when the National Socialists seized power. They saw this institution as embodying the epitome of what they called "cultural Bolshevism". They not only turned against modern architecture and art, but against the entire

modern world. They promised their supporters an exit from history, a stable "Thousand Year Reich". National Socialist architecture was based on antiquity, and included a tendency, which had existed since the turn of the century, to the excesses of an increasingly coarse neo-Classicism. Gigantic elongated buildings, usually clad in limestone and strictly symmetrical, with rusticated ground floors, enormous projections and endless rows of high pillars and windows, were intended to convey a cold sense of majesty and intimidate the observer.

Unlike the dynamism and transience demanded of modern architecture, the requirement here was for stasis and permanence. Thus, the "ruin value" of the buildings had a role to play: Hitler had his head architect Albert Speer produce drawings which showed the Reichsparteitag complex in Nuremberg half ruined and overgrown.

The Nazis applied the same intention to plans for the conversion of most large German cities that they had applied to individual buildings. The high point of this project consisted of the plans for the redesign of Berlin as the capital of the Reich, "Germania". The "north-south" axis, a gigantic prestigious avenue, was to extend from the biggest railway station in the world via a triumphal arch designed by Hitler to the "Great Hall", on the dome of which would sit (at a height of 290 metres) the National Socialist eagle with the globe in his claws.

Social or similar perspectives had no part to play in this form of urban planning. The sole aim was to stage a gigantic architectural show of strength. The likelihood of war was taken into account, however, in severely restricted public housing activity. Designs exist for rows of houses in which the staircases and one room per flat are built as air-raid shelters. Technical and design regulations were also defined in terms of war: the use of steel and reinforced concrete was prohibited from the mid-1930's, as these materials

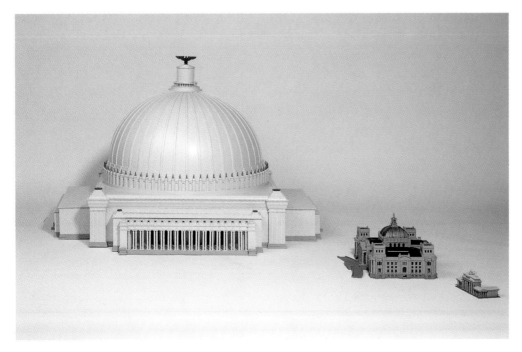

Erik Gunnar Asplund: *City library*,
Stockholm, 1920–28

The central cylinder of the city library is
surrounded by three lower cubic wings
arranged in the shape of a horseshoe.
With its imaginative neo-Classicism, the
Swede Asplund demonstrates that
Swedish architecture was well on the
way to Modernism in the 1920's.

were required for the construction of weapons and
bunkers. Natural stone which is self-supporting had
no economic value in the context of war.

The National Socialists were not unique in their
support of neo-Classicism. The age of the artistic
avant-garde in the Soviet Union ended in 1932,
when a monumental, massive and Historicist
design won the competition for the Soviet Palace.
In the following years, pompous residential
complexes – "workers palaces" – were built. These
were similar to the megalomaniac architecture of
the Nazis in their distribution of mass and
presentation, but were often veiled with Historicist,
pathetic ornament.

In Italy, by contrast, where the Fascist dictatorship
had been in power since 1922, the most sober
Rationalism was not merely tolerated but even
used for party buildings. Giuseppe Terragini's "Casa
del fascio" in Como (1936) is the most famous. Like
the Olivetti works by Figini and Pollini in Ivrea near
Turin, the cube with its wide gridded façade,
smooth white wall surfaces and flat roof, shows the
same external style as, for example, Le Corbusier's
Unité d'Habitation in Marseilles (1947–52). In Italy,
which had become industrialised considerably later
than its European counterparts, the Fascists saw
themselves as part of a thoroughly "modern
movement". To this was added the influence of
Futurism, which originated in 1909 and glorified the
industrial age, machines and speed. Its most
prominent spokesman Marinetti was appointed
Minister for Railways under Mussolini. It was not
until the mid-1930's, when the Italian Fascists
became more and more embroiled in the ideology
of the German Nazis, that they began to turn their
backs on Rationalism.

By contrast, in liberal Scandinavia architects sought
a synthesis between modern architecture and
regional traditions. The most important of them, the
Finn Alvar Aalto, declared that the previous
approach of Rationalistic architecture was too
strongly influenced by "technical functionalism",
and too little by the specific needs of the people
who use the buildings. It was essential to examine
these needs very closely as a background to every
design; for example the manipulation of light in a
library as realised by the Swedish architect Erik
Gunnar Asplund in Stockholm. According to Aalto
"Functionalism [is] only justified when it is
expanded and also includes psycho-physical
concerns. This is the only way in which architecture
can be humanised" – a long neglected option.

Modernism goes to America

American architects did not initially develop any
new visions but continued to base their work on the
European stylistic canon from the turn of the
century. Thus some of the buildings constructed
were carbon copies of Speer's work, e.g. the US
Ministry of Defence, the Pentagon (1941/42) and
the San Francisco Mint (1937). The Superior Court
built by Cass Gilbert in 1935 and the Trade Ministry
of 1932 – both of which stand in Washington – are
by contrast pure Classicist buildings. Art Déco
remained a seminal influence in the cities, above all
for skyscrapers and other commercial buildings.
This was a style which emerged from the 1925
Paris exhibition "Exposition des Arts Décoratifs
Modernes" which was consequently known as the
"1925 Style". Art Déco became extremely popular,
particularly in interior design. In Europe it mixed the
elegance of Rationalism and the pure, precious
materials favoured by Mies van der Rohe with a play
on rectangular surfaces reminiscent of de Stijl. It
betrayed a fondness for streamlining as well as
eclectic borrowings involving Babylonian or Ancient
Egyptian ornament. The cool, bare, completely
rectangular spatial structures and glass curtain
façades of an architect like Mies van der Rohe were
not impressive or monumental enough to assert
their influence on commercially oriented
architecture.

The visionary approach of the Chicago School had
long since disappeared and had found few disciples
in the USA. Even Sullivan's pupil Frank Lloyd Wright,
who had given rise to controversy before the First
World War with his "prairie houses" and open
plans, designed little of note in the 1920's.

This situation first changed when many of the most
important European architects emigrated to the
USA, due to the political situation in Europe and the

hostility towards modern architecture in Germany and the Soviet Union, two of the most important avant-garde countries. One of the first to arrive was the Viennese architect Richard Neutra, whose Lowell Beach house of 1926 still stood out on a limb stylistically. Neutra worked for Frank Lloyd Wright, whose house above a waterfall – "Falling Water" – with its asymmetrical layered concrete cubes separated by window bands, was clearly inspired by the immigrant.

It was also an American who pushed the entire development of modern architecture to its limits and almost to its culmination, just at the point when Modernism had reached an unchallenged position in most countries. Philip Johnson reduced colour, form and material to the limits when he built his "Glass House" in New Canaan in 1949. He was clearly inspired by the work of Ludwig Mies van der Rohe; for example, the Crown Hall in Chicago which had been designed earlier than Johnson's house but was not built until later. It would have been impossible to build something more minimalist than Johnson's design with its thin, dark, rectangular steel frame. It is completely glazed, has no walls and only a cylindrical brick container which houses various technical installations. It would be impossible to push any further the boundaries of what had been standard for thousands of years of architectural history. However, the challenge to the users of such a building had also been pushed to the limits: the idea of living in a "glass box" is simply unacceptable to most people up to the present day.

Frank Lloyd Wright: *"Falling Water" house*, Pennsylvania (USA), 1935–39

Wide projecting concrete terraces intersect above the waterfall in Wright's "Falling Water" house. To achieve maximum differentiation of the parts of the building, Wright broke the closed contours of the cube and turned the horizontal levels against each other. The architecture confronts its natural surroundings powerfully and asserts itself with elementary power.

Philip Johnson: *Glass House*, New Canaan, Connecticut (USA), 1949

Philip Johnson pushed the dematerialisation of architecture to the limits in his Glass House. The glass exterior walls take their cubic contour from the thin steel frame, and provide maximum transparency for the space beneath the trees. Johnson initially worked as director of the architecture department at the Museum of Modern Art in New York. He had promoted the "International Style" in books and exhibitions before he began to study architecture in 1940 under Walter Gropius and Marcel Breuer, who was famous for his tubular steel furniture. With the Glass House, Johnson marked the culmination of the search for permeability and flexibility in European Modernism. The skeleton structure could not be developed any further.
In his subsequent projects he worked with Mies van der Rohe before adopting a polemical distance from the strict principles of Modernism in the 1960's.

The failure and revision of Modernism

THE SECOND HALF OF THE 20TH CENTURY

since 1945

THE TRIUMPH OF MODERN ARCHITECTURE

Modern architecture = freedom

The hour of modern architecture arrived with the end of the Second World War. Many of its most important representatives, who had been refused commissions and planning permission for their work, sought and found refuge in the USA. America, which had been spared the destruction and desolation of war, was now the richest and most modern country in the world. The Soviet Union may have been able to offer some competition in terms of political and military strength. However, when it came to issues like living standards and cultural influence it remained hopelessly in the shadow of the USA, which had been the geographical embodiment of hope and freedom for centuries.

Shortly after the end of the War, when Stalinism was still at its height in the Soviet Union, a neo-Classical architectural style – similar to that elevated to an ideal in Nazi Germany – was still being promoted there. Attempts to link up with the modern architectural tradition of the inter-war years, which had been strongly influenced by Socialism, were positively outlawed in the Soviet Union and its satellite states, on the basis that this style was "formalistic", "cosmopolitan" and "alien to the people". In the West meanwhile, massive, monumental, Historicist, i.e. very "un-modern" architecture was considered both outdated and unsuitable due to its associations with totalitarian ideologies. For this reason, despite regional resistance and variations, the only style which could really be considered for public and large company buildings was a more modern style. With its reduced forms and colours, lightness and transparency, dynamism and asymmetry, Rationalism had become the symbol of progress, freedom and democracy.

The last director of the Bauhaus, Ludwig Mies van der Rohe, had emigrated from Germany to the USA in 1938. In the mid-1920's he had designed a daring memorial to the assassinated Socialists Karl Liebknecht and Rosa Luxemburg in Berlin. It consisted of asymmetrical layered brick blocks, projecting and receding on top of each other, and emblazoned at one end by the star, hammer and sickle. He now became the leading architect for the design of commercial buildings. In 1948–51 in Chicago, he finally managed to realise his vision of a skyscraper sheathed in glass, which he had designed some thirty years earlier for a competition, for a skyscraper project beside the Friedrichstrasse railway station in Berlin. His Lake Shore Drive apartments take the form of two box-shaped skyscrapers, supported by a steel frame, set at right angles to one another. Their exterior consists of a curtain wall consisting of completely identical windows extending the full length of each floor. I-shaped beams act as projecting "glazing bars", covering the perpendicular assembly area between two windows. Together with the exposed steel members on the façade they provide the vertical articulation, whilst the intermediate floors provide a

---

1946: Foundation of the United Nations (UN).

1949: The Federal Republic of Germany and the German Democratic Republic are founded along the border between the East and West blocks.

1950–53: War-like confrontation between communist North and capitalist South Korea resolved by the superpowers.

1953: Workers' revolt in the GDR on June 17th.

1956: Anti-Stalinist revolt in Hungary

violently suppressed by Soviet troops.

1957: The first artificial satellite (Sputnik) circles the earth.

1959: Günter Grass writes his novel *The Tin Drum*.

1962: Cuban crisis. Krushchev declares willingness to remove Russian rockets to Kennedy. Première of Benjamin Britten's *War Requiem*.

1963: US President J. F. Kennedy is murdered in Dallas.

1964: Première of Robert Stevenson's film *Mary Poppins*.

1965: The Cultural Revolution begins in China.

1966: Student unrest starts in

the West with protests against the Vietnam War.

1967: Six-Day War between Israel and Syria, Jordan and Egypt.

1968: The Prague Spring in Czechoslovakia is crushed by Warsaw Pact troops.

1969: The Americans Neil Armstrong and Edwin Aldrin are the first men to walk on the moon.

1975: The Vietnam War ends (started 1963).

1979: The Nobel Peace Prize is awarded to the Catholic nun Mother Theresa.

1985: Mikhail Gorbachev as General Secretary of the USSR introduces perestroika.

1989: The Berlin Wall is breached.

1990: First elections are held in all of Germany since the War.

"That's one small step for a man, but a giant leap for mankind": Neil Armstrong on the moon.

1991: UN troops defeat Saddam Hussein's regime in Baghdad.

1994: The Black majority wins the first free elections in South Africa.

1995: Christo and Jeanne-Claude "wrap" the Reichstag in Berlin.

Potsdam Conference (17th July to 2nd August 1945): Churchill, Truman and Stalin during a break from negotiations.

horizontal accent. The ground-floor columns are free-standing and the completely glazed entrance hall is somewhat recessed. This emphasises the unique capacity of the skeleton structure to support large masses resting on a few columns.

The design of this building is radical and modern. External form is reduced to two upright cubes, and the façade – which no longer has a load-bearing function – is completely glazed. Form is mainly revealed through the elimination of all ornament. "Less is more" was the architect's most famous maxim. "As simple as possible no matter how much it costs", was another. This building consists solely of straight lines and right angles, with no added decoration and no colours – except for the natural colour of the materials. The façade structure is completely dictated by function and the overall structure, hence it is completely rational. The grid is dictated by the load-bearing skeleton, or the glass infill of the windows. A degree of variation and movement is provided by the blinds and curtains, with which individual residents cover their windows.

The Seagram Building in New York was the first office building to which Mies van der Rohe, working in collaboration with Philip Johnson, applied his skyscraper vision. As the site was wider and the building higher than in previous schemes, what emerged was a high rectangular slab rather than a tower. Glazing bars on the curtain façade were faced in bronze and the glass is bronze-tinted. The constantly changing pattern produced by the residents' curtains and blinds, which also defined the exterior of the Lake Shore Drive apartments, is absent here. The impenetrable mirrored façade is covered by a regular grid.

This rectangular slab stands like a gigantic monolith from another world, on Park Avenue. Its effect is cool, elegant, refined, unapproachable and sublime, further underlined by Mies's insistence that the building be moved back from the street. This was, however, also necessary so that it could comply with New York building regulations and retain its completely straight façade without recessing. Its position allowed a small courtyard in front of the building, which the architect designed as a flat, granite-paved podium with a rectangular fountain on the left and right.

Opportunity for a new beginning

Although Modernism in the West was ideologically rooted in the 1920's, it was also based on economic necessity. The economic perspective could no longer be ignored – particularly in the area of housing. In the aftermath of the worst war in human

history, vast areas of Europe and East Asia now lay in ruins. Whereas the main concern had previously been to improve living conditions in the interests of social equality and public health, the priority now was simply to find a way of putting a roof over the heads of millions of people as quickly as possible. Many architects and town planners regarded the devastation left by the War with barely concealed delight: they had always dreamed of tearing down the old cities and building new ones. Now the bombing squadrons and artillery battalions had done it for them – Hans Scharoun even spoke of "mechanical dispersal". Grandiose plans proposing the radical re-design of cities and demolition of the old city fabric were presented at every opportunity. After all, everything was to change and improve after this war; faith in the ability to provide happiness for all through planning was unshakeable.

Ludwig Mies van der Rohe and Philip Johnson: *Seagram Building*, New York, 1954–58

New York is reflected in the Seagram Building on Park Avenue, yet the skyscraper slab gives the impression of a closed withdrawn form which barely communicates with the city. The monochrome façade, consisting of specially manufactured bronze structural elements and tinted thermal windows, has the appearance of a tranquil surface which is emphasised by the addition of floor bands. Mies van der Rohe's first venture into commercial architecture, this building, with its ingenious technological solutions and luxurious materials, proved to be good advertising for both the client and the architect. The plaza or square in front of the entrance provides a visual counterpart to the elegant skyscraper, relieving the impression of weight from its volume.

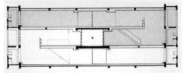

Le Corbusier: *Unité d'Habitation*,
Marseilles, 1945–52. Section through one
unit consisting of three floors

Le Corbusier expressed his opposition to
"de-urbanisation", or as he put it the
"madness of the single-family home",
with his plan for a collective residential
system. He pledged his support for
skyscrapers as integrated urban design
units, with precisely defined functions to
fulfil and a specific role to play. The dream
of the garden city was to be fulfilled
through the allocation of a precisely
defined space to all community services.
There would also be sufficient room at
the foot of each skyscraper for extensive
parks.
The roof terrace of the "unité" has
several sports facilities and a nursery.
There are shops, a doctor's surgery and
laundry inside the building. The section
shows how two flats with gallery levels
interlock, giving space at the centre for an
interior access.

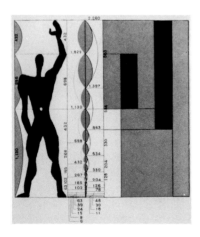

Le Corbusier: *Modulor*, theory of
proportion based on the human figure

Le Corbusier, who had lived in German-occupied
France during the War, was now given the
opportunity to realise his dream of a "residential
unit" in Marseilles. The idea behind this scheme
was that in this modern age – which was so radically
different from everything that went before –
it was necessary to design for living in a completely
new way. Le Corbusier believed that accom-
modating the living space in a smaller physical
space would lead to a greater collectivisation of life,
in the sense of residential and more general
activities. Behind the idea of the "machine for
living" was the belief that an artificially created
world, completely planned and designed by man,
had to be better than a natural one created by
random forces. Le Corbusier's planning was
extremely thorough and detailed. Using his
"modulor" system of proportion, which defined the
average height of the human body as 1.75 metres
and was based on the Classical Golden Section
system of harmony, he calculated that the ideal
height for a room was 2.26 metres.

A total of 337 flats with different interlocking plans
was accommodated in the enormous reinforced
concrete cage of the Marseilles "unité", like wine
bottles slotted into a wine rack from both sides. Half
way up the slab there is a broad two-storey
shopping arcade which extends right across the
135 metre-long building. The "unité" also has a
nursery school, function rooms, a restaurant,
laundry, roof garden with a playground and
gymnasium, and other communal and supply
facilities. Other "unités" were built in Nantes, Berlin
and Brie-La-Forêt. However, the future-oriented
standard model for new housing developments,
which the French government had sought when it
commissioned Le Corbusier to design the Unité
d'Habitation, was mainly identified by its external
architectural form: enormous horizontal reinforced
concrete slabs soon began to appear everywhere,
not just in France. The heavy shading elements,
which were intended to protect the flats from the
direct southern sunlight in the Marseilles building,
were also widely copied. Together with the
coloured design of the inside walls of the balconies,
they were later used to liven up façades, especially
in the asymmetric designs later favoured by Le
Corbusier himself.

Architects like Kenzo Tange were responsible for
the spread of Le Corbusier's style to places as far
flung as Japan. However, the architect's wish that
the "unité" would become a prototype for entire
complexes of such buildings remained unfulfilled.
Despite innumerable plans and competitions, hardly
a single European city was ready to implement such

a radically new approach. Firstly, the immediate
need for new housing was too great, and later the
reconstruction of houses along the old street
alignment had progressed too far. A "generous"
new approach to design, with extensive open
spaces, could simply not be afforded in the town
and city centres.

Beyond the building of new residential estates,
mostly the size of small towns, the only places to
show any interest in grandiose new urban design
concepts were some future-oriented "developing
countries". For example, Chandigarh, the capital of
the Indian state of Punjab, with 500,000 inhabitants,
was built from 1950 onwards based on plans by Le
Corbusier. Brazil, which at the time was defined as a
"threshold country", i.e. on the brink of attaining the
economic power and affluence of an industrialised
state, created its capital Brasilia along the same
lines. The location selected for the city was a
sparsely populated mountain plateau in the
country's interior, which has a tropical mountain
climate. The location was rather inhospitable but
was selected on the strictly rational grounds that it
was at the geographical centre of the country. What
was created here was a "drawing-board city",
which mostly corresponded to Le Corbusier's
ideas for the division of urban functions, with
separate transport and pedestrianised areas.
It was a beautiful, new, entirely artificial concrete world, with buildings in the cool elegant style
of Mies van der Rohe standing on vast empty
spaces.

Despite adhering to a strict Rationalism, the
Brazilian architect Oskar Niemeyer, who was
primarily responsible for the planning of Brasilia and
its main public buildings, also felt a need for
symbolism. Thus he gave the city plan the form of
an aeroplane – an expression of the progressive
dynamism with which Brazil was supposedly
heading towards a happy future. The parliament
building has a funnel-shaped hall for the
parliamentary assembly and a domed room for the
upper house or senate. Both of these sit on the roof
like two saucers, one the right way round and the
other inverted. Skyscrapers housing the parliamentary deputies' offices stand between the two
saucers and provide a vertical accent. The impression of monumentality is emphasised by the
strongly symmetrical complex at the centre of the
six-kilometre-long north-south axis, which is lined by
various government and cultural institutions. As a
symbolical gesture, the supreme court and
president's palace were built beside the parliament
building, giving rise to the "Three Powers Square".
Due to its sterility and cold majesty, Brasilia never

succeeded in asserting its identity like the old, lively and chaotic capital of Rio de Janeiro.

The loss of faith in progress

After the appearance of the Seagram Building, in a drive for self-promotion, numerous other companies and corporations also wanted to have such impressive buildings as their headquarters. By 1960, Mies van der Rohe's extremely reduced, severe style had become the main fashion in architectural taste. Legions of architects were now imitating the style he had created thirty years earlier, with the German Pavilion for the World Exhibition in Barcelona. All over the world, buildings appeared which consisted almost exclusively of straight lines and right angles. They were wide and bright with the elevations glazed from top to bottom. The only decoration both inside and outside was the pure effect of the materials used: shining chromed or dark anodised metal, raw brick walls, unvarnished timber, bare concrete, and polished or relief-style crude natural stone. Due to their simple skeleton structure and open plans, Mies-style buildings were endlessly adaptable, whether in the form of skyscrapers based on the model of the Seagram Building, or low flat buildings. One example of the latter is "Crown Hall" with its large, open column-free space, which was built for the Illinois Institute of Technology in Chicago in 1956. Entire architectural practices specialised in imitating this style. One of the most successful was Skidmore, Owings and Merill (SOM), which with the New York Lever House erected a building in this style as early as 1952, and with the Sears Tower in Chicago designed the tallest office building in the world in the 1970's.

Material effects and "dematerialisation" were the main features in demand at this time. As Le Corbusier had done in the 1920's, buildings were raised on stilts to create horizontal open spaces underneath, or in the middle of the building as "air floors". Stairs were constructed using steel or re-inforced concrete beams, on which individual steps were balanced. Windows had very thin frames and often took the form of "pivoted windows", which were opened by being turned vertically or horizontally on their own axis. Doors consisted of large, unframed glass panes on to which hinges, locks and handles were directly fitted. Everything was meant to seem transparent and unforced.

However, in many cases this spare reduced style was merely seen as an excuse to build cheap undecorated boxes quickly with a superficially modern appearance. Where Mies had used expensive onyx or marble, chipboard covered with cheap patterned plastic film was supposed to achieve the same effect. Façades did not conceal spacious open-plan flats but tiny, cell-like rooms. This was particularly widespread in the area of social housing, which was subject to strong financial restraints. The pioneers of modern architecture had dreamt of houses which not only functioned like machines but which could be produced by them: the Modernist buildings of the 1920's and 1930's were supposed to look as though they had been produced by machines, whereas in reality they were often the product of intricate manual work. And when houses were finally produced in large numbers from mechanically produced parts, it quickly became apparent that this resulted not only in unrelenting monotony,

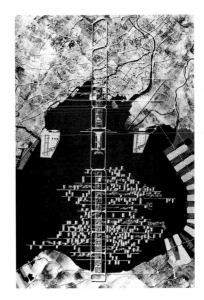

Kenzo Tange: *Plan for the extension of Tokyo Bay*, 1960

The rapid expansion of Tokyo was the motivation behind Tange's plan to extend the city on piles over Tokyo Bay. The catastrophic daily levels of traffic congestion led him to plan a system of rapid transit roads into which flexible residential units would be integrated. The Tokyo project is one of a series of similar schemes developed by young Japanese architects. In the "Sea City", K.. Kituake featured submerged housing for 3,000 people in cylinders, while K Kurokawa's "Helix City" had transport tracks perched on concrete ribs, between which residential cells were spanned like a spider's web. The architects were inspired to these Utopian structures by the search for a flexible system which would be equipped to accommodate future changes.

Oskar Niemeyer: *Parliament building, Senate and Administration skyscraper on Three Powers Square*, Brasilia, 1957–64

Three Powers Square is like a surreal collage taken straight from revolution architecture's box of tricks.
Despite being a complete product of the drawing board, the plan for Brasilia was not characterised by Rationalism but by symbolical form. The planners had to take account of neither history nor historical plans in this completely new city located in a remote landscape.
This apparently new historical beginning is emphasised by the universalistic formal language of the Brazilian architect Oscar Niemeyer. The saucer-shaped roof of the house of representatives is reminiscent of an open funnel in which the people's votes are collected, whereas the closed form of the senate dome represents concentration. Both forms potentially complement each other to form a sphere, the symbol of perfection.

Eero Saarinen: *Supporting member from the Trans World Airline Terminal*, New York, 1956–62

Y-shaped beams support the curved roof shells of the TWA terminal by Eero Saarinen: they evoke the image of a bird opening its wings in preparation for flight. Compared with the reduced rationalist buildings popular at the time, Saarinen's architecture represents the regaining of an individual profile and corporeality. Dynamic curves were applied consistently throughout the design and included the advertising boards and check-in counters, giving passengers the impression that they were setting off into a futuristic era.

but also in an extremely low quality of both finish and form.

This failure, in which euphoria and enthusiasm for the future and faith in human omnipotence and its beneficial effects eventually culminated, was gradually acknowledged from around 1970 – mainly in the West. Disillusionment was mostly linked with developments in town planning; the way in which many towns and cities had been re-designed after the Second World War or extended through the addition of new estates. The extent of the destruction they had suffered during the War played a minor role in the decision to implement a radical new approach to planning. To have a newly constructed flat was the greatest conceivable happiness at the time. Modern town planners and architects were firmly convinced that new, completely planned towns and cities, with wide streets and abundant parking spaces which made them more suitable for cars, and with functions "divided" into zones, filled in with parks and green belts, had to be infinitely preferable to the random chaos of the old towns and cities.

However, "functional zoning" of the city, on the basis of which people lived in one place, worked in another, and shopped and pursued their leisure activities in others, resulted in the disintegration of what the "city" had previously embodied. Entire neighbourhoods disintegrated over time. This was combined with the effect of the new architecture which was perceived as monotonous and smothering in its never-ending, uninspired, schematic imitation. In his film "Playtime" of 1965, at the height of the Mies-van-der-Rohe-style imitation,

French film director Jacques Tati depicted a car-friendly Paris consisting only of such buildings, full of traffic noise and the humming of air-conditioning systems and fluorescent lights, and looking as if Le Corbusier's "Plan Voisin" of the 1920's had been transformed into reality.

Due to the fast, cheap and careless way in which these new estates were built, they quickly disintegrated into substandard condition and a state of disrepair. Architects and planners had failed to take into account that that the communal parts of these enormous buildings, such as staircases, lifts and entrance halls, would be subject to considerably greater wear and tear – due to the fact that they were used by a considerably larger group of residents than was the case with smaller buildings. The 1960's plans outlining solutions to the housing crisis even contained dreams of the construction of so-called "mega-structures" – series of enormous buildings which would partly or completely replace an entire town. Moshe Safdies's "habitat" complex, shown at the World Exhibition in Montreal in 1967, was an example of how this concept might look in the real world: identical residential units of up to eleven floors in height, piled "higgledy piggledy" on top of each other. The absolute height of impersonality, crude design and cold technology had finally been reached. It was not long before a movement emerged which opposed this radical rationalistic faith in technology, which celebrated the abolition of the milk bottle as progress, and measured the degree of civilisation of a society on the basis of the number of cars it had and the scale of its energy consumption. People

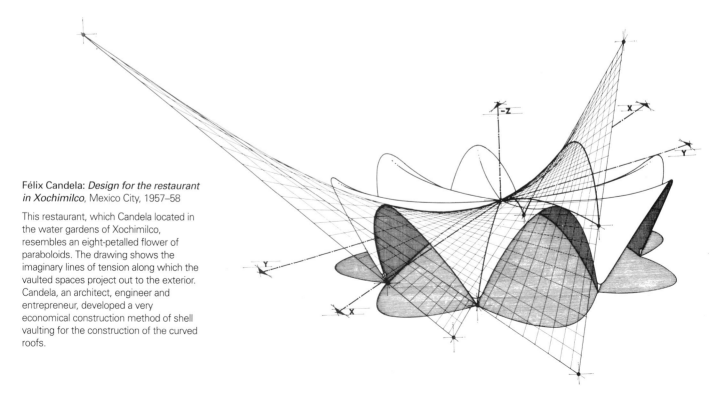

Félix Candela: *Design for the restaurant in Xochimilco*, Mexico City, 1957–58

This restaurant, which Candela located in the water gardens of Xochimilco, resembles an eight-petalled flower of paraboloids. The drawing shows the imaginary lines of tension along which the vaulted spaces project out to the exterior. Candela, an architect, engineer and entrepreneur, developed a very economical construction method of shell vaulting for the construction of the curved roofs.

Hans Bernhard Scharoun:
Philharmonie, 1960–63, Berlin

The contour of the roof silhouette of the
Philarmonie is defined by three curves.
They reveal the form of the hall ceiling
from the outside, which is actually the
most characteristic feature of the interior
hall. Daylight penetrates the foyer through
a glass roof on the west side of the
building. The acoustic waves of the music
seem to have inscribed their lines in the
staggered structures of the stalls and the
graduated ceiling. With the Philharmonie,
Scharoun developed a spatial concept
which had preoccupied him in expressive
drawings since the 1920's. He was
looking for a curved contour to restrain
the expansive force of the space. He
understood the collective experience of
listening to music as the restraining of
energy, to which he gave a physical form
with his architecture.

began to talk about the "desolation of the cities",
expressing their opposition to large-scale plans for
the demolition of existing structures to make way
for the construction of more and bigger roads.

In 1972, the Club of Rome produced a controversial
study on the "Limits of Growth", a notion which
had previously seemed inconceivable. The advent
of the oil crisis one year later saw the demise of the
economic basis for unrestrained consumerism
which had been criticised by members of the
younger generation. After some two hundred years,
enthusiasm for the advantages created by technical
progress and human behaviour, which had started
with the Enlightenment, finally died.

This development was accompanied by a fear of
the future and a desire to escape from reality.
Esotericism and other equally irrational political
ideologies had been gaining in popularity from the
late 1960's onwards. This development was
reflected aesthetically in the popularity of bright
colours, extreme patterns, nostalgia and the
rediscovery of Art Nouveau.

The city of the 19th century underwent a surge in
popularity and appreciation. In 1975, the European
Year of the Preservation of Monuments, it was
discovered that more architectural monuments had
been destroyed since 1945 in West Germany than
were actually destroyed during the Second World
War. This was despite the fact that up to the mid-
1970's few 19th and 20th century buildings were
actually classified as historical monuments, i.e. the
term applied almost exclusively to castles, churches
and town halls, and not to factories, cinemas,
workers' housing and railway stations.

When the estate of Minosu Yamasaki in St. Louis –
which had been lauded as an ambitious and
progressive project two decades earlier – was
demolished in the summer of 1972 because the
houses were seen as neither habitable nor capable
of being salvaged, it was seen by many as a sign of
the end of modern architecture.

SCULPTURAL ARCHITECTURE

Swaying, hovering, organic forms

In view of the lessons learned from the above-
described experiences with certain forms of
modern architecture, and from the construction of
new cities like Brasilia and Chandigarh, it is not
surprising that serious doubts should emerge as to
whether strictly rationalistic architecture could ever
adequately express freedom and democracy.
"Organic" forms, which represent freedom of
expression in their rounded, swaying and asymmetrical dynamic, remained an equally lively force in
post-War architecture. This movement, which is
also known as "organic architecture", was based
on Plato's theory of proportion, which also had
a strong influence on the development of
Renaissance architecture. The perception of man in
relation to the building was once again to become
the main criterion for architecture. At the same
time, buildings were no longer to be treated as
isolated structures, but should aim to create
harmony between the landscape and architecture
through their form.

Attempts to achieve dematerialisation, which had
dominated the architecture of the 1950's, occasionally assumed bizarre forms. The most famous
example of this forced effort to achieve something
unforced is the kidney-shaped table, which came to
epitomise 1950's taste.

However, this desire to give form an expression of
its own was not only evident in developments in
interior design. It can be seen, for example, in Eero

Frank Lloyd Wright: *Guggenheim Museum*, New York, 1956–59

Plans for the Guggenheim Museum, which rises from a circular plan in the shape of a spiral, had been created in 1943. The ramp, which is wound around an empty space, is impressive as architecture which has become sculpture. However, it competes with the exhibited art for the attention of the visitor. The series of curved wall spaces restricts the scope for the functioning of the museum. Wright had already used the motif of a rolled strip in his Johnson Building in Racine, Wisconsin (1936), which is reminiscent of interlocking cylinders: the entrance located in the interior was accessed from a driveway. The ramps and spirals of America's drive-in culture of gas stations, snack bars and cinemas had come to embody a signpost for mobility since the 1930's. These architectural structures allowed space to pass by the observer like the reels of film which present the viewer with a series of images. In the Guggenheim Museum, Wright elevated this cipher of popular culture to a modern artistic form.

Saarinen's terminal for Trans World Airlines (TWA) at John F. Kennedy Airport in New York. A similar dynamic, occasionally exaggerated symbolism can be seen in Jörn Utzon's Sydney Opera House. Whereas in New York the curved swaying forms were intended to evoke wings, in Sydney the sail-shaped, stacked saucers open up as symbols of heightened festivity.

By contrast, the Philharmonie in Berlin, the main work of Hans Scharoun, one of the most important representatives of "organic" architecture, is reminiscent of a large tent. The audience stalls are arranged around the music area – which cannot really be described as a stage – like terraces in a vineyard. Their different shapes and heights are derived from the plan of three pentagons which are arranged against each other at different levels. Above all this rises the ceiling which, for acoustic reasons, is also graduated to shield the hall from external noise. For the same reason, the ceiling is actually a three-shelled structure and the exterior walls are for the most part devoid of windows. Just as the external form is dictated by the internal organisation of the building, and this in turn is "organically" developed from the functional requirements and the location of the music at its centre, the exterior reflects the character of the building and the events which take place inside it.

The renewed desire to treat buildings as sculptures played an important role in this context. The French "revolution architects" Ledoux and Boullée had been unable to realise comparable ideas two

centuries earlier. Erich Mendelsohn had to resort to a conventional masonry structure for his Einstein Tower in the early 1920's, which with the help of cement encasing was then made to look like a concrete sculpture. During the 1950's architects were no longer forced to resort to such subterfuge, as reinforced concrete and other new technologies were more widely available.

This material, which was actually patented in 1886, takes account of the discovery that fine hairline cracks (which arise in concrete due to the tensile stress absorbed by the steel reinforcements) can be avoided if the concrete is "pre-stressed" during building. This made it possible to use reinforced concrete structures to support greater loads or span greater widths. Above all, it allowed the construction of slimmer, more elegant, load-bearing elements, which were more in line with the taste of the 1950's.

The use of reinforced pre-stressed concrete shells, i.e. single or double, curved self-supporting elements which are very thin but at the same time very stiff, became equally popular. They are particularly suited to the roofing of large halls, and had been used for this purpose by the Italian architect Pier Luigi Nervi since the 1940's.

During the 1950's, however, it was more important that their curved, voluminous form could accommodate dynamic, bizarre and contradictory-looking designs like those created by Felix Candela. For example, his restaurant in Xochimilco in Mexico City has a wafer-thin roof which undulates up and

The contours of the pilgrim church of Notre-Dame-du-Haut are as soft as sand dunes formed by the wind and weather. The roof arches over the rounded walls like the head of a mushroom on its stalk. The external openings of the irregularly distributed windows are small. In the interior, however, they expand to form caves embedded in the thick walls. The atmosphere is defined by a sense of secrecy and intimacy, which at first glance would seem the furthest thing possible from Le Corbusier's Rationalism. The church holds up an image of familiar security to the social organisational form of the city. It is, however, possible to find one thing which links the reproducible grids of the "machines for living in" and the solitary moment of the church in Le Corbusier's pictures and sculpture. Over the years he developed a vocabulary of organic forms which he could use to achieve the integration of man and mechanical forms. In a restless never-ending search for the reconciliation of technology and nature, he had tried out forms which did not yet seem plausible as spatial structures.

down in a continuous line. Despite the fact that it rests on minuscule supports, it projects extensively. This light hovering impression is the opposite of the more monumental symbolism evoked by Le Corbusier's pilgrim church of Notre-Dame-du-Haut at Ronchamp, the form of which is reminiscent of an arch. Among other things, the architect used double shells to give the building, with its apparently heavy burden-like roof, a certain earthiness and containment.

Frank Lloyd Wright's revolutionary spiral ramp, which provides the exhibition space in the New York Guggenheim Museum, is another excellent example of the way in which architects responded to the demand that buildings be seen as sculptures. In many instances, however, unusual designs created in the name of organic architecture, dynamic symbolism and the treatment of the house as a sculpture became an end in itself. A building like Saarinen's TWA terminal, for example, guaranteed the company a high degree of recognition, particularly as the airline's logo was repeated in the curved form of the building.

Large-scale housing projects, which are usually subject to the constraints of extremely limited funding, were no longer the central design focus of the architects of the 1950's – in contrast to the concerns of their Modernist colleagues during the inter-War years. It was primarily commercial buildings and cultural buildings, such as museums and concert halls, which attracted attention and yielded generous fees.

HIGH-TECH ARCHITECTURE

Building as an expression of the communications society

In addition to the concept of organic architecture, the 1960's saw the emergence of the idea of the building as a technically organised work of art. This so-called "high-tech architecture" is historically rooted in Joseph Paxton's Crystal Palace of 1851 and other 19th century industrial buildings. However, the former approach of deriving the form from the fulfilment of structural requirements and the accentuation of character was only continued by a few architects after the Second World War. These included the above-mentioned Nervi who, among other things, built halls from prefabricated concrete elements, just as Paxton had built the Crystal Palace from prefabricated iron elements.

Since the construction of that pioneering building, the maximum realisation of the external wall as a glass skin had remained the dominant topic in high-tech architecture. This also includes extremely thin membrane structures, as developed by the German engineer Frei Otto and used with the architect Rolf Gutbrod for the German pavilion at the 1967 World Exhibition in Montreal. He collaborated even more spectacularly with Günter Behnisch on the Munich Olympic Stadium in 1972. The tent-like roof structure of the latter is reminiscent of a spider's web. Otto developed his structures in empirical experiments: he used setting agents to stiffen spider's webs which had been dampened with

Foster Associates, Ove Arup and Partners: *Hong Kong and Shanghai Bank*, Hong Kong, 1979–86

Turned inside out: 139 modules for technology and installations are fitted externally to the building, which is supported by eight masts. The bridges on which the office "sets" hang divide its structure. The high-tech design is the bank's trademark and is also symbolic of the economic power of Hong Kong, which is based on the production of electronic parts.

Günter Behnisch, Frei Otto and Wolfgang Leonhardt: *Olympic Stadium*, Munich, 1968–72

The earliest sketches for the Munich Olympic Stadium banished all angular and rectangular forms: soft forms poured into the space. Working with a landscape architect, the Behnisch office developed a complex on an abandoned airfield in which the architecture and the landscape flow into each other. Functional essential buildings and sporting arenas disappear into hollows in the landscape and below ground. Permeable framework structures blur the lines between the interior and the exterior. Thousands of trees were planted and a lake was built. The roof hangs on massive supports like a cloud over a sports field. Whilst the translucent covering made the idea of "sport in the open" possible, the roof also provided protection from the rain and weather. The abundance of natural light also facilitated the recording of the games by the media.

drops of water, and then placed the resulting structure upside down. He was also inspired by soap bubbles, on the basis of their optimum ratio of material to membrane tension.

The English architect Norman Foster, one of the main proponents of high-tech architecture, attached long narrow perpendicular glass panels to the projecting floor corners of the Willis Faber & Dumas office building in Ipswich. As the panels also stiffened the glass skin (structural glazing), it was possible to fully glaze the gently curving elevations produced by the irregular site without the need for a metal frame.

One of the most famous high-tech buildings, the Centre Pompidou in Paris, oscillates between the desire for multi-purpose expansive spaces and accentuation of the technical and structural elements. In this cultural centre, which was built between 1971 and 1977, Richard Rogers and Renzo Piano moved all the building technology to the exterior. They displayed sanitary modules, escalators and lifts in open form, completely glazed or accentuated through the use of colour. Rogers used the same principle a second time in 1986, in his design for the new headquarters of the insurance group Lloyds of London. The architectural duo created technical building machines, whose entire aesthetic is based on the ambivalence of structure and style.

Another favourite topic of the high-tech architects was implemented in an exemplary manner by Norman Foster in the 1980's, with the administration building for the Hong Kong and Shanghai Bank: prominent externalisation of the structure which is, if possible, placed in front of the façade. The approach was justified in this case:

Foster compiled the building using "bridges" located beside and above each other, which carried "sets" of office floors. Therefore, in view of the extremely high price of building land in Hong Kong, this made it possible to use the site to its maximum potential without interrupting traffic during construction – which had to be completed in the shortest possible time. This structure also made it possible to comply with the requirement that the ground floor level be left open.

However, ingenious structures developed on the basis of functional requirements were often taken over by structural exhibitionism. Structural experiments were reduced to the level of functionless games played for their own sake. For example, Foster opted for a roof structure for his Renault Centre in Swindon (1983) which is far more complex than was actually necessary. It is, however, particularly distinctive and prominent, a feature desired by the company for image and advertising purposes. High-tech architecture tends only to be applied in office blocks, large halls and similar structures, not least because of the high costs arising from such extreme designs.

The Centre Pompidou could be said to embody the high and end point of modern architecture. In the late 1960's and early 1970's, high-tech tendencies were often linked with "Brutalism" (from the French "brut" = crude), a term which had been applied to Le Corbusier's style of the 1950's. Excessive accentuation of building technology (in the interior also, with, for example, exposed pipes on ceilings) was combined with increased use of exposed-aggregate concrete (pebbled surface). Above all, exposed concrete showed the marks from formwork which was supposed to produce a

Renzo Piano and Richard Rogers:
Centre Pompidou, Paris, 1971–77

In the beginning was the shock. When first approached, the Pompidou Centre looks like something which has landed from outer space and crashed into the mature fabric of the city. The glass skin which covers the 40-metre high steel structure is concealed behind a network of frames, ventilation pipes, corridors and escalators. It quickly becomes obvious, however, that this gigantic cultural machine is merely flexing its technical muscles like a performer.
Despite the high-tech costume, the architecture is actually more imitative of an organic structure. One moves through the glazed pipes of the staircases and escalators which provide a view of the service pipes. As long as the programme of exhibitions, readings, music, film and new media remains attractive, the architecture of Rogers and Piano continues to function as a cultural supply station.

"natural" effect as weathering left its mark. Combined with the massive forms which had already been introduced by Le Corbusier, and which became as popular as bright colours during the 1970's, this led to extremes of ugliness and clumsiness which had little in common with the refined elegance of classical Modernism.

POST-MODERNISM

Return to the styles

"Organic-Romantic" architecture, with its curved surfaces, soft roofs, oblique columns and walls and forms borrowed from nature, based on Art Nouveau and particularly the work of Antonio Gaudí, exercised a certain influence on the general development of architecture in the 20th century. More influential, however, was "Post-Modern" architecture which has its roots in the 1960's. American architect Robert Venturi's "Guild House", an old people's home in Philadelphia, is acknowledged as the foundation building of the Post-Modern era. Many typical elements of this style can be seen here; the symmetrical solid masonry façade, the entrance on a central axis which is emphasised by a column, a large segmental arch window, and a non-functioning television aerial as a decorative ornament and symbol of the main occupation of the residents.

The pioneers of Post-Modern architecture dismissed their predecessors with the same gusto as Modernists had rejected theirs. Balanced asymmetry was replaced with a return to Classical symmetry, the transparent wall was replaced with a return to the traditional "pierced façade" featuring increasingly small windows, and the absence of decoration was replaced with a return to applied ornament.

Mies van der Rohe's maxim "less is more" no longer applied, and was replaced instead with Venturi's pronouncement that "less is a bore". Venturi expressed his general criticism of Modernist architecture in his book "Complexity and Contradiction in Architecture". His work "Learning from Las Vegas", which was compiled between 1972 and 1978, and in which he celebrated the advantages of trivial, popular architecture, was even more influential. In this book, written together with his wife Denise Scott Browne, he pleaded for the "decorated shed"; the conventional building (as opposed to the modern focus on progressive construction techniques) to which decorative forms were added, culminating in a show façade which had nothing to do with the building interior or the structure. Ultimately the Gothic cathedrals and Early Renaissance palaces worked on the same principle. In adopting this approach, Venturi and many others overlooked the fact that some things had actually changed since the Middle Ages, such as the revolution brought about by reinforced concrete construction. The outcome was that form and decoration, and the ever-popular game involving quotes from historical buildings, became increasingly random. The Post-Modern architects produced little more than an unoriginal counter-programme to Modernism, in which they hailed the glorious pre-modern times. In doing this they overlooked the fact that Boullée and Ledoux, whom they declared as their heroes along with Gaudí and Palladio, were forward-looking and not retrospective in their approaches.

SOM (Skidmore, Owings & Merill):
Sears Tower, Chicago, 1969–73

SOM is one of the biggest construction companies in the USA, with branches and heads of design in many US centres. From the 1950's onwards it exercised a key influence on the architecture of the USA, through the development of a building type for the administration buildings of large companies. It played an important role in the war of the skyscraper cities – New York and Chicago – by perfecting the skeleton structure and developing a pipe structure which allowed the construction of extremely high buildings. The Sears Tower held the record as the world's tallest building for a long time.

Richard Meier & Partners: *Bridgeport Center*, Bridgeport, Connecticut, 1984–88

The familiar image of the skyscraper as a backdrop is intensified in the interlocking masses of Richard Meier's Bridgeport Center. The central tower looks as though it has been swallowed up by the two corner buildings. The red granite and steel panelled facing not only emphasises the organisation of the building, but the return to a closed façade using precious materials. Like the window bands, the façade shows strong axes and a rectangularity which is sculpturally emphasised on the roof. Access to the Post-Modern architecture via a five-floor atrium is an attempt to compensate for the loss of public space by providing an arena for communication in the interior.

Michael Graves, one of the most important developers of the Post-Modernist formal vernacular, built his Portland Building in Portland (1979–82) as a conventional cube, to which he added a pierced façade and gigantically excessive decorative "quotes", such as garlands, pilasters and similar elements. The builder's question "the house is ready, which style do you want it in" echoes once again. With his Bridgeport Center, Richard Meier actually built several buildings at once, which he placed beside each other but failed to connect as though he were unable to decide whether the building should be round or angular, brown, white or with a metallic sheen.

This all culminated in the reconstruction of entire historical buildings which had long since disappeared from the face of the earth, and an architecture which is a direct copy of 19th century Historicism. As the main criterion was mass taste, the quality of design deteriorated correspondingly. The fleeting or uneducated observer understands as little about Venturi's and other Post-Modern

architects' "decorated sheds" as he/she does about Rembrandt's paintings. He merely recognises something. Art cannot be subjected to general approval but is always based on what is recognised at a given moment. When the Impressionists exhibited in Paris for the first time, they were violently attacked by the public for their "crazy" pictures. Today, these same works enjoy enormous popularity and Impressionist exhibitions are hugely successful events.

The desire to win the approval of the fleeting observer led the Post-Modern architects to produce increasingly pandering, coquettish and showy designs. Given that the function of the architectural profession to provide a service is denied by this style, and individual vanity is prized above functional fulfilment, Post-Modern buildings are often pleasant to look at but difficult to use. Architects increasingly indulged in more and more bizarre and senseless games: merlons on top of residential buildings, staircases leading nowhere, arches which could be neither walked nor driven through, living spaces with slanting walls, or completely chaotic plans which had been forced into abstruse structures. This was combined with a certain fondness for intimidating monumentality, as can be seen in Ricardo Bofil's residential complexes "Les Arcades du Lac" near Paris (1975–81) and "Arena" in Marne-la-Vallée (1980–84). The latter was intended as a "Versailles for the people", constructed using prefabricated elements with monstrous column orders which extended across ten floors, and flats with windows wedged between enormous cornices. The fine line which exists between Post-Modern architecture and megalomaniac Stalinist architecture is obvious.

By contrast, Aldo Rossi based his work on the Italian Rationalism of the 1930's which, with its symmetry, stereometric forms and endless repetition of the same elements, ultimately culminated in a kind of neo-Classicism. He remains, however, imprisoned in Post-Modern. For example, he created the Teatro del Mondo for the 1979 Venice Biennale; it uses the historical repertoire like a wardrobe of costumes and includes towers, walls, castle, palace and market stall. As a provocative piece of party architecture which never aimed to provide anything but a stage, the theatre sustained a poetic levity. After the Biennale the theatre was welded to a raft and shipped to Dubrovnik.

The Swiss architect, Mario Botta, created formative works of the Post-Modernist style in his houses in Pregassona (1979–80) and Stabio (1980–82), which is also known as "Casa Rotonda". In the latter, a perpendicular glazed incision penetrates to the depths of the building and lacerates the otherwise windowless façade, which consists of masonry strips.

Despite the fact that Post-Modernist architecture sought refuge in the old, Romantic forms as a reaction to the demise of belief in future progress and the beginning of the computer age, it also utilised some modern formal elements. These include flat or saw-tooth roofs and undulating glass walls, as can be seen in James Stirling's Neuer Staatsgalerie in Stuttgart. This building also has natural stone veneers, high-tech elements such as a glazed lift, romantic-anecdotal elements such as garage ventilation openings in the form of "openings broken through the wall", and other bizarre features like an "Egyptian tomb entrance" which leads to the hall used for temporary exhibitions. The total lack of uniformity of colour, form and material seen here is a typical feature of Post-Modernism.

In general terms, however, the intellectual substance behind this style proved so fragile that it could only provoke controversy for a short period of time until the late 1980's. Now, less than a decade later, it all seems rather boring and silly. Highly contemporary jokes and extreme fashion should be avoided in architecture, because for economic reasons alone its products cannot be changed at the same rate as furniture, clothes or hairstyles.

DECONSTRUCTIVISM

A new Modern movement?

Around 1990, Post-Modern architecture was replaced as a focus of media attention by "Deconstructivism". This style was named after an exhibition entitled "Deconstructivist Architecture" organised in New York by Philip Johnson, which aimed to establish the new style. Representatives of this new style developed an elite formal language based on the philosophy of Jacques Derridas. This took the abstraction of Modernism to the extreme

Aldo Rossi: *Residential Building, Kochstrasse*, Berlin, 1989

James Stirling, Michael Wilford & Associates: *Extension to the Staatsgalerie*, Stuttgart, 1977–84 (terrace with the glass façade of the entrance hall)

Inspired equally by Le Corbusier, Schinkel, Weinbrenner and Semper, the English architect Stirling designed a monumental structure for the extension to the Stuttgart Staatsgalerie. It combines modern-technological with Classical-Romantic formal language. Although he found contemporary German architecture boring, he welcomed the opportunity to work in Stuttgart with old-fashioned reliable craftsmen. The particularly finely polished sandstone surfaces contrast starkly with the shining pink and blue balustrades. The architectural collage, which is overflowing with references, works with set pieces from all centuries of architectural history. For example, the enormous rotunda in the interior courtyard would appear to have been built for the staging of ancient dramas. Architectural critics praised Stirling's capacity to arouse curiosity, his wit and the virtuosity with which he created additional possibilities for the presentation of the Stuttgart collection.

Behnisch & Partners: *Hysolar Research Building, Stuttgart University*, Stuttgart, 1987

Initially it was planned to build a temporary structure for the Hysolar research institute using containers. The improvised temporary image of the building is a legacy of this idea of architecture on call. What is being staged here is a test case for structural performance. How far can the individual element go without destroying the functional cohesion of the structure? Oblique glazing frames, corners which defy the heart bond and parts of the roof which open out like the wings on a windmill combine to create a turbulent, dynamic and broken contour. The mandatory space for communication disintegrates into individual elements, the balance of which can only be restored by their users.

Bernhard Tschumi: *Folie P7*, La Villette, Paris, 1982–90

The "Folies", are red pavilions which cover the Parc de la Villette in Paris like a grid consisting of a broken composition of cubic elements and containing cafés and restaurants. With these pavilions, Tschumi evokes the machine culture of the Constructivists and spells out the constitutive elements of an architectural language, the text of which can no longer be decoded.

and mainly worked on the principle of exaggeration of familiar motifs. The movement is assigned by its interpreters to the intellectual context of Modernism and is thus also known as the "New Modernism".

However, like the Post-Modernists the Deconstructivists also seek a prominent, spectacular form, which expresses their opposition to structural and decorative norms and does not take into account the fulfilment of functional requirements. The motto for Deconstruction "form follows fantasy", which was coined by Bernhard Tschumi and derives from Sullivan's famous maxim "form follows function", could ultimately also have been used as a battle cry for Post-Modernism.

The Deconstructivists identified a further source of inspiration in Russian avant-garde artists of the early 20th century, i.e. the Constructivists and the Supremists.

From all of this, a concept of "disturbed perfection" was developed: the whole often looks like somebody has been playing with building bricks, an extremely varied model construction kit or match sticks and accidentally bumped into the table. This caused everything to slip and shift, and the resulting form was then used as a model. Delicate filigree elements are often found next to monstrous oversized elements, with the result that the chaotic structure appears weak, as if it were liable to collapse at any minute. The architecture of Deconstruction tries to use all these means to upset the unquestioning daily perception of architecture, and through this alienation make architecture capable of being experienced in a new and more direct way as art.

The British architect Zaha Hadid, who was born in Iraq, designed a fire station for the Vitra company in Weil am Rhein in Germany, which seems to be partially submerged in the ground and has an expressive, largely functionless roof protruding like a wedge into the sky. The central of the three columns is oblique and looks as if it has almost fallen over. The projecting roof and oblique column are two popular Deconstructivist motifs.

Another example of this architecture can be found in the Hysolar Institute for Solar Energy at the University of Stuttgart, which was designed in 1987 by Günter Behnisch. The rooms of this building seem randomly stacked on top of each other. The surface of the first floor is inverted with respect to the ground floor and this is directly reflected in the exterior form of the building. A prominent red functionless pipe sways from the upper edge of the glass roof down to the ground.

A similarly imaginative game involving various parts of a building is played in the new roof structure built onto an old house for the Schuppich legal practice in Vienna in 1989. The structure was designed by Wolf Prix and Helmut Swiczinsky, whose office is known as COOP Himmelblau ("COOP sky blue"). Seemingly chaotic and disorganised, his new roof structure seems to tear up the old structure and pushes far over the façade of the house. The architects' vision of an inverted clap of lightning or spanned arch is impressively realised.

Another popular feature of this style is the creation of an impression of something temporarily put together, using correspondingly cheap and casual materials. Thus in the conversion of his house in Santa Monica (1978), the American architect Frank O. Gehry used lathing, corrugated iron, wire mesh and other cheap materials. This produced the image of a barracks building which evokes playful reminiscences – even if they are borrowed from other design contexts.

Like Gehry and Hadid, Bernhard Tschumi belongs to a group of architects which met in the 1970's in the London Architectural Association. Tschumi's "Folies" or pavilions, built on a strict grid in the Parc de la Villette on the periphery of Paris, seem unfinished or distorted – their steel structures resemble ruins. Here too there is a certain pleasure in destruction, a symbol of over-satiation. Such impressions would have been unthinkable in the Post-War era when there were enough ruins around without architects having to make a special effort to create them.

This has nothing to do with the severity and clarity of classical Modernism. Structures are veiled and functions squeezed into forms. The architectural scene is dominated by spectacular individual schemes.

Thus, for example, it remains to be seen whether the Jewish Museum in Berlin, which was designed in 1989 by Daniel Libeskind with a crooked spatial structure and oblique walls, will really be suitable for use as an exhibition building. However, this is not the aim of such architecture. It declares itself "autonomous" from purpose and the necessity to take account of anything, be it functional requirements, the urban context or the natural world. (Zaha Hadid wanted to level an entire range of mountains for her scheme for "The Peak" club in Hong Kong which won a competition but was never built.) It is interesting to note, however, that Libeskind's museum has completely conventional cohesive spaces underground.

TRENDS

Lessons learned from mistakes?

Whilst Post-Modernism and Deconstructivism have monopolised the headlines, rationalistic streams based on Classical Modernism continue to exist to the present day. Frequent attempts have been

COOP Himmelblau: *Roof conversion for a legal practice*, Vienna, 1983–84

COOP Himmelblau's roof conversion shimmers blue and silver like a cloud which has landed on the city. The steel backbone of the structure consists of an arch which connects the open multi-faceted structure and points down to the street. It is from here that the energy originates, to which the COOP Himmelblau group – who could be identified as the Punk group on the architectural scene – gives form. They have developed dancing forms and chaotic figures from a critical comment on the existing situation. Their radical intervention in the old house and its surroundings does not seek reconciliation but exposes the discrepancies in the layers of time.

James Stirling, Michael Wilford & Ass. with Walter Nägeli *Braun AG Works*, Melsungen, 1985–92

This team of architects won the commission to build a factory complex for a pharmaceuticals manufacturer with a convincing concept based on the division of the structure. They created an ensemble based on the organisation of production processes which fuses impressively with the surrounding landscape. The curved administration building (seen here from behind) continues the topography of the surrounding hills. It is enclosed by two black monoliths which contain the lifts and staircases. A green shimmering socle is covered with copper scales and thus evokes the impression of a prehistoric reptile skin: this part of the building contains the company's computer centre. This impression is heightened by the strange window insertions. The copper plates were pre-coated in a controlled process of aging to achieve uniformity of colour.

Zaha Hadid: *Vitra Fire Station*, Weil am Rhein, 1992–93.

made to retract the excesses and mistakes, and link up with the exemplary architecture of the early 1920's, with its purity of colour, form and materials. A building like Tadao Andos's "Church on the Water" in the Japanese town of Tomamu (1985–88) is a highly aesthetic example of this approach. He uses exposed concrete, as he had done previously in his chapel on the mountain Rokko in Kobe (1985–86). The back elevation of this simple church is completely glazed so that the observer's eye falls not on the altar but on a cross standing in the water. The severity of the forms and the materials are not exclusive to Andos's religious buildings: he aims to cling to asceticism on an everyday basis, and insulates his buildings against the noise of the big city (and thus against modern life) with the help of closed concrete walls, building his houses without thermal insulation or heating.

Thus the aesthetic elements of classical Modernism coincide with their educational claims and an anti-modern flight from reality. This is typical of the lack of uniformity and cohesion which has characterised the development of international architecture since the late 1980's. Did the modern era culminate in the demise of the belief in progress and the loss in significance of classical industry, or has it merely taken on a different form with the transition to a computerised, communications and service-orientated society? Is Mies van der Rohe modern although not functional? Or is the modern facet of his buildings the very fact that they are multi-functional and thus can be used again and again in different ways, which is important at a time when the functions of a building often change more rapidly than its substance? Is it regressive to want to link up to classical Modernism? Is Deconstructivism the actual beginning of modern architecture, as Zaha Hadid claims? Or is this merely a slightly different version of Post-Modernist lack of function, addiction to decoration and architects' vanity? The multiplicity is made all the more confusing by the fact that some architects have changed their design principles on several occasions. For example, Philip Johnson and Oswald Mathias Ungers over the years have shifted from a very severe Modernism to Post-Modernism and then back to Rationalism.

Some critics like to describe current trends as "modern pluralism", but all this ultimately says is that modern architecture is now like popular music or hair fashions: there are a few trends which are particularly prominent but few architects adhere to them and instead simply do what they want.

What has remained from Post-Modernism is, at least, a sensitivity for the environment and existing structures, an estimation of the traditional city fabric and the use of materials and forms which do not actually go together. Modern technology is used to make environmentally friendly architecture feasible; for example, through thermal insulation or the use of solar panels. And individual set pieces from the formal language of Deconstructivism also continue to be used, although the style as a whole seems to have failed to assert itself. In general, architecture is tending more and more towards a very strict Rationalism which includes one or other of the above-described forms – a "revised Modernism".

The multiplicity of building tasks created over the last few years not only allows this stylistic pluralism to thrive but actually demands it. The rise in populations and expectations means that the volume of buildings required is still increasing steadily. Thus it is necessary to build faster and more rationally; it is not possible to invent a new style every week. To this is added the desire of individual clients for exclusivity – exclusivity for all is, however, a contradiction in itself. What is ultimately decisive is the question as to whether buildings fulfil the requirements made of them. Their appearances will always be similar to this or that other building, whether the design is pure and simple or overflowing with decorative details. Despite the use of innumerable stylistic set pieces, a certain randomness must emerge – it is part of our time and our society.

The built environment has long since ceased to be subject to the will of individual architects or planners. The functional zoning of cities which was stipulated by the Charter of Athens, and implemented at great cost in many places after the War, no longer requires any state intervention. It is implemented through market forces and is dependent on individual investors and lobbyists who can no longer take account of the urban context in their plans.

In Berlin, where the War and re-design plans of the various political systems and urban design ideologies left not only enormous wastelands in the middle of the city, but led to the destruction of once pulsating city neighbourhoods, an attempt is now being made to recreate the mixed city which existed up to the mid-20th century. This would involve creating places for living, shopping, pleasure and working, in offices and industries which create neither noise nor air pollution. This is clearly impossible. It is impossible to recreate the old urbanity and liveliness, and where it still exists it is visibly disintegrating. What was once enthusiastically demanded by the pioneers of modern architecture and the modern city has long since been achieved – without the necessity for a political programme. This is because modern architecture and the modern city, which is more an enormous divided residential space than a city in the original sense, reflect our modern times.

Gerkan, Marg & Partners with
H. Nienhoff: *Trade Fair Hall*, Leipzig, in
construction since 1993

Abbey A monastery which is run by an Abbot or Abbess. The Abbot's house which is linked to the monastery often has its own chapel which sometimes has its own cloister.

Agora Open space in a Greek town used as a market-place or general meeting place.

Alternating system of supports Alternation of pillars and columns in the nave of a Romanesque basilica, technically defined in the crossing square plan.

Abutment Solid masonry structure which counteracts the lateral thrust of an arch or vault.

Altar A structure on which offerings to a deity are placed or sacrificed. The altar in Christian churches is a table or slab on supports, consecrated for the celebration of the sacraments.

Apse In ancient Roman architecture: semicircular space built onto or above an elevated main space. In Christian architecture: usually semicircular termination of a rectangular longitudinal structure; important component of church buildings.

Aqueduct Ancient Roman water conduit whereby the town's water supply was carried through an open or concealed water channel consisting of an elevated masonry or brick structure supported on several storeys of arches.

Arcade The arrangement of several arches in a row is called an arcade. Arcades can be built alongside each other or on top of each other along several floors of a building (arcade floor). The triangular area on the point above the supports is called the arcade spandrel.

Arcaded walk (loggia) Open, vaulted arcaded hall or passage in or in front of a building. A common feature of Italian Renaissance palazzos and public buildings.

Arch Vaulted structure in a wall opening or hall. The arch offers the only way in which to span large spaces in stone structures as it absorbs the load and distributes it among the

supports. The first stone in an arch is called the springer; the keystone is the wedge-shaped stone at the highest point or crown of the arch. The inner curve or surface of an arch forming the concave underside is called the intrados. Most arch forms are developed from a circle or several segments of a circle: the round arch is semi-circular, the pointed arch is produced from two curves, each with a radius equal to the span and meeting in a point at the top.

Architrave In ancient architecture and the styles which developed from it, the horizontal lintel of a temple which lies on the columns and is supported by them. The architrave itself supports the upper structure.

Atrium Central courtyard in the Roman residential building. In Early Christian and Medieval architecture a courtyard in front of a church (paradisus).

Ashlar Natural stone which is cut into regular rectangular blocks.

Axial plan/view/orientation (longitudinal plan) Plan based on the axes in a building. An axis is an imaginary straight line which can be drawn longitudinally or horizontally through a building or part of a building. Opposite of centrally-planned building.

Balustrade A parapet consisting of rows of small columns (balusters).

Baptistery Independent religious building where Christian baptisms are held. The water font in which the person to be baptised was fully emerged stood in the centre of the room.

Basilica Hall of commerce and justice in the Roman empire. Building type adopted by the Christians. In Christian church-building tradition it is a multiple-aisle building with a longitudinal axis and a nave which is higher than the side aisles and lit by clerestory windows.

Base The bottom of a column or pillar.

Bauhütte German name for associations of church builders

and artisans in the Middle Ages.

Bay Area of a vault which is divided from the adjacent bay by a band. The bays of a building are counted along the longitudinal axis.

Bifora Window divided by a column to form two separate arched openings.

Blind arcade, blind arch, blind window The elements of an arch or window applied to a wall without any aperture for decorative and articulation purposes. Several blind arches form a blind arcade.

Bracket A stone protruding from a wall which serves as a base for balconies, figures and arches and is often decorated.

Buttressing/ flying buttress/ pier buttress Skeleton structure which is a particularly common feature in Gothic churches. Pier buttresses are used in the reinforcement of high walls and to counteract lateral thrust. They are found either on the exterior or along the side aisles and are linked across the roof through the flying buttresses. The buttressing functions by dispersing the lateral thrust from the roof and the vaults.

Campanile Free-standing bell tower in Italian church complexes.

Camposanto Italian name for a cemetery.

Capital Head of column or pillar with ornamental, plant or figurative decoration.

Caryatid Sculptured female figure used as a column to support an entablature or similar member.

Cathedral Bishop's church in a town or city, sometimes called a minster.

Cell One of the four compartments of the groin vault (cf. vault).

Cella Windowless main chamber of the ancient temple which contains the cult image.

Centrally-planned building Plan in which all parts relate to a central point and which is based on a geometrical figure (circle, ellipse, square). The Roman Pantheon was seen as the highest achievement in terms of centrally-planned ancient buildings. The centrally planned rotunda with dome embodied

the ideal in Renaissance architecture.

Central perspective Optical impression whereby parallel lines converge as they recede towards a single point on the horizon level with the viewer's eye (vanishing point). The central perspective and its theoretical foundation was developed during the Early Renaissance period.

Chapel Small independent space for religious worship or ceremonies which is added on to a church (e.g. baptistery, palatine chapel, etc.).

Choir Originally the term for the elevated area in Christian churches where the divine service is sung. The area beyond the nave has been known as the choir since the 8th/9th century.

Choir ambulatory A passage surrounding the choir which is created through the continuation of the side aisles and is usually separated from the choir by arcades.

Clerestory (windows) Upper area of the walls of the nave in a basilica which is pierced by windows.

Cloister A passage surrounding a square open courtyard in a monastery where the Stations of the Cross are held.

Cloverleaf cf. trichora

Column figures cf. jamb (figures).

Column orders Ancient system of form and proportion whereby the column, capital, architrave and cornice relate in such a way that they have a defined "order". The Doric column has no base and a fluted shaft and a slab as capital. The Ionic column is more slender than the Doric column and it has a base, fluted shaft and capital which curves in a snail-like scroll or volute at each end. The Corinthian column differs from the Ionic column in that it has a richly decorated capital of acanthus leaves and volutes at the corners.

Colonnade Row of columns with vertical entablature (architrave) as distinct from an arcade. The colonnades in St. Peter's Square in Rome are a well known example.

Colossal order Column order whereby the columns rise from the ground through several – usually two – floors, sometimes also called a giant order. The colossal order was developed by Michelangelo and Palladio.

Composite capital A capital consisting of combinations of the Classical orders.

Corinthian The youngest of the Classical Greek styles (cf. column orders).

Cornice Horizontal strip projecting from a wall which differentiates the horizontal sections of a building (e.g. socle, floors, roof) from each other and encloses the perpendicular architectural elements (e.g. column, pilaster).

Crenellation (battlement) Parapet with alternating indentations or embrasures and raised portions or merlons.

Crepidoma Foundations and usually three-stepped base of a Greek temple.

Crocket Projecting ornament, usually in the form of curved foliage, used in Gothic architecture to decorate the outer angles of pinnacles, spires and gables (pinnacle, triangular gable).

Crossing Square or rectangular space which is created by the intersection of the nave and transept in a church.

Crossing tower A tower which sits on the crossing of a church.

Crossing-square plan Common plan in Romanesque basilicas which is based on the crossing square. One square in the nave corresponds to two squares half its length in the side aisles.

Crypt In Early Christian times the tomb of a martyr in the catacombs. In the Middle Ages half underground space beneath the East choir of the church used for the storage of relics and as a burial place for saints and dignitaries.

Donjon Central tower in French castles containing living quarters (cf. keep).

Doric The oldest of the Classical Greek styles (cf. orders).

Double-ended church plan Church plan with an East and West choir.

Drum cf. tambour.

Dwarf gallery A wall passage with small arcading and delicate columns on the outside of a building. A popular decorative

form found in Romanesque buildings, it has no structural function.

Early Christian basilica Church with a longitudinal plan and several aisles with a nave which is higher than the side aisles and clerestory windows above the nave.

Enfilade French system of aligning internal doors in a sequence so that a vista is obtained through a series of rooms when all the doors are open.

Entablature 1. The upper part of an ancient order consisting of the architrave, frieze and cornice. 2. All of the beams which combine to form a ceiling structure.

Entasis Slight convex curve on Greek and later columns to correct the optical illusion of concavity which would result if the sides were straight.

Fan vault A vault composed of a number of concave conoidal sections springing from the corners of the vaulting compartment, often decorated with ribs which radiate like the framework of a fan.

Finial A foliated ornament which terminates the peak of a spire or pinnacle.

Flamboyant style Late Gothic style in France. In Flamboyant tracery the bars of stonework form long wavy divisions.

Floor, storey A vertical section of a building which is separated by floors and ceilings.

Flutes/fluting The ridges along the shaft of ancient columns.

Flora/forum Roman market place and assembly place.

Fresco Painting technique whereby water-based paint is applied to lime plaster. Already known in ancient times. Frescos by Raphael, Michelangelo and Tiepolo are acknowledged as the highest achievements in this technique.

Frieze Horizontal band for the articulation and decoration of a wall. A distinction is made between an ornamental frieze and a figurative frieze.

Gable 1. Triangle which terminates the narrow side of a saddleback roof (cf. tympanum). 2. Triangular area at the top of windows and portals in Renaissance and Baroque architecture.

Gallery 1. In church architecture, an upper storey over an aisle, opening on to the nave, which is used to accommodate specific groups in the congregation (e.g. women, royalty) and, more importantly in design terms, an important feature in the articulation of the wall surface (cf. wall structure). 2. In secular architecture, a platform or mezzanine supported on columns or brackets and overlooking the main interior space of a building, e.g. a theatre. In Renaissance and Baroque palaces, a long room, often on an upper floor, for recreation or entertainment, e.g. Galerie des Glaces in Versailles.

Girder Large beam of wood, iron, steel or concrete.

Groin vault A compound vault formed by the perpendicular intersection of two vaults forming arched diagonal arrises called groins. Also known as a cross vault.

Hall church Church with a longitudinal plan with aisles of (almost) the same height as the nave and which often has a single roof covering both the nave and the aisles.

Hall choir Choir consisting of several aisles of the same height.

Haram Columned prayer hall in a Mosque, the columns of which initially consisted of palm trunks.

Hipped roof A form of roof which is created when the gables of a saddleback roof are substituted by sloped roof surfaces.

Illusionism The use of pictorial techniques to create an illusion of three-dimensional space and form on a two-dimensional surface.

Inlay Alternation of layers of coloured and plain stone; for example, light and dark marble.

Ionic Second oldest of the Classical Greek styles (cf. orders).

Jamb (sculpture) Surface created by the oblique insertion of a window or portal into a wall. In Gothic and Romanesque architecture, portal and window jambs are often richly decorated with sculptures (jamb sculptures).

Keep Defence tower and living quarters in English-Norman

architecture (cf. donjon).

Keystone Central stone of an arch or rib vault, sometimes carved.

King's Gallery cf. royal portal.

Lacunar Panelled or coffered ceiling, the sunken panels of which can be filled in with ornaments, colours or paintings.

Lantern Circular or polygonal turret with windows all around it which crowns a ceiling or vault opening, usually on top of a dome.

Leaded glazing System of glazing whereby the individual panes which combine to form large windows are enclosed with metal strips – a technique used by the Romans.

Lean-to roof Roof form with only one slanting surface.

Longitudinal plan cf. axial plan.

Lucarne A dormer window.

Madrasa Islamic school in a Mosque, combined school and prayer room grouped around a courtyard.

Masonry Structure built using natural or artificial stone joined using either mortar or without binding (dry masonry).

Masonry spur A short piece of masonry which projects from a wall.

Mastaba Ancient Egyptian tomb in the form of a massive brick or stone mound with battered walls on a rectangular base. The sarcophagal chamber was deep under the ground below the structure. Developed into a Pyramid after the Old Kingdom (2850–2052 B.C).

Mausoleum Name used to describe a monumental tomb.

Megaron Main hall of the Greek residence with stove and anteroom. The Greek temple was developed out of the megaron.

Merlon Raised portions on a battlement or crenellation.

Mihrab Focus for prayer in a mosque, usually a niche in the centre of the qibla wall.

Minaret Tall, slender tower connected with a mosque from which the muezzin calls the people to prayer. Originally a separate structure, it was later integrated into the general mosque complex and some mosques were surrounded by several minarets.

Mosaic Geometric or figurative surface decoration for walls, domes and floors. Coloured pieces of glass or stone are joined in a bed of mortar.

Mosque, Columned Mosque, Domed Mosque The name given to the Islamic place of worship. The mosque was developed from a simple place of prayer and does not require a standard structure. Early mosques nearly always consisted of a courtyard surrounded by arcades and a colonnaded prayer hall (columned mosque). In Syria and Turkey, where the Islamic rulers had not yet developed their own architectural style, Christian domed buildings were often converted to mosques from which the domed mosque developed in the 14th century.

Mouchette Curved dagger motif found in Gothic tracery, particularly popular in England.

Mullion Vertical post or other upright dividing a window or opening, cf. tracery.

Nave In churches with axial or longitudinal plans the elongated section of the building which links the façade and the transept or choir.

Obelisk Tall, tapering rectangular stone pillar which ends in a pyramidal top.

Octagon Octagonal structure which is built on a regular octagonal plan

Pendentive A concave spandrel leading from the angle of two walls to the base of a circular dome.

Peripteral temple Greek temple, the cella of which is surrounded by columns.

Peristyle Colonnades surrounding the courtyard of an ancient residence or temple.

Perpendicular Style Specifically English version of the High Gothic style with an extreme perpendicular accent in the tracery, walls and windows.

Pier church Single-aisle church with internal pier buttresses between which there are chapels instead of the side aisles.

Pilaster Vertical pillar with base and capital projecting from a wall.

Pilaster strip Vertical strip of masonry which projects slightly from the wall surface and has no base or capital but has an articulating and load-bearing function.

Piloti French name for free-standing column at ground-floor level of buildings favoured by Le Corbusier.

Pillar Free-standing upright member on a rectangular or polygonal plan which can be articulated in the same way as a column.

Pinnacle Slim pointed turret. Decorative element typical of the Gothic style where it usually features as a termination crowning spires, buttresses, the angles of parapets, etc.

Pointed arch cf. arch.

Portal Decoratively designed entrance. The Roman triumphal arch is the model for the Western portal.

Portal jamb cf. jamb.

Portico A porch on the façade of a building with a roof supported by columns (less commonly pillars) leading to the entrance of the building.

Pronaos Area in front of the cella of a Greek temple which is open to one side.

Protorenaissance Italian Gothic style, particularly prominent in Florence, which showed the emergence of many of the features which became typical of the Renaissance style.

Pseudo-basilica Hall church with a raised nave which does not, however, have any clerestory windows.

Pylon 1. Trapeze-shaped tower-like gate structure from Egyptian art. 2. Pillar or mast onto which the structural framework of a building or bridge is hung (e.g. Olympic Stadium in Munich).

Pyramid Tomb of the Egyptian Pharaohs. Structure with sloping triangular sides built on a square plan which converge on a single point.

Qibla wall Wall in a mosque which indicates the direction in which Muslims must face when praying, i.e. Mecca.

Rayonnant style Gothic style most common in France named after the radiating arrangement of lights in rose windows.

Respond A half-pier bonded into a wall and carrying one end of an arch, often at the end of an arcade.

Rib Strictly speaking a rib is a load-bearing structural element of a ceiling or vault. At later stages in the development of the vault, the rib became a visible projecting band and was purely decorative.

Rose/rose window Circular window in Gothic cathedrals decorated with tracery.

Rosette Rose-like ornament in which petals are arranged around a circular core.

Round arch frieze Cf. arch & frieze.

Royal portal A series of royal figures depicted above the portal on the façade of Gothic cathedrals which probably represent Christ's predecessors or French kings.

Rustication/rusticated Masonry cut in crude massive blocks. Particularly common in Early Renaissance buildings in Tuscany.

Saddleback roof (pitched roof) Roof consisting of two gables at both ends.

Saw-tooth roof Series of pitched roofs, one slope of which is glazed and steeper than the other, allowing large volumes of light to flood the space below (frequently used in museum buildings and halls).

School General term used to describe a group which uses the same architectural style, usually combined with a geographical name, e.g. Chicago School.

Secular building "Unconsecrated" architecture without religious purpose, e.g. palace, castle, housing, etc.

Series of structures Group of structures, the location of which is determined by each other (e.g. palace complex). In the Middle Ages, such groups were combined on the basis of an additive principle, according to which the necessary individual parts of a church were grouped together selectively. Some combinations were regional features and characteristic individual solutions can also be found.

Side aisle Space in a church running parallel to the longitudinal axis which is separated from the central aisle by columns or pillars. Side aisles usually come in pairs, one on each side.

Single-aisle church Church whose interior is not divided by supporting members.

Shaft The trunk or rump of a column which can be either smooth or ridged (fluted). It can taper downwards or upwards, have a swelling (entasis) or be of a consistent girth.

Shell Massive, curved load-bearing structure with minimal strength which can be used to span extensive widths.

Skeleton structure Structural method based on a wood, stone, steel or reinforced concrete frame imposed on a grid system. The skeleton assumes all the load-bearing functions and can be visible (Gothic buttressing) or concealed.

Socle Base or pedestal of a building, column or statue.

Spandrel An approximately triangular surface bounded by the outer curve of an arch and the adjacent wall. This term is also applied to the surface between two arches in an arcade and the surface of a vault between adjacent ribs.

Stereometry, stereometric System for the measurement of volumes and other metrical elements of solid figures. Hence a stereometric structure is one which is characterised by a readily measurable solid form or volume.

String course Cornice which separates the individual floors of a building.

Stave church Scandinavian timber church, the walls of which are constructed using posts and masts.

Stalactite Ceiling ornament in Islamic architecture formed by corbelled squinches made of several layers of brick, scalloped to resemble natural stalactites.

Stucco (work) Sculptural decorations made of stucco (mixture of plaster, lime and sand).

Tambour/drum Cylindrical or square structure on which a dome rests which is usually pierced by windows.

Tectonics Organised structure of a building whereby the individual technical and formal elements form a uniform artistic unit.

Terracotta Fired unglazed clay used to make wall coverings and ornamentation, e.g. reliefs, architectural sculptures.

Thermal baths Roman bathing complexes which were centrally heated through hollows in the walls or hollow brick floors.

Thrust (lateral thrust) The horizontal forces within the wall created by the weight of the arches or roof structure. Thrust is countered by reinforcing the walls (cf. I).

Tracery Ornamental work of branchlike lines, especially the lacy open-work in the upper part of a Gothic window. Originally developed for decorating the pointed arch of large windows, it was later also used in the articulation of wall surfaces.

Transept The horizontal structure which is built between the nave and the choir which can have one or more aisles. The transept gives the church plan the form of a cross.

Transverse arch Arch which separates one bay of a vault from the next.

Trichora/cloverleaf plan Church with three apses (cf. apse) facing three directions.

Triforium A narrow arcaded wall passage open to the nave under the clerestory windows of the nave, transept and choir in Romanesque and Gothic churches. Its purpose is mainly articulatory.

Triglyph Blocks which separate the metopes in a Doric frieze. Each has two vertical grooves or glyphs in the centre and half grooves at the edges.

Turret Slim (wooden) tower on the ridge of the main roof of a church.

Tympanum 1. Gable area in an ancient temple. 2. Arched area above Romanesque and Gothic portals.

Vaulting shaft In Gothic architecture, semi or three-quarter column on a wall or on a composite pillar.

Volute Architectural element with spiral-shaped scroll, e.g. on the Ionic capital.

Westwork A projecting, almost square, structure at the west end of Carolingian and Early Christian churches. From the outside, the westwork often takes the form of a wide tower which is sometimes flanked by raised stair turrets.

Ziggurat Artificial stepped hill with ramps or steps on which the "residential tower" of the god stood.

LIST OF ARCHITECTS

Numbers in bold refer to page numbers with illustrations

Aalto, Hugo Henrik Alvar (1898–1976) Finnish architect whose buildings are characterised by functionality, adaptation to a human scale and requirements, regional architectural forms and original sculptural ideas. *93*

Abbot Laugier, Marc-Antoine (1713–69) French Jesuit priest and theorist of Classical architecture who glorified antiquity. *63*

Alberti, Leon Battista (1404–72) Italian architect, architectural theorist, universal genius. In his church of St. Andrea in Mantua he predicted the typical spatial form of the Baroque church. His "On Painting" and "Ten Books of Architecture" are basic texts of art theory. *44, 45, 49*

Anthemios of Tralleis (6th century A.D.) Greek architect and scholar. Commissioned by Emperor Justinian to design the Hagia Sophia in Constantinople, the main work of Byzantine architecture. He understood architecture as "the application of geometry to solid material". *15*

Asplund, Gunnar (1885–1940) Important Swedish architect who by using light metal elements, glass and free roof forms completed the transition from Classical to modern architecture. *94, 94*

Barry, Sir Charles (1795–1860) Early Victorian English architect who studied international architecture during a three-year study trip (1817–20). He designed in Neo-Renaissance style with the help of sketches made on his travels. His main work is the Houses of Parliament on the banks of the River Thames in London. *70, 71*

Behnisch, Günter (1922) The most famous works of the Behnisch & Partners office are the sports buildings in the Munich Olympic Park which were built in 1966. Behnisch is one of the best known contemporary German architects specialising in public buildings. *103, 104, 108*

Behrens, Peter (1868–1940) German architect and industrial artist. From 1907, architect and artistic advisor to AEG in Berlin. His factory buildings are among the first architecturally significant industrial buildings. *84, 86*

Bernini, Gian Lorenzo (1598–1680) High Baroque architect and sculptor. His main works in Rome include the semi-circular colonnades surrounding St. Peter's Square and the church of Sant'Andrea al Quirinale. His ideal was to achieve a perfect fusion of architecture and sculpture to a dynamic whole. *47, 54, 55, 56*

Bon, Giovanni (ca. 1355–1443) **and Bartolomeo** (ca. 1374–1467) Leading sculptors and architects of the early 15th century in Venice. Builders of the urban palace Ca' d' Oro (Gold House), a masterpiece of the Venetian Late Gothic. *41*

Borromini, Francesco (1599–1667) Italian architect and *Bernini*'s rival who, with his complicated spatial interlocking and dynamic plans, was responsible for the introduction of the Late Baroque to Rome. His main works include the Roman churches of San Carlo alle quattro fontane and the university church of Sant' Ivo della Sapienza. *54, 55*

Boullée, Etienne-Louis (1728–99) Leading French neo-Classicist architect strongly influenced by Romanticism. His "philosophical buildings", in which he promoted an architecture of feeling and exercised an important influence on his contemporaries, are among his most important works. *63, 64, 102, 105*

Bramante, Donato (1444–1514) Architect of the High Italian Renaissance period who worked in Milan and then in Rome. The clarity and harmonious beauty of his buildings represent the perfection of the High Renaissance style. His plan for the reconstruction of St. Peter's and his circular temple of San Pietro in Montorio in Rome are his most significant works. *44, 46, 49*

Brunelleschi, Filippo (1377–1446) Revolutionary Italian Renaissance architect who saw his main task in the application of the laws of perspective, the linear organisation of space and application of clear proportions. From 1420–36 he built the cathedral dome in Florence using new technical methods. *43, 44, 48*

Bulfinch, Charles (1763–1844) Affluent Bostonian architect who went on an extended study trip to Europe where he found inspiration. His buildings included the most authoritative public edifices in America, where he was also involved in the construction of the Capitol in Washington. *66*

Burnham, Daniel Hudson (1864–1912) North American architect who worked in partnership with J. W. Root. In 1891 they built the Masonic Temple, which at the time was the highest building in the world, and in 1902 they built the Flatiron building, the first skyscraper in New York. *78, 79*

Candela, Felix (1910) Spanish architect who lives in Mexico and is acknowledged as one of the most original concrete engineers. One of his most important buildings is the Church of the Miraculous Virgin in Mexico City (1953–55), an extreme example of a mid-20th century "expressionist" church building. *100, 102*

Cesariano, Cesare di Lorenzo (1483–1543) Milanese architect, painter and writer whose most important work is his translation of *Vitruvius* and commentary. *41*

Chicago, School (Jenny, Sullivan, Burnham, Root, Adler, *inter alia*) Influential formal language developed by American architects for 20th century commercial buildings. The Chicago School style was established in 1884 with the introduction of the metal skeleton structure, which gave architects new possibilities and enabled them to design buildings which were not necessarily based on borrowings from historical styles. 77, *78, 79, 82, 94*

COOP Himmelblau (Wolf D. Prix, 1942; Helmut Swiczinsky 1944) With the "Viennese Super Summer" of 1976, this architectural practice, founded in Vienna in 1968, presented aggressive alternatives to the standard approach to urban design. Their trade mark consists of exciting, heady architectural projects. *108, 109*

Cornelius Floris de Vriend (ca. 1514–75) Sculptor and architect from Antwerp who drew attention to himself mainly on the basis of his complex use of ornamentation. His system of decoration became very popular as the "Floris style" in the Netherlands during the second half of the 16th century. *50*

Delamair, Pierre-Antoine (17th/18th century) Royal director of building in Paris. *56*

Dientzenhofer, Family (17th/18th century) Baroque architectural dynasty active in France and Bohemia. They introduced the dynamic spatial design of Italian architects (*Borromini, Guarini*) to Germany, and developed an excellent synthesis of Italian-German Baroque architecture. Their church buildings are acknowledged as the most important of their time. *59*

Durand, Jean Nicolas Louis (1760–1834) French architect and recipient of several prizes for architecture. Durand became famous for his engravings of important Paris buildings and as an architectural theorist. He exercised a lasting influence on the 19th century. 67, *68*

Ehn, Karl (1884–1957) Architect attached to the Vienna urban authority during the 1920's and early 1930's who was responsible for social housing. *91*

Eiffel, Alexandre Gustave (1832–1923) French engineer and entrepreneur famous for the Eiffel Tower which he built for the World Exhibition of 1889 in Paris, and which at 300 metres was the tallest building in the world. *75, 76*

Fischer von Erlach, Johann Bernhard (1656–1723) Appointed imperial court architect of Vienna following an extended study trip in Italy. As the first great architect he founded a national German Baroque architecture. In his work he wanted to visually express the idea of the empire, and his style is correspondingly expressive and pathetic. *59*

Foster, Sir Norman Robert (1935) British architect, head of the London practice Foster Associates. He is one of the most consistent representatives of modern technology, his main building type is the large neutral spatial tent. *104*

Garnier, Charles (1825–98) French architect, travelled in Rome and Athens and in 1861 won the competition for the Paris Opera. The building acted simultaneously as a context for artistic and social events, which is also true of Garnier's casino building in Monte Carlo. *72*

Gaudí y Cornet Antonio (1852–1926) Spanish architect who created a unique imaginative style which combined Late Gothic and exotic forms. His main work is the church of the Sagrada Familia in Barcelona which was begun in 1884 and never completed. *81, 86, 105*

Gerkan, Meinhard von (1935) **Marg, Volkwin** (1936) and **Partners** Architectural practice founded in 1965 which won numerous competitions for large projects in the Federal Republic of Germany. Its areas of activity extend far beyond mere architecture to include general planning, engineering calculations and transport infrastructure. *111*

Gibbs, James (1682–1754) London's most influential church builder in the early 18th century, studied architecture and painting in Rome and developed his repertoire of forms there. The church of St. Martin in the Fields is seen as his main work and has often been imitated. *61*

Gilly, Friedrich (1772–1800) Great architect of German Classicism and teacher at the Berlin Academy of Architecture. His best works were not realised. His work is characterised by clear spatial forms. *67, 68, 69*

Golosov, Ilya (1883–1945) Russian Constructivist architect and professor. He aimed to combine historical tradition and the new socialist self-image in his buildings. *85*

Gropius, Walter (1883–1969) Architect and founder of the Bauhaus. His architectural style is characterised by a clear functional form. As a teacher of art, he promoted a shared basic training for artists and craftsmen in form, colour and material qualities. 84, *86, 88, 89, 92, 95*

Guarini, Guarino (1624–83) Italian architect of the Late Baroque period. He brought the church to the height of mathematical experiment. His spaces interlock and blur all clarity of structure. *53, 59, 60*

Guimard, Hector (1867–1942) Teacher at the École des Arts Decoratifs in Paris, French Art Nouveau architect. He used metal, faience and glass tiles in a particularly imaginative way. *82*

Hadid, Zaha (1950) British architect born in Iraq influenced by Russian Constructivism. She designs technically highly complex structures from partly eccentric perspectives. Hadid is acknowledged as one of the contemporary avant-garde and her projects are seen as leading the way into the 21st century. *109, 110*

Hardouin-Mansart, Jules (1646–1708) French architect at the court of Louis XIV who was involved in the extension of Versailles from 1678 onwards. His main work in a powerful Baroque Classicism is the Church of the Invalides in Paris. *56, 57, 61*

Haussmann, Georges-Eugène (1809–91) Ruthless Alsatian civil servant appointed by Napoleon III to implement his sweeping plans for city improvement in Paris. His main motifs are the long straight boulevards which meet in the shape of stars at the "rond-points". *74*

Holl, Elias (1573–1646) Augsburg municipal architect

who developed a classically balanced Renaissance style based on *Palladio's* formal repertoire and was responsible for the transformation of German gable façades. *50, 51*

Horta, Victor (1861–1947) Belgian architect. With his Hôtel Tassel he created one of the most daring Art Nouveau buildings and joined the ranks of the avant-garde of European architecture of his time. *82*

Ictinus (5th century B.C.) One of the most important Greek architects of his time and builder of the Parthenon on the Acropolis in Athens. *11*

Isidorus of Miletus (5th century B.C.) Collaborated with *Anthemios of Tralleis* in the design of the Hagia Sophia in Constantinople. *15*

Jefferson, Thomas (1743–1826) Scholar, third President of the USA and architect. He studied the villa architecture of ancient Rome and *Palladio*. His Jeffersons Virginia State Capitol (completed in 1796) became the model for public buildings in the USA. *65, 66*

Johnson, Philip Cortelyou (1906) American architect, first director of the architecture department at the Museum of Modern Art in New York. During the 1930's he promoted avant-garde European architecture in the USA. His buildings are increasingly characterised by spectacular effects and breath-taking "glazed" elegance. *94, 95, 97, 102, 107, 109*

Jones, Inigo (1573–1652) Far ahead of his time, he was responsible for the sudden flourishing of English Renaissance architecture following a long stay in Italy. His buildings are impressive in their formality and strict Classicism, which is based on *Palladio's* models. *51*

Juan Bautista de Toledo (died 1567) Spanish architect who initially worked as court architect in Naples. In 1563 he was commissioned by King Philip II to build the castle and Augustinian monastery of El Escorial. After his death, the project was taken over by his pupil, Juan de Herrera. *48*

Juan de Herrera (ca. 1530–97) Pupil and assistant of *Juan Bautista de Toledo*. *48*

Klenze, Leo von (1784–1864) The Munich court architect of King Ludwig I made a decisive contribution to the city's image with his Classical and Italian Renaissance-style buildings. His best known work outside Munich is the Walhalla near Regensburg. *64, **67**, 69*

Labrouste, Henri (1801–75) French architect who following six years in Rome opened a teaching atelier in Paris which became a centre for Rationalistic ideas. He promoted the consistent use of iron in architectural form. ***77***

Langhans, Carl Gotthard (1732–1808) Trained as a Baroque architect, he became one of the earliest representatives of German Classicism. His most famous remaining work, the Brandenburg Gate in Berlin, is based on the ancient Greek model. *67*

Latrobe, Benjamin H. (1764–1820) American architect who, through the construction of the Bank of Pennsylvania, was responsible for the revival of Greek Classicism in America. From 1803 he worked on the completion of the Capitol in Washington. ***66***

Le Corbusier (Charles Édouard Jeanneret) (1887–1965) Influential, highly inventive French-Swiss architect, painter and writer. His main concern was the new objective style of housing design and town planning. After the Second World War he developed an anti-rational style based on a complex system (known as "modulor"), the most famous example of which is the pilgrim church at Ronchamp. *11, 32, 63, 84, 88, 89, 91, 93, **98**, 99, 100, **103**, 104, 105, 107*

Ledoux, Claude-Nicolas (1736–1806) Main representative of the French "revolution architecture". His style is based on geometrical bodies which do not fuse but interpenetrate in an expressive way as immobile blocks. *63, 66, 102, 105*

Lenné, Peter Josef (1789–1866) German landscape architect who, following an apprenticeship in France, was appointed General Director of the Palaces and Gardens in Potsdam and Berlin, where he designed famous garden complexes (Sanssouci palace gardens). *68, 74*

Le Nôtre, André (1613–1700) One of the greatest landscape architects, he is acknowledged as the founder of the geometric garden complex. He created his masterpiece, the enormous palace gardens of Versailles, for Louis XIV. *57*

Leonardo da Vinci (1452–1519) Universal genius of the Italian Renaissance who was an extremely talented artist and scientist. Leonardo left behind numerous plans and designs including a model for the dome of Milan cathedral. *Bramante* was influenced by his interest in centrally-planned buildings. *41, 44, 47, 50*

Levau, Louis (1612–70) French Baroque architect. With other artists he created the style "Louis quatorze" in Versailles and implemented the Baroque variety impressively. In 1657 he was commissioned to design his masterpiece, the country residence at Vaux-le-Vicomte. *57*

Lissitzky, El (1890–1941) Russian painter and architect of the Constructivism movement. His abstract compositions consist of simple geometrical forms from which he developed spatial structures. *85*

Lodoli, Carlo (1690–1761) Venetian priest and architectural theorist. His Classical and functionalistic ideas were very popular among his contemporaries. *63*

Loos, Adolf (1870–1933) Austrian architect who was mainly involved in the design of products and functional housing. In his writings he vehemently opposed the Viennese Art Nouveau movement and formulated trail-blazing ideas for subsequent generations of architects. *83*

Maderna, Carlo (1556–1629) An important representative of the Roman Early Baroque whose main work was the nave of St. Peter's with its porch and façade. With his façade design for the Roman church of Santa Susanna, Maderna developed an individual, clear and strongly dynamic style. *52, 55*

Malevich, Kasimir (1878–1935) Russian painter and one of the founders of abstract art, which aims at a limitation of art to pure forms from the context of geometry. He formulated his influential theories in his book "The non-objective world" (1927), which he published at the Bauhaus. *85*

Marinetti, Filippo Tommaso (1876–1944) Italian writer, founded with other artists and intellectuals the Futurist movement in Italy in 1908, which proclaimed a complete break with tradition. Characteristics of the movement include the "leitmotif" of dynamism and simultaneous movement. *85*

Maurice de Sully (died 1196) Archbishop of Paris from 1160; an influential church client, he laid the foundation stone for Notre Dame in 1163. *34*

May, Ernst (1886–1970) In 1925–30 as municipal director of building in Frankfurt am Main he introduced the social housing programme. In his urban design and housing projects he combined the principle of the English satellite town with the formal language of the new Rationalistic architecture. *90*

Meier, Richard (1934) One of the most popular contemporary American architects and important proponent of purist Modernist forms. His buildings embody the logical and consistent development of modern architecture.

Mendelsohn, Erich (1887–1953) His daring ideas of an architecture which is understood as sculpture were influenced by the Expressionism of the 1920's. The main idea was the stream-line form. He later emphasised the structure of his buildings and simplified the forms. *86, 87, 102*

Meyer, Adolf (1881–1929) German architect, colleague of *W. Gropius*, teacher at the Bauhaus then municipal director of building in Frankfurt am Main. His architecture is characterised by a geometrical, rational style. *84, **86***

Michelangelo Buonarotti (1475–1564) Sculptor, poet, architect, the epitome of the artistic genius. During the last two decades of his life he worked increasingly on architectural projects in Rome (re-design of the Capitol square, completion of the Palazzo Farnese, supervision of St. Peter's Church). Michelangelo did not create "rooms" but modelled walls and surfaces. *42, 44, 46, **47***

Mies van der Rohe, Ludwig (1886–1969) Initially worked in Germany, and in the USA after 1938. His buildings are characterised by cubic order, strict rules of measurement and proportion, and perfect precision of detail. Mies van der Rohe is one of the most influential architects of the 20th century; his design elements were often imitated. *82, 84, 86, 91, **92**, 94, 96, **97**, 98, 105, 109*

Morris, William (1834–96) British theologian who turned to architecture. Dissatisfied with the architectural and interior design style of his time, he founded his own company through which he became the pioneering force in modern design (Arts and Crafts Movement). *82*

Muggenast, Josef (1680–1741) Cousin and pupil of *Prandtauer* and his successor as the client of Melk monastery. Muggenast showed his originality in the conversion of the Benedictine monastery at Altenburg where he built one of the most beautiful libraries. *59*

Neumann, Johann Balthasar (1687–1753) Engineer and architect. As court architect to the Schönborn family he built his main work, the Residenz in Würzburg. His main architectural ideas consisted of the freely moving vault and dynamic, rhythmic space. His church buildings are impressive in their complicated interaction of spaces. *59, 60*

Neutra, Richard Josef (1892–1970) Austrian architect who worked under *Loos* and with *Mendelsohn*. In 1923 he emigrated to the USA where he disseminated the modern ideas of European architects. *94*

Niemeyer, Oscar Soares Filho (1907) Brazilian architect, actively involved in the foundation and design of Brasilia, the new capital of Brazil, from 1957 onwards. *98, 99*

Odo von Metz, Master (7th/8th century B.C.) Architect of the Palatine Chapel in Aachen (consecrated in 800). This octagonal structure is the first major completely vaulted stone structure to be built north of the Alps. *22*

Oud, Jacobus Johannes Pieter (1890–1963) Municipal director of building in Rotterdam from 1918 to 1933 and director of housing. Oud is one of the main proponents of modern architecture in Holland who aimed to build severe, clear and functional buildings. Co-founder of the artists group de Stijl. *88, 89*

Palladio, Andrea (1508–80) The most important architect and architectural theorist of the Late Italian Renaissance, who exercised an important influence on posterity. He developed a feeling for symmetrical structures and particularly harmony of proportion from his studies of antiquity. *48, 49, 50, 51, 61, 66, 105*

Paxton, Sir Joseph (1801–65) Originally a gardener, in 1850–51 he presented his design for a glass and iron exhibition building for the London World Exhibition. This "Crystal Palace" was revolutionary. It involved the use of mass-produced elements which were then assembled on site. *75, 103*

Piano, Renzo (1937) Italian architect, whose buildings are exemplary in their aesthetic quality, user-friendliness and technology-oriented design. He built the Parisian cultural centre, the Centre Pompidou, in collaboration with *Rogers* (1971–77). In 1992, Piano won the competition for the Daimler Benz building on Potsdamer Platz in Berlin. *104, 105*

Prandtauer, Jakob (1660–1726) Important German Baroque architect. His main work is the monastery at Melk. Prandtauer used all the advantages available to him in linking the unusual location of the monastery above the Danube with Baroque majesty. *59*

Rietveld, Gerrit Thomas (1888–1964) This self-employed furniture-maker came into contact with the architect *Oud* and the Dutch artists group de Stijl in 1919. He designed villas, exhibition pavilions and terraced houses of extreme simplicity and elegance, always giving a

central role to the interior design. *88*

Rogers, Richard (1933) Important defender of functionalistic architecture; form and function are central to his buildings. With *Piano* he built the Centre Pompidou in Paris. His architectural practice works on a broad international level. Rogers won the most important German architectural awards during the 1980's. *104, 105*

Rossi, Aldo (1931) Controversial Italian architect who developed an individual formal language and radically reduced it to a handful of typical elements. He derived his principles and visions from a historical preoccupation with traditional urban design. *107*

Saarinen, Eero (1910–61) Finnish-American architect, his father designed the main railway station in Helsinki. Saarinen combined technology and his own original ideas in his buildings. These are characterised by a highly personal style and a dynamic spatial quality. *100, 102, 103*

Sansovino (Jacopo Tatti, known as Il Sansovino) (1486–1570) Originally a sculptor, he brought the High Renaissance style to Venice and became one of the city's leading architects. His works combine architecture and sculpture in a new way. *Palladio* described Sansovino's library on St. Mark's Square as the most perfect building of post-antiquity. *46, 49*

Sant'Elia, Antonio (1888–1916) Italian Futurist architect. His designs, which demonstrate his vision of the industrial and commercial metropolises of the future, remained unrealised. *85*

Scharoun, Hans (1893–1972) German architect who promoted the idea of "organic architecture", which rejects any kind of uniformity, in his buildings and writings. A large number of his designs were not built. The crowning achievement of his late work is the Philharmonie in Berlin. *97, 101, 102*

Schinkel, Karl Friedrich (1781–1841) The most famous architect of the Classical period in Germany. Thanks to major commissions (mainly in Berlin), he was able to develop his style which was greatly influenced by

the Classical and Gothic models. His buildings combine function with harmonious clarity of form. *68, 69*

Schlüter, Andreas (ca. 1660–1714) Educated in Gdansk, Schlüter came to Berlin in 1694 as a sculptor. Following study trips through Italy and France, he took over construction of the Zeughaus and was involved in the construction and conversion of the Berlin palace, the two main works of North German Baroque. *59*

Schütte-Lihotzky, Grete (1897) Designed the "Frankfurt kitchen" for the "Praunheim Estate" in Frankfurt am Main (1926–30), the director of which was *May*. The Frankfurt kitchen is a purely functional kitchen where everything is reduced to minimum proportions. *90, 91*

Scott, Sir George Gilbert (1811–78) English architect, specialised in Gothic churches. His motifs were taken from High French and English Gothic. *77*

Semper, Gottfried (1803–79) Widely travelled German architect and professor of architecture. His buildings are characterised by the economic use of historical forms. The harmonious proportions of the Italian Renaissance were his model *71, 107*

Skidmore, Owings & Merill (SOM) Architectural practice founded in 1937, which developed new design elements for buildings for the American business world. SOM's strength lies in the ability to process predominant social trends with originality and formal brilliance. By 1980, SOM had worked itself up to the number one international position among architectural and engineering practices and set decisive standards. *105*

Smirke, Sir Robert (1781–1867) Leading architect of English Classicism who built in the spirit of Greek antiquity (Greek Revival). His main works include the British Museum in London *65*

Soufflot, Jacques-Germain (1709–80) The greatest French Classical architect. He educated himself in Italy on the basis of ancient models and the work of *Palladio*. He designed the

church of Ste. Geneviève in Paris which was known as the Panthéon. *64*

Speer, Albert (1905–81) Speer attracted Hitler's attention with his design for the National Socialist Party headquarters in Berlin (1932). As General Building Inspector for the capital of the Third Reich, he planned numerous gigantic state buildings which were never built. *93, 94*

Stirling, James (1926–92) British architect who tried to achieve a precarious balance between Modernism and Classicism in his buildings. His numerous public buildings are impressive in terms of their functional precise forms and a spatial division based on strict rules. *107*

Suger, Abbot (ca. 1081–1151) Important client for the comprehensive conversion of the monastery of Saint-Denis near Paris. Suger had a strong input into the planning and realisation of the project. He is given significant importance in the development of the Gothic style. Up to the 19th century, he was regarded as the inventor of Gothic architecture. *30, 31, 32, 33*

Sullivan, Louis Henry (1856–1924) American architect who worked on the development of the steel skeleton for the construction of skyscrapers. He developed the model for the modern commercial building and department store in the USA. Teacher of *F. L. Wright. 78, 79, 94, 108*

Tange, Kenzo (1913) Leading Japanese architect who modelled himself on *Le Corbusier*. His buildings are characterised by dynamic, urban design methods and overt symbolical forms. He built a number of public buildings and became the leading personality in the Modern movement and in the search for a new Japanese architecture. *98, 99*

Tatlin, Vladimir J. (1885–1953) Founder of Russian Constructivism. His works consist of simple geometrical forms and reject any reference to objective motifs. *85*

Taut, Bruno (1880–1938) One of the pioneers of modern architecture in Germany. His main contribution lay in the reform of housing estate architecture and in urban design, where he was particularly involved in the use of colour as a design element. *63, 88,* **90**

Tessenow, Heinrich (1876–1950) German architect and professor in Vienna, Dresden and Berlin. He promoted objectivity, clarity and simplicity in architecture. His residential buildings became popular models in Germany. *83*

Thornton, William (1759–1828) Emigrated as a doctor from the West Indies to the USA and in 1793 won the competition for the Capitol in Washington. His plans were, however, subject to strong alterations. **66**

Tschumi, Bernhard (1944) Internationally renowned architect whose main ideas emerged under the influence of modern media and contemporary philosophy. He sees his architectural concepts in terms of his image of reality as controllable, fragmentary, endless and deconstructive. His fame is based, among other things, on his buildings in La Villette, a science and media park in Paris. *108*

Van de Velde, Henry (1863–1957) Belgian architect and craftsman. His functional and material-based forms exercised a decisive influence on the development of Art Nouveau. *81*

Venturi, Robert (1925) American architect and architectural theorist. He tries in his buildings to transform psychological perceptual motifs such as multiplicity of meaning, memory capability and contradiction. In his writings he analyses the contradictions of European and American architectural history. *105, 106*

Vignola, Giacomo Barozzi da (1507–73) Leading architect and architectural theorist in Rome following the death of *Michelangelo.* His main work is the church of Il Gesù (begun in 1568) with which he was responsible for the further development of the Baroque church. *48, 49, 52,* **53**

Vitruvius Pollio, Marcus Roman military technician and engineer. He compiled the 10 books of "De architectura", the only remaining work of architectural theory from antiquity. *9,* **41,** *43, 48, 49, 64*

Wagner, Martin (1885–1957) Municipal building advisor of Berlin where with *Bruno Taut, Walter Gropius* and *Ludwig Mies van der Rohe* he built housing estates and trade fair complexes etc. **90**

Wagner, Otto (1841–1918) Austrian architect and professor who is acknowledged as one of the pioneers of modern art. The artistic clarity and economy of his compositions had a decisive influence on subsequent Viennese architects. *82*

Wallot, Paul (1841–1912) Won the competition for the Berlin Reichstag building in 1882, his only famous work. *72,* **73**

Weinbrenner, Friedrich (1766–1826) German architect, whose life's work was the conversion of Karlsruhe into a Classical town. He designed a number of buildings in the town as part of this project. *67, 107*

Wesnin, Leonid, Viktor, Alexander (19th/20th century) Russian architects and engineers. The brothers' collaboration began in 1918. Influenced by Constructivism, they designed functionalist-oriented structures which were intended to portray the essence of the "ideal socialist" city. **85**

Wren, Sir Christopher (1632–1723) English Classical architect. Following the Great Fire of London (1666) he was commissioned to rebuild the city as royal building administrator. His main work is St. Paul's Cathedral, an impressive domed structure which is based on St. Peter's in Rome. *61*

Wright, Frank Lloyd (1869–1959) Famous American architect whose basic tenet was that architecture should be developed from the inside out. He created organic buildings, the structure and materials of which corresponded to the features of the surrounding landscape and their function. His design for the spiral-shaped Guggenheim Museum in New York (1956–59) originates from 1943. *94,* **95, 102,** *103*

Zimmermann, Dominicus (1685–1766) South German architect. His pilgrim church at Wies in Upper Bavaria is one of the main works of the Baroque and Rococo. **60**

PICTURE CREDITS

The publisher would like to thank the institutions, archives and photographers for permission to reproduce illustrations, and for their kind assistance in the preparation of this book.

Joaquin und Fernando Alvarez Ordoñez: 100 below

ANA: 29 above (Jobin), 105 above (Sigurd Thorson)

Anthony Verlag: 51 above (Eder), 58 (Hetz), 60 below (T. Beck)

Arcaid: 28 above right (Colin Dixon), 36 above (Mark Fiennes), 37 above (Mark Fiennes), 66 below, 77 below (David Churchill), 82 above (Richard Bryant), 103, 104 above (Richard Bryant)

Archiv für Kunst und Geschichte, Berlin: 10 (Erich Lessing), 13, 15 above right, 20 (Erich Lessing), 25 above left (Erich Lessing), 35 (Jürgen Sorges), 36 below (Erich Lessing), 42, 45 above, 52 (Erich Lessing), 54 below (Ulrich Zillmann), 59 above, 61 above, 62, 66 above, 67 (Hilbich), 69 above, 70, 73, 75, 76 above, 77 above (Erich Lessing), 78 (Waldemar Abegg), 80, 82 below (Erich Lessing), 84 (Dieter E. Hoppe), 87 above right (Erik Bohr), 90 below (Dieter Hoppe), 96 both

Maurice Babey: 98

Central A.A. Bachrushin State Theatrical Museum, Moscow: 85 above right

Badisches Landesmuseum, Karlsruhe: 16

Achim Bednorz, Cologne: 25 below, 26 below, 28 below, 44 all, 47 above right, 47 below left

Bibliothèque Nationale, Paris: 63 above (both)

Bildarchiv Foto Marburg: 14 below, 39 below, 45 below, 51 below, 54 above, 61 centre, 63 below, 76 below, 91 below

CESA, Cölbe (Stefan Drechsel): 17 below, 19, 23, 24, 25 above right, 28 above left, 34 above, 53, 57 below, 65, 86 above, 108 below.

Deutsches Historisches Museum, Berlin: 57 above

EDIFICE: 29 below (Lewis)

Faksimile Verlag, Lucerne: 33 above right

Klaus Frahm, Hamburg: 86 below, 89 below, 92, 92, 107 below, 108 above, 110, 111

Manuela Fugenzi, Grazia Neri: 14 above

© Jeff Goldberg, Esto Photographics: 106

G + J Fotoservice: 99 below (Schmidt-Luchs)

Hirmer Verlag: 31 and 34 below (Albert Hirmer and Irmgard Ernstmeier-Hirmer), 33 above

left (Max and Albert Hirmer)

SMPK, bpk: 30

SMPK, Kunstbibliothek Berlin: 41 below (D. Katz), 68 (D. Katz), 87 above left

Landesarchiv, Berlin: 93 below (Markus Hawlik)

Landesbildstelle, Berlin: 69 below, 90 above

© Dieter Leistner/Architekton: 110 unten

Steve Leonard, Black Star: 105 below

Christopher Little: 95 above

© Norman McGrath, New York: 95 below

G. Paolo Marton, Treviso: 46 above, 49 all.

Bernardino Mezzanotte, Milano: 27 centre

Frank den Oudsten, Amsterdam: 88, 89 above

Uwe Rau: 107 above

Pablo de la Riestra, Marburg: 48

Caroline Rose, © CNMHS/ SPA-DEM: 64

Paul Rosner: 79 all

Vittorio Savi: 93 above

Bildarchiv Steffens: 7 (Hans-Joachim Rech), 8 above (Hans-Joachim Rech); 9 all (Ralph Rainer Steffens), 11 all (Ladislav

Janicek), 12 above (Nigel Blythe), 12 below (Markus Haefke), 15 above left (Walter Allgöwer), 17 above (Ladislav Janicek), 18 above (Dieter Klöppel); 18 below (Uwe Vierkotten), 22 above (Ralph Reiner Steffens), 27 above (Dirk Waldeck), 37 below (Ralph Rainer Steffens), 38 (Pieter Jos van Limbergen), 39 above (Dirk Waldeck), 40 (Ladislav Janicek), 41 above (Ladislav Janicek), 43 (Walter Allgöwer), 46 below (Walter Allgöwer), 50 above (Walter Allgöwer), 50 centre (Ralph Rainer Steffens), 55 (Walter Allgöwer), 59 below (Walter Geiersperger), 60 above (Peter Jos van Limbergen), 71 (Ladislav Janicek), 74 (Friedrich Mader), 81 (Dieter Klöppel), 101 (Dieter Klöppel), 104 below (Thomas Bauer)

Wolfgang Steinborn, Karlsruhe: 91 above, 97, 100 above, 102

State Tretyakov Gallery, Moscow: 85 centre left

© Gerald Zugmann, Vienna: 83, 109